DOWN IN THE DARKNESS

THE SHADOWY HISTORY OF AMERICA'S HAUNTED MINES, TUNNELS & CAVERNS
BY TROY TAYLOR

- A Whitechapel Productions Press Publication -

BOOKS IN THE HISTORY & HAUNTINGS SERIES BY TROY TAYLOR
Book I: The Haunting of America (2001)
Book II: Into the Shadows (2002)
Book III: Down in the Darkness (2003)

This book is dedicated to those writers and adventurers who inspired me to seek out the mysteries of which I had only previously read -- to Sir Arthur Conan Doyle, Harry Houdini, Charles Fort, Harry Price, Richard Winer, Sir Richard Burton, Colonel Percy Fawcett, Wade Davis -- and others I have forgotten over the years.

And also to Anastasia, who will likely manage the company one day, to Orrin, who will handle the artwork and to Margaret, who will accompany me on my adventures and one day take my place. And of course to Amy, because no book could ever be written without her!

Original Cover Artwork Designed by
Michael Schwab, M & S Graphics & Troy Taylor
Visit M & S Graphics at www.msgrfx.com

This Book is Published by
- Whitechapel Productions Press -
A Division of the History & Hauntings Book Co.
515 East Third Street - Alton, Illinois -62002
(618) 465-1086 / 1-888-GHOSTLY
Visit us on the Internet at www.prairieghosts.com

First Edition - April 2003
ISBN: 1-892523-31-0

Printed in the United States of America

THE HISTORY & HAUNTINGS SERIES

Welcome to the third book in my "History & Hauntings Series". The series was first conceived a few years ago as a way to combine my two greatest literary interests. I have long been of the belief that no great ghost story can exist without a rich history to back it up. The events of yesterday truly give birth to the hauntings of today.

The book that you now hold in your hands is but another installment in an ongoing series of ghostly titles. In future volumes, I hope to continue to delve into the darker side of American history and to take you along on a continuing journey into the haunted corners of our country and to the farthest reaches of your imagination!

Happy Hauntings!

TABLE OF CONTENTS

DOWN IN THE DARKNESS · 5

- INTRODUCTION -

DOWN IN THE DARKNESS

What is it about the underground chambers of the earth that so fascinate us? Like so many others, I have had a lifelong interest in not only natural caverns, but tunnels, mines and the mysterious shafts that appear in legend and lore and within the pages of books. And, if you are like me, you don't want to just read about these locations either. I never fail to take a roadside detour when I am traveling and see a sign (no matter how lurid) that advertises a commercial cave of any sort. Such side trips have led me to some wonderful and unique locations over the years, including one haunted cavern that appears in the pages of these books.

The first cave that I can remember visiting as a child was a place called Meramec Caverns in Missouri. Growing up in Central Illinois, I often saw signs and roadside markers (usually painted on the roof of old, decrepit barns) that advertised the cave as "Jesse James Hideout", which made it even more appealing to a young boy. As an adult, I know that Jesse's connection to the cave is a little tenuous but it is still an appealing place. The cave had been initially discovered in the 1700's by a Frenchman named Jacques Renault, although Native Americans had used it for shelter for centuries prior to this. Renault took advantage of the cave's greatest resource, saltpeter, which was used to make gunpowder. During the Civil War, the cave was allegedly used by Missouri guerilla fighters, which Jesse and Frank James were among. Legend has it that they returned to the cave in the 1870's because it afforded a secure hideout for them after bank and train robberies. Meramec Caverns was opened to the public as a tourist attraction in 1935 and the notoriety of the James gang remains an important part of the cave's appeal today.

After Meramec Caverns, I was hooked and became a devoted cave visitor. As mentioned, I rarely pass by a roadside marker that offers a cave and fail to stop. But commercial caves are not the only passages beneath the earth that I have traversed. Perhaps even more fascinating are the unfinished caves that are only partially explored. I have been lucky enough to slide, crawl and slither through the muddy corridors of a number of "wild" caves over the years as well.

There is nothing quite like the feeling of passing through a narrow portion of a cave and realizing that the only way to turn back is to wriggle along backwards for who knows how many yards! Or when the difference between making it through a gap is one deep exhale, which allows your ribcage to shrink just enough for you to pass through. It's not a hobby for the faint of heart but if you ever get the chance to try your hand at spelunking, you are liable to be as enthralled with it as I have been.

My interest has even stretched beyond caves. While traveling out west, I had the chance to go inside a couple of old, abandoned mines, now barren shafts that had long since played out. The mines of the Old West, as well as the coal mines of the east and Midwest, were places that saw the destruction of many men's hopes and dreams -- as well as their lives. In the mines I visited, the timbers, rails and discarded tools of yesterday remained as memories of another time. It was not hard to imagine that ghosts lingered here. In this book, I will chronicle some of my adventures in the mines and abandoned mining camps of Utah for the first time. I have never forgotten my experiences at these places, where so many dreams -- and so many men -- died.

American mines have long had a history of labor strife, conflict and death. Once again, memories from my childhood played an important role in my perception of mines, especially when it came to tragedy and disaster. I grew up in a small Illinois town called Moweaqua. One of the most important events in the history of the town was the disaster that took place in the local coal mine on Christmas Eve of 1932. Almost every family in Moweaqua was affected by the loss of life at the mine and even more than 50 years later, I had friends whose families had suffered from the deaths of fathers, grandfathers, nephews and brothers.

Coal had been discovered in Moweaqua in 1889and a company was formed to take it from the ground by James G. Cochran of Freeport, Illinois. The Moweaqua Coal & Manufacturing Company opened in 1891 and the first vein was reached about five months later, in April 1892, and by June 1893, there were 54 men at work in the mine. Within a year, the mine had claimed its first injuries when four men were badly hurt in an explosion. The first death occurred in 1897 when Jacob Spitz, a German immigrant, was killed and not long after, four Italians were injured in a fire.

By 1899, the Moweaqua mine was setting new productions records and an electric plant was built near the shaft to illuminate the mine and to supply electricity to many of the townspeople. Three electric mine machines were put into use and electricity was also used to power a rail car in the main shaft. It was used in conjunction with mule-driven cars since there were eight of the animals working in the mine at that time. The mules were taken down in the cage about one month prior to their use in order for them to get used to the darkness of the mine. They were stabled below and generally well-treated by the drivers. Later, when the mine was closed down during the summer months, the mules were taken to a nearby farm and were kept inside of the barn for a month, until their eyes became used to the light again.

As time passed, the mine claimed more lives. The second to die was Charles Karloski, a German miner who was killed when a portion of ceiling collapsed on him. The third death was that of mine superintendent John Cairns, who was crushed and nearly decapitated when some boilers that were being delivered to the mine shifted positions on a flat car. A fourth death occurred in 1905 when Thomas McCray was crushed between two mine cars.

In 1909, a number of deaths occurred, including the deaths of eight mine mules, which were killed in a fire that was started by a faulty wire connection to a water pump. Another man, Stephen Potsick, was killed by falling rocks. Tony LeCount died of powder burns. Joe Nanni was crushed to death, again by falling rock. Jacob Newman died from injuries suffered when the elevator cage fell on him.

In spite of what seems like one death after another, the mine was actually doing very good business, providing coal for the railroad and for over a hundred wagons and trucks that came each day to be filled. The average payroll in 1924 was $10,000 and the average daily output from the mine was about 650 tons of coal. At that time, there were 150 men employed at the mine. By the end of the 1920's though, the mine owners began cutting back on the hours and men, choosing to close down over the summer months and re-hiring the men in the autumn. This practice was followed until 1930, when the mine closed down.

Just a short time before the mine was closed, a strange event took place that was reported in the local newspaper, the *Moweaqua News*. According to the story, a large block of coal was found in the middle of a vein one afternoon that was found to bear the figure "6666" in two inch-high letters. They looked as if they had been carved there and yet no one had an explanation for what could have caused this phenomenon to occur. Some took it as a bad omen though and perhaps they were right -- it did seem to be a foreshadowing of things to come.

As America entered the Great Depression, the owners decided that the Moweaqua mine was no longer profitable to operate and they closed it down. As can be imagined, this was a disaster for the small community, as there were no other jobs to be found in the area. Debate raged throughout the village and finally, a cooperation was formed by the miners and the townspeople and money was obtained through subscription to reopen the mine. On September 17, 1931, the mine opened again, this time as the Moweaqua Coal Corporation. Tragically though, its days were numbered.

The death knell sounded for the Moweaqua mine, and for 54 of the miners, on Christmas Eve 1932. At 8:15 in the morning, a methane explosion swept through the mine and killed the men who had just reported for work. Only two men who were inside were spared, the cage operators, whose work kept them close to the bottom of the shaft. The other miners were going toward other areas of the mine to work when they were caught by the explosion. An exact cause of the disaster has never been determined but it is believed that an unusual drop in barometric pressure caused gas that was already present in the mine to be forced from the unused areas and into the main corridors of the mine. A spark was probably set off by a miner throwing a light switch or by one of their lamps coming into contact with the gas.

Word quickly spread of the disaster and the mine manager summoned workers from a mine in Pana, Illinois. The crew arrived in less than two hours and mine rescue teams around the state were also alerted. Not knowing if any of the men in the mine were still alive, miners from the surrounding area flooded into Moweaqua to offer their services. They set to work trying to gain passage into the mine, as the entrance had been filled with fallen rock, and to rebuild the walls that had collapsed. The rescue teams worked continuously through the day and into the night. On Christmas Day, they discovered a passageway that was littered with the bodies of 12 of the imprisoned men. All of them were dead and hope began to dim that any of the miners could still be alive. On Monday morning, 27 more bodies were discovered and late that night, the battered corpse of Tom Jackson, the town Santa Claus, was found. The rest of the bodies were brought up out of the darkness over the next several days, with the last being found on December 29.

The scene at the surface was chaotic. Rescue squads constantly came and went while trucks and wagons moved back and forth near the cluttered mine entrance. The Red Cross set up a headquarters at the site and supplied food around the clock. Every newspaper for miles around sent reporters to the scene and it was estimated that 10,000 people were in the little town during the week after the disaster. Meanwhile, the families of the trapped miners kept a silent vigil a short distance away, too shocked and stunned to notice the activity around them.

The mine stayed closed for six months and then re-opened for a short time, with cleaning and repair work being done by miners who worked without pay. By December 1933, coal was again being removed from the mine. It remained in operation for two more years and then closed down for good. There was some talk of opening the mine up again in the years that followed, but the plans were never followed through. Eventually, the main shaft was filled, the buildings razed and the Moweaqua mine became an open field on the edge of town. Its physical presence was gone but the mine itself remains a haunting memory in this little town, even today.

But I don't suppose this has provided an explanation as to why caves and mines hold such a fascination for me and for many others though. Perhaps it is something about the mystery that awaits all of us in the subterranean regions of the earth. Mankind has always been curious about what lies beneath. In a previous book, I recounted some of the stories and legends of the so-called "hollow earth" and the lost civilizations that were alleged to be located there. It just might be this mystery, this lingering unknown, that draws us into the shadows.

Or could it be the darkness itself? For no place on earth will we find the utter blackness that awaits us in a cave. If you have ever ventured into the passageway of a cavern, only to have your guide shut off all of the lights, you soon realize what complete and total darkness is -- when you very literally cannot see your hand in front of your face. Is this enveloping darkness the appeal to those of us who seek out such places?

I have to confess that I do not know what draws me to caverns and underground chambers and have yet to find another with the same interests who can answer the question either. It remains a mystery to me. However, I encourage the reader to go and seek out those answers for himself -- to explore, wander and brave the shadows that wait in America's deepest and darkest caves. Hopefully, this book will provide a sort of guide for you of places worth visiting and to what hauntings and mysteries remain to be discovered.

In the pages ahead, I have tried to collect not only some of the strangest and most mysterious caves and caverns, but haunted ones as well. You'll also find a collection of haunted mines, shafts and spirit-infested railroad tunnels before ending up at what has been called "the largest haunted place in the world", the renowned Mammoth Cave in Kentucky. I have tried to provide you with the information to seek out these locations on your own and where possible, have provided directions and assistance so that you can find them.

Remember though, and with all ghosts aside, caves and abandoned mines and tunnels can be dangerous places for the careless. I never recommend that you enter a mine shaft or tunnel without permission and never enter a commercial cave without a guide or without paying admission. Should you have the opportunity to enter a wild cave, remember that all caves are very fragile. Their features may be thousands or perhaps even millions of years in the making and should never be touched or handled. Both cave features and cave life can be destroyed by people who do not understand how delicate underground life can be. Irresponsible people have taken stalactites from caves and they will never grow again. They have killed off bats by disturbing habitats at a time when food supplies are low. Caves are wonderful places for adventure and discovery but should be entered with caution. You can learn more about caving by contacting the *National Speleological Society at 2813 Cave Avenue, Huntsville, Alabama, 35810-4431.*

Here is also some information that you will need should you decide to explore a cave.

- Caves are always dark and every spelunker should always carry three sources of light including carbide lamps, electric headlamps, flashlights, plumber's candles and matches. If a caver should get lost in the darkness, it could mean death, so this is an important rule.

- Helmets and knee pads are recommended for cave exploring to protect against ceiling scrapes and rock falls, as well as from damage to the knees while climbing or entering small passages.

- The caver's pack should contain food and supplies for about 24 hours of exploration, even if you don't plan to be in the cave that long. It should hold extra batteries, flashlights, candles, a first aid kit, rope, canned food, water bottles and anything else that might needed.

Getting lost in a cave is a horror that has been imagined by most us since reading Mark Twain's *The Adventures of Tom Sawyer*. In most caves, this is unwarranted but large caves can be so confusing that even experienced spelunkers can get lost. Even without "Injun Joe" pursuing us, the dangers of cave exploration are many and range from falling rocks to tumbles into unseen holes. Caves can be deadly, there is no question about it, so always be cautious. There is no way to know just what awaits us, natural or supernatural --- down in the darkness.

Happy Hauntings!
Troy Taylor
March 2003

I. MYSTERIOUS SITES AND ANCIENT AMERICAN MYSTERIES

Mysterious sites come in many forms, from locations that have strange feelings associated with them to places where unusual events have happened. Mysterious caves and tunnels have fascinated Americans almost since our first arrival on these shores. There are many unusual sites along the back roads and in the desolate regions of the country, which have yielded more than their share of mysteries over the years. Various caves, mines and tunnels have even managed to be built and explored when the parts of the country they are located in were thought to be uninhabited. Such is the case with the thousands of worked copper mines that are located in northern Michigan. The mines were discovered by French missionaries in the 1500's but they reported that the local Indians knew nothing of their origins. Modern research shows that these mines were first worked more than 4,000 years before their "discovery", when no one was believed to even live in this region.

Other tunnels and shafts of similar vintage have been discovered elsewhere in America. Along a trail that skirts a mountain ridge in northern New Jersey and southern New York State is a series of exploratory tunnels that may have been dug by someone seeking ore. No one knows who cut the tunnels but they are believed to have been carved in prehistoric times.

In addition to these, there are a number of other complex underground tunnels and shafts found throughout North America. Many of the islands that lie along America's east coast have been associated with tales of hidden treasure that date back to the days of the pirates who plundered along the shores here. Perhaps the most famous is the strange shaft and tunnel system located on Oak Island, off Nova Scotia. For well over 200 years, researchers have been trying to figure out who built it, when and how it was dug and why it was created in the first place. The complexity of it remains an unsolved mystery and leads many to believe that untold riches lie somewhere within the shaft.

Many of these sites can be linked to unknown ancient visitors to the

Americas, or so many believe. There is an ongoing controversy between professional archaeologists and many amateur researchers about the possibility that the Native Americans and their culture were influenced by prehistoric explorers from the Old World. Most academic archaeologists and historians dismiss these theories and ideas, but have so far been unable to explain the strange tunnels, mysterious sites and script-like markings that have been found that seem to resemble various old languages. Even more unusual are the strange artifacts that are sometimes found -- which also remain unexplained.

In the pages to come, we'll take a look at some of these mystery sites, from mysterious places that remain intriguing and unexplained, to sites where the unknown has been discovered over the years.

BEEHIVE CHAMBER & TUNNELS
Petersham, Massachusetts

Located off a desolate dirt road in Central Massachusetts is an underground, beehive-style chamber from which several stone-lined tunnels exit in various directions. Where they actually go and what their function may have been remains a mystery.

The land where the chamber and tunnels are located was once the territory of the Nipmuck Indians, who deeded the region to Daniel Spooner, one of Petersham's original settlers in the middle 1700's. The land was later farmed by Charles Dudley and John Cornell and in 1907, was purchased by industrialist James Wilson Brooks. He accumulated large tracts of land here to protect the Swift River Valley and he donated 2,000 acres of land to Harvard University to establish the Harvard Forest. Much of that original land became the Brooks Woodland Preserve.

The tunnels are located a few miles from the Petersham town center and have been an enigma to local residents for years. Very little exists in print about them and no one in town is aware of any legends concerning their origins. They were accidentally discovered in 1940, when a tractor hauling lumber was driving across the site and the ground collapsed under it. When workers went to see what had happened, they found the underground chamber and the tunnels.

Entrance to the chamber is gained by dropping down into a hole that is about five feet deep. This passageway is made from large fieldstones and has been capped by even larger granite slabs. A few feet away from the opening is the round room, which often has water standing on the floor. A tunnel leads off from the right side to the surface and below is another small tunnel that leads off to another location. The site has never been excavated so know one has any idea just how many tunnels are here or where they might lead. The stonework is complex and seems to pre-date anything else in the area. Thanks to this, the purpose of the chamber and the tunnels remains a mystery.

Some researchers have tried to make the case that they were used as a hiding place of sorts in the 1700's, and although there was a colonial-era farm located here, an examination of the tunnels easily dispute this. The stone passageways are so small that even a child would have trouble passing through them, let alone an adult who might have been hiding from anything. Most believe that the stonework was in place long before the colonial settlers were present in the area. As to what purpose it served -- no one knows.

The chamber and the tunnels are located outside of Petersham, Massachusetts, about 70 miles west of Boston. from the town center, travel east on East Street for a little over two miles, then turn left (north) onto Glasheen Road. This is an unpaved, dirt road. An opening path will be on the left about a quarter mile along the road and the chamber and tunnels are directly up the path.

FLAGSTONE TUNNELS
Goshen, Massachusetts

Along a hillside near the center of Goshen, Massachusetts is a stone-lined shaft that plunges down into the ground. Looking down on it from above, the shaft appears to be nothing more than dry, stone well but buried down 16 feet below the surface is a complex of stonework tunnels that are perhaps a part of a greater mystery in Goshen. Near the bottom of the main shaft, two tunnels, lined with stacked flagstones, vanish outward for no apparent reason. One of them only travels about 16 feet but to the other snakes out into the underground of the hillside for 68 feet before narrowing into a collapsed sand pile. Strangely, this tunnels runs beneath a cemetery that was started centuries after these tunnels were likely created.

There are a number of theories as to why the tunnels were built. Some locals once believed that they were started by an early settler who planned to grown silkworms in them. Others thought that they had been used as passages for the Underground Railroad and still others surmised that they had been dug by the colonials as an escape route from Indian attacks. However, James Whitall, director of the Early Sites Research Society, excavated the tunnels in the 1980's and stated that they had been there for over 5,000 years. Like everyone else, he had no answers as to what they had been used for.

As the excavations were carried out, the team uncovered one mystery after another. Above a capstone in the tunnel, they found a carefully made, round disk that was about seven inches in diameter. It had been carefully placed there in position and had been delicately made by someone who pressed and worked the stone with a blunt instrument, causing telltale indentations along the edges. Although the function of the artifact is unknown, similar stones had been recovered at several New England Indian sites dating to a period about 5,000 years before.

The researchers also had to contemplate the riddle of the north tunnel, which traveled 68 feet and then stopped. It was almost as if the builders had just decided to give up, however they had quarried into the rock to keep the tunnel level, leading some to think that perhaps they had been interrupted before the passage could be completed.

Perhaps the greatest mystery though is the suggestion that the tunnels are part of a larger complex of underground chambers and shafts that have yet to be discovered in the area surrounding the village. Aerial photographs of the area have revealed long and straight soil discolorations near the tunnels. These disturbances may be the outline of a foundation for a structure that once stood here. If so, then it had to be nearly six times the size of a modern house though and over the last 300 years, nothing of that size has been recorded to exist in Goshen. In addition to the vanished structure, there are other ancient stoneworks in the area, including a strange underground chamber in a ridge west of the tunnel site, a 6-foot high stone pile in Ashfield (about seven miles away), a stone house made from massive slabs of granite atop Hanging Mountain (about seven miles south) and a standing stone near the town of Cheshire (about 20 miles away) that was in place before the first settlers came to the region. No one had any idea what it was used for but local Indians considered it evil -- and refused to go near it.

The Goshen Tunnels may be part of a much greater puzzle but at this point, are enigmas all on their own. No one knows who built them, why they built them, or where they vanished to before the work could apparently be completed. While the stone disk found here is similar to disks found at other Native American sites in New England, there has never been a suggestion that the Indians built anything like the tunnels. Could the stonework be a remaining remnant of some strange and mysterious culture that disappeared from America long ago?

The tunnels can be found in Goshen, Massachusetts, about 90 miles west of Boston. The present owners of the property have placed a large boulder over the entrance to prevent injuries and lawsuits but the site can be viewed from the cemetery, which is located in Goshen, just before the intersection of Route 9 and Route 112.

CARVED MYSTERY TUNNELS
Ellenville, New York

Carved into the side of a mountain here is a system of tunnels that were created using an ancient form of pick and wedge mining. Although theories exist as to who made the tunnels and what they may have been used for, scholars admit that they are stumped when it comes to proving any of them.

The first recorded explorations that carried reports about what riches could be found in this part of the world date back to Henry Hudson in 1609. Within a few days after Hudson entered New York harbor, he reported that the Indians had "yellow copper". Expeditions that followed brought settlers up the Delaware River and they quickly reported that the area was rich in ores, including copper, iron and lead. Along the east bank of the Delaware River, there once existed a 104-mile dirt path known as the Old Mine Road. The road, which has long since been paved and rerouted, is still a major artery in northwestern New Jersey known as Route 209. The Old Mine Road became so well known from the fact that it was the oldest trade highway in America. Local legend has it that it was built by the Dutch in 1650 to transport heavy loads of copper ore from mines in the Pahaquarry Township of New Jersey to Kingston, a Hudson River port city.

Historians do not believe that any mining was done by the Dutch in this area prior to 1650, but strangely, the evidence of mining along the ridge at Ellenville points to the fact that it was done long before that. It is also thought that the Old Mine Road dates back to an era before this as well. In all probability, the road was an ancient Native American trail that cut through the forest, following the ridges and contours of the land. This trail may have been used by ancient people who were involved in rock and ore exploration.

Throughout this area are more tunnels and what also appear to be mines. There are numerous shafts that have been dug into the mountains and at least seven of them were worked by people using hand tools. Stone masons believe that the larger mines would have taken at least ten months to dig using primitive implements and look much different from examples of Dutch mineral exploration. The Dutch, and just about everyone else who searched for ore during the colonial days, used gunpowder to blast away the stone. It was cheaper and saved time, as the explorers could not spend nearly a year in one place searching for mineral veins. However, no trace of gunpowder or evidence of blasting has ever been found in the mines around Ellenville.

The Ellenville tunnel, located at the foot of the Shawangunk Mountains, is on of the best known of these mystery tunnels. The shaft goes back into the mountain for 515 feet and at the end of the passage is a water spring.

Further south along the ridge are lead mines and are small in comparison to the original "mystery tunnel". All of these mines (which were likely Dutch excavations) were accounted for on maps of the 1600's, except for the original Ellenville tunnel. There was no historical mention of it until it was discovered in 1905. Two years later, in 1907, a water-bottling company purchased the land leading to the tunnel, built a large brick plant and began marketing their water. A small railway was built into the tunnel to satisfy the curious who came to see this mysterious site. They also built a concrete Roman archway at the tunnel's entrance, hoping to add charm to the place, and arranged a formal garden outside. Today, all of this has fallen into ruin although the stone archway --- as well as the mystery of who dug this mine and what they were looking for --- remains.

Ellenville is located in southeast New York State and the tunnel can be found off Berne Road. Just past a ball field, turn into a long, paved driveway in front of red brick factory building. There is a store on the site. Park at the left side of the parking lot and take the trail from the northeast corner of the lot. Follow it for a few minutes and cross a stream and you will soon see a concrete-faced opening with water coming out of it. This is the original mystery tunnel and you will get wet while trying to get inside. Be sure to request permission at the store before visiting the tunnel. Permission is usually granted to all of those who are courteous with their request.

CAVE VALLEY CAVE
Humboldt National Forest, Nevada

One of the most mysterious caves in the West is one that is located along the eastern border of Nevada, almost into Utah. It has been the source of many weird legends over the years and was first described by the Mormon settlers back in 1858. It remains a dangerous place and visitors are advised to approach it with much caution.

As mentioned, the modern history of the cave dates back more than 150 years to the time of the early Mormon occupation of Utah. On March 20, 1858, a young Indian interpreter, explorer and guide named George Washington Bean was sent from Provo, Utah by Mormon leader Brigham Young to seek out a hiding place for the Mormon colony in case of invasion by the United States Army. He was to set out into the Nevada desert and find a suitable place to shelter the settlers and he eventually found a large cave west of the Schell Creek Range in Cave Valley.

He stumbled onto the cave almost by accident and found that the main shaft boasted a number of smaller branches leading off in many directions. Three small pools of water were also found inside, as well as the "thousands of tracks of human beings and also the appearance of fires being lighted in many places, throughout the entire length of the cave." Bean was unable to learn who had been living in the cave in years past, for when he questioned the local Indians about the place, they refused to enter the cave. They told him that it had been considered a forbidden site for several generations.

The Indians told Bean that the cave was a source of a legend. According to the story, two young women entered the cave many years before and remained inside for almost six months. When they had gone inside, they had been naked but had returned in fine buckskin. The women reported that they had found a large, beautiful valley inside with timber, water and filled with game. They also discovered a band of Indians living in this valley who were in an advanced state of civilization and who dressed like white men. The Indians told Bean that the tracks he and his men had found inside of the cave had been made by these subterranean inhabitants. Bean believed that the tracks had instead been made by some of the more ancient inhabitants of the region, who had ventured into the cave looking for clay to make pottery with or perhaps even some much later arrivals than the clay seekers. He referred to it as "an old Spanish mine", which the Mormons had a tendency to do when they discovered the ancient diggings of the region. Even though it had been explored long before the earliest explorers crossed the Rocky Mountains, it was easier to label the site as something much more recent.

Eleven years later, in 1869, Lieutenant George M. Wheeler led a survey team of U.S. military engineers into the same valley during a mapping expedition. The men again explored and mapped the cave that the Mormon expedition had found. Wheeler described the cave as being much larger than Bean had and added that the expedition stopped their journey at a pit that was "found impracticable to explore for lateral connections, that may, for all that is known, extend in any direction."

Both of the accounts, from Wheeler and Bean, seem to indicate that this cave is an unusual place and the accounts also leave a number of unanswered questions behind. Who were the strange white men that the Indians believed were living in the cave and why was it then a forbidden place? If the tracks discovered by Bean in the cave had been made by earlier inhabitants seeking clay, then why did the Indians stop using this source? And if the cave was inhabited at one time, where did the inhabitants go?

Cave Valley is located in the Humboldt National Forest and from Ely, Nevada can be reached by taking Route 93 south to Route 486. Take Route 486 (Steptoe Creek Road) until turning east onto a small campground road. Look for signs for the Cave Creek Reservoir. The cave is about a mile ahead on this road. Remember, this can be a very dangerous cave and if you plan to visit, contact the National Park Service at Great Basin in advance of your trip.

Throughout the history of the land that came to be known as America, underground caverns have always been recognized by the indigenous people as places of great spiritual power and often as a gateway to the underworld or a passageway for earth spirits. Aside from the obvious elements of darkness and mystery associated with caverns, why have such places become the focal point of legends? Some have speculated that fissures in the earth may in some way influence the human neurological network and that the changes in the natural magnetic field caused by these openings may affect our perception in some way. Could these be what attracted the ancient people to them?

Tales and speculation about ancient inhabitants, strange tunnels and mysterious mines may be odd --- but in the pages ahead, things are going to get even stranger.

A LOST EGYPTIAN CITY?
Grand Canyon National Park, Arizona

For years, the Grand Canyon in Arizona has been considered a place of great beauty and mystery but for many researchers and amateur archaeologists, it is also a place that is shrouded in secrecy. Many believe that within the depths of the canyon, there exists a place that would turn American archaeology upside down and would be one of the most amazing discoveries in history --- an underground city of Egyptian origin that is hidden with away inside of one of the Grand Canyon's many walls!

In 1893, the Grand Canyon was declared a national forest preserve and in 1908, a National Monument. It finally became a National Park in 1919 and today is visited by more than 3 million visitors each year. Very of these visitors are aware of the mysteries that continue to plague the Grand Canyon, including what may be one of the greatest archaeological mysteries in American history.

In 1909, a lengthy article appeared on the front page of the *Phoenix Gazette* newspaper. According to the story, an explorer and hunter named G.E. Kinkaid, who had spent "thirty years in the service of the Smithsonian Institution", had reported an amazing discovery within the depths of the Grand Canyon. Kinkaid claimed to have found, about 2,000 feet above the Colorado River, a vast underground city that had been carved from solid rock. His employer, Professor S.A. Jordan, wanted the find to be further investigated as it was deemed to be of major importance and in 1909 was allegedly doing just that.

The newspaper went on to say that "the archaeologists of the Smithsonian Institute, which is financing the expeditions, have made discoveries which almost conclusively prove that the race which inhabited this mysterious cavern, hewn in solid rock by human hands, was of oriental origin, possibly from Egypt, tracing back to Ramses."

According the report, the city was found to be nearly a mile underground and accessible by way of a long, main passage. This led to a massive chamber from which other passages radiated outward like the spokes of a wheel. Kinkaid claimed that the team from the Smithsonian had explored several hundred rooms and had discovered weapons, copper instruments, carved idols, urns of copper and gold and carved inscriptions that appeared to be hieroglyphics of Egyptian origin. In one chamber, they found a large crypt that was said to contain many well-preserved mummies. Each of them had been entombed with weapons, leading the explorers to believe that the chamber was a burial site for soldiers.

The explorers theorized that upwards of 50,000 people could have lived in the immense underground city and that possibly the ancestors of the Indians who resided in the area in 1909 may have been slaves or servants of those who lived in the cave. The civilization, they believed, existed thousands of years before it was generally thought such a culture could have lived in America.

"Professor Jordan," Kinkaid was quoted as saying in the newspaper article, "is much enthused over the discoveries and believes that the find will prove of incalculable value in archeological work."

A story like this must have been stunning in 1909! The Grand Canyon city could be regarded as the oldest and most unusual archeological discovery in American history and yet today, it is largely forgotten. The Grand Canyon is filled with places and geological formations that have been given Egyptian names but no one in authority can explain why. So why is this city never mentioned in textbooks, especially with a formidable authority like the Smithsonian Institution involved in its discovery?

Largely because the Smithsonian now claims that neither the discovery, nor its discoverers, ever existed! Many ask how such a thing could be possible; especially after the extensive newspaper coverage the site was given? The *Phoenix Gazette* claims that the story must have been a hoax and the Smithsonian discourages any inquiries on the subject. In fact, they claim to have no records that G.E. Kinkaid or Professor S.A. Jordan ever worked for them at all! Could the story have been a complete fabrication --- or could it be that the discovery was so monumentally important that it was covered up?

Author David Hatcher Childress, who has written scores of wonderful books including *Lost Cities of North and Central America*, became intrigued by the story of the Grand Canyon's Egyptian City several years ago and decided to look into it. The first thing that he did was to call the Smithsonian Institution and explain that he was researching the 1909 newspaper story about the rock-cut vaults and the Egyptian artifacts. He wondered if anyone could provide him with further information. A staff archaeologist informed him very quickly that not only had no Egyptian artifacts ever been found in North or Central America, but that the Smithsonian had never been involved in any such excavations. Neither she nor anyone else that Childress spoke with could find any record of the discovery or of explorers Jordan and Kinkaid.

Of course, it can't be ruled out that the entire story was an elaborate newspaper hoax, but the fact that it was on the front page of the paper and continued on for several pages, named the prestigious Smithsonian and gave a highly detailed account, does lend a great deal to its credibility. It does seem hard to believe that such a story would come out of thin air.

Many then ask the question as to whether or not the Smithsonian is covering up this remarkable revelation? If the story were true, it would radically change the ideas of pre-Columbian settlement in America. Is the idea that ancient Egyptians came to America thousands of years ago so preposterous that it has to be erased from all records? Could the Smithsonian be more interested in maintaining the recognized standard than in releasing information that could change all of the ideas that currently exist?

You might believe though that only "conspiracy nuts" would think the Smithsonian Institution was trying to engineer a cover-up of the Grand Canyon's

Egyptian city. You might believe that, but don't be too quick to judge. A look at a hiker's map of the Grand Canyon does reveal that much of the area on the north side of the canyon, as already mentioned, has Egyptian names. The region around Ninety-four Mile Creek and Trinity Creek has points and formations with names like "Tower of Set", "Tower of Ra", "Horus Temple", "Osiris Temple" and "Isis Temple". And while this is not so strange if you consider the idea that perhaps the early explorers of the area were inspired by the discoveries that were taking place in Egypt at that time, it's not the most unnerving part of the puzzle. What is strange is that this part of the Grand Canyon is totally off-limits to hikers and visitors "because of dangerous caves". It's interesting that the exact same area that was described in the 1909 articles by Kinkaid is now a "forbidden zone", where no one is allowed inside!

Is something being hidden away within the shadowy confines of the Grand Canyon? Or are the tales of an underground city and Egyptian relics merely part of an elaborate hoax from the last century? Perhaps only time will provide the answers to another historical, unsolved mystery.

The Grand Canyon is located in north-central Arizona and the south rim is about 70 miles north of Flagstaff on U.S. Highway 180. As mentioned, the area where the cave was allegedly discovered in 1909 is off limits to visitors.

THE SOUTHWEST TUNNELS
Region around Victorio Peak, New Mexico & Parts of Arizona

The legends and lore of South America are filled with stories of tunnels that run for hundreds of miles beneath countries like Chile and Peru but some historians believe that a similar set of tunnels also exists beneath Arizona and New Mexico. At the turn of the last century, when the United States Army was pursuing Geronimo through the southwestern deserts, he and his men sometimes reportedly rode into box canyons, with the army in close pursuit --- only to mysteriously vanish. A day or two later, it would be reported that Geronimo had turned up in Mexico, a few hundred miles away. This happened not one time, but several and some have surmised that he was using an ancient system of tunnels that was unknown to the Army. Certain members of the Indian tribes knew about the passages, it was thought, but kept them a closely guarded secret.

One such tunnel was believed to have been discovered years ago in western New Mexico, near Victorio Peak. In 1937, a half-Indian podiatrist named Doc Noss happened upon a cache of Apache gold on what is now the White Sands Missile Range. The gold had been hidden away there around 1880 and was a combination of Aztec and Spanish treasure that had been stolen over the years. Much of it was in the form of gold bars, as well as statues, cups, jewelry and even artifacts like swords and armor. Noss was shot to death by his partner,

Charlie Ryan, in March 1949 and what became of the treasure is unknown, but most believe that it was confiscated by the government when they took over White Sands. Prior to this, Noss had removed as many as 88 gold bars from hidden tunnels in the mountain.

In 1968, an article about the cache appeared in *True Treasure* magazine and sparked a renewed interest in the treasure and the mysterious tunnels. A prospector named Harry Snow was approached by several ranchers in the area to the west of Victorio Peak because he had spent more than 25 years exploring the area where White Sands was now located. Because he knew the area so well, it was thought that he could lead them past the Army patrols and into the region where the treasure was found.

However, Snow believed that the cache was not on Victorio Peak, but on nearby Hardscrabble Peak, which was also government property. He had met a cowboy years earlier who told him that he had seen Doc Moss disappear into a cave on Hardscrabble Peak and then emerge hours later with loaded pack mules. The cowboy claimed to go into the cave to find carved stairs that led down underground. He followed them downward for a short distance but did not go to the bottom, fearing that Noss would return and kill him.

Snow took the ranchers to Hardscrabble Peak in November 1968. They searched the mountain for two days, looking for any sign of the cave, before running out of supplies. After re-stocking, the ranchers returned to the mountain and left Snow there, planning to return for him in three days. The veteran prospector then began to comb the mountain on his own.

According to his account to author David Chandler, he found the cave on the second day. He descended an estimated 1300-1400 steps before reaching the bottom of the staircase the cowboy had described to him years before. Interestingly, the last step was rounded so that if you stepped on it, it would roll. It was then connected to a bow and arrow by a strip of rawhide, designed to trigger an arrow that was aimed at the step as an ingenious booby trap. Luckily for Snow, the rawhide had long since rotted away.

At the bottom of the staircase, Snow began following a small stream that ran along an old earthquake fault. He followed along it, entering carved room after carved room, until he began to find small stacks of gold, copper and silver. Beyond this, he found a large room, with smaller tunnels and branches leading off from it. As he explored, he often had to get down on his hands and knees but always stayed on the east-west tunnels, staying away from the smaller branches. He continued on, rationing his water and supplies, for two days and two nights. According to his story, he followed the tunnel for 14 miles. He eventually emerged in an area of the White Sands range called the Jornada.

Snow did admit to Chandler that he had made an exciting discovery in the tunnels but would not reveal exactly what it was, whether it was bodies or some strange artifacts. He did tell him that he later made additional trips into the first rooms and removed some of the metal bars. As it turned out, the story itself was incredible enough that Snow did not feel the need to embellish it further by explaining what he had found there.

The location of the tunnel, thanks to the fact that this now a military preserve, remains a mystery and there are other aspects of this case that remain just as odd. The area around Victorio and Hardscrabble Peaks, both in the Hembrillo Basin area, were constantly guarded by Apache war parties. At one point, the Apache chief Victorio held off the American cavalry at the Hembrillo Basin spring for two days. It was unusual for the Apache to fight this way, as they normally used practiced fight and run guerilla tactics, but they fought so well in this position that eventually the Army had to battle its way to the spring because they were out of water. They didn't know at the time that the spring, and the mountains around it, were the Apache's secret headquarters. The entire area was honeycombed with tunnels, cave and secret entrances -- at least according to Harvey Snow's later story. His account would certainly explain the changes in tactics by the Apache in this battle.

On a side note, there was also a huge mural that was painted on rock wall at Hembrillo Spring that was connected to the tunnels and the gold cache. According to Chandler, the mural was dynamited by the military in 1973 because it contained a cryptic map to the tunnel entrance. The mural, as it has been described, apparently came from two time periods. The older, underlying mural had faded colors and showed two figures wearing skirts and pointing at smaller figures. There were also a number of other designs like suns, moons and snakes as well. Painted on the same ledge, but not obscuring what was apparently prehistoric artwork, was a newer, more vivid mural. It showed a large Indian warrior leading smaller warriors in an attack on a wagon train. Between the attackers and the wagon train was a ghost-like object that was taller than the giant warrior and which was enveloped in an aura of light.

Some historians believe this figure may have been Quetzalcoatal, the mysterious Mexican god who was said to be a bearded white man that lived among the Aztecs, but the presence of a wagon train seems to place the mural in the 1800's. The figure was likely the "Gray Ghost" instead, a strange character who was seen in the mountains in the 1860's. According to the legend, he always rode alone and "could never be approached". Eventually, while being pursued by the Army, he was led to a secret tunnel by Apache braves and escaped to become a friend of the Apache. The Gray Ghost stayed with them for many years, learning the language and living among them. He was said to have told Victorio that he was a "chief from toward the rising sun" and one day he departed, riding on to the west. Most believe the Gray Ghost was a Confederate officer who was in the west on some mission when the Confederacy fell. He was apparently adopted into the tribe and he became a mystical figure to later generations of the tribe.

Unfortunately though, with the mural destroyed and all routes to the tunnels obliterated, we will never know for sure.

Victorio Peak and the White Sands Missile Range are located in south-central New Mexico, just outside of Alamogordo. The area is absolutely closed to the public.

LEGENDS OF WINGATE PASS
Death Valley, California

America is riddled with caves and strange tunnels about which claims are made of them connecting to secret cities and underground civilizations. Even the most ancient records of past societies tell of reasonable people who have wandered into holes and tunnels, where they find artifacts and paintings pointing to some subterranean world.

The idea that we could somehow gain access to these "forbidden" worlds has intrigued man for centuries. One such desert civilization could allegedly be accessed through treacherous Death Valley, the lowest and hottest place in America. According to Native American legends, there existed near an area called Wingate Pass, the entrance to a city that the Indians called "Shin-au-av". It was said to be inhabited by fair-skinned people who spoke an unknown language and who lived in hidden caverns that were illuminated by green light.

Some time around 1920, a Native American guide named Tom Wilson claimed that his grandfather had stumbled into the caverns and had become totally lost. He ended up stumbling into an underground city, where he found white people who wore shiny leather clothing. They spoke a language that he had never heard before but did show him a way to get out of the tunnels and back to the surface. The guide told the tale after meeting a prospector named White who claimed to have fallen through the floor of an abandoned mine and found various chambers that contained bars of gold and mummies dressed in leather clothing. The prospector said that he went back to the cave several times with his wife and a partner named Fred Thomason to see the mummies (and likely to haul away some of the gold) but when he tried to lead an archaeological team to the site, he was unable to find it.

The cavern was again lost for many years -- or was it? Many people in the area speculated as to the source of wealth enjoyed by an eccentric old prospector named Walter Scott. He built a "castle" in the valley and a racetrack that still exists today. Those who knew him stated that when his funds were running low, "Death Valley Scotty" as he was known, would disappear for a few days and would return with some suspiciously refined-looking gold that he claimed he prospected. Many believe that the old man, who spent millions on his castle, got his gold from the stacks of bars that were hidden in the caves beneath Wingate Pass.

The cavern remained lost until 1931 when an amateur archaeologist and physician named Dr. F. Bruce Russell literally stumbled onto it again. He soon made an announcement that he had discovered a variety of strange artifacts and eight foot-tall mummified bodies, along with 32 similar caves within seven miles of the original site. He spent the next 20 years exploring the caverns and trying to generate interest in them and funding for a major dig. After putting the money together, he issued invitations throughout the academic community to accompany him to the caves and to bring back artifacts that could be studied scientifically. All of those he invited refused to come. They would only go to the site after first seeing the artifacts. Discouraged, but not hopeless, Dr. Russell returned to Death Valley to bring back proof of his discovery.

He was never seen again.

The mysterious caverns were forgotten until 1947 when a new announcement came from a man named Howard E. Hill, an amateur archaeologist who claimed to have re-discovered Dr. Russell's lost caverns. He stated that the caves contained mummies of men and animals and implements of a culture that was thousands of years old but "in some respects more advanced than our own." In a newspaper report, Hill admitted that Dr. Russell had discovered the caves and that he "tried for years to interest people in them, but nobody believed him."

According to the report, Hill and his team found one cave that seemed to contain a ritual hall with designs and markings similar to Freemason design. A long tunnel from this temple took the group into another room, where they found the preserved remains of dinosaurs, saber-toothed tigers, elephants and other extinct beasts. The animals had been placed in pairs as if on display. He believed that perhaps some sort of catastrophe in the past had driven the civilization into the caves and they had left all of the implements of their culture behind, including household utensils and stoves "which apparently cooked by radio waves".

The story made the newspapers and then mysteriously vanished. If it was true though, whatever became of the artifacts and mummies? The stories were apparently too hard to believe and the Los Angeles County Museum, which at first apparently expressed interest in the find, soon broke off contact with the group when the story grew too incredible. And once again, the caverns were lost.

Interest in them was revived in the 1960's, thanks to the attention of cult leader and alleged killer Charles Manson. He came to believe that a water-filled cavern entrance in Wingate Pass was a passageway to the underground civilization from the earlier tales about the area. He was arrested here in 1969 before he could lead his followers into the portal to the other side.

While such interest in the site is questionable (at best), there have been many others who have come to believe there may be more to the area than meets the eye. Since Manson's brush with Wingate Pass, at least two people have died trying to swim through the hundreds of feet of water that blocks the entrance to the cavern. One has to wonder what they hope to find inside? Relics of some forgotten, ancient culture --- or the entrance to another world?

Death Valley National Park is in San Bernardino County in California. The Devil's Hole is located just over the state line from Death Valley Junction at Highway 127 and Highway 190. The entire Wingate Valley was made part of the China Lake Naval Weapons Center a few years ago and permission must be obtained before entering the area.

THE MYSTERY SKELETONS
Near Lovelock, Nevada

A strange discovery took place in 1911 near the town of Lovelock, Nevada. Two miners began working the rich bat guano deposits in Lovelock Cave, digging into areas in the cavern that was as much as 15 feet deep in places. The men had removed several carloads of guano before coming upon a collection of Indian relics and animal bones. Soon afterward, they also discovered a mummy --- a six and a half foot-tall person with "distinctly red hair". According to the legends of the local Paiute Indians, a tribe of red-haired giants (called the Si-te-cahs) had once lived in the area and had been the mortal enemies of the other tribes. They had finally all banded together to drive the red-haired ones away. A mining engineer from Lovelock, John T. Reid, became convinced that the discovery of the mummy substantiated the Paiute legend and spent years collecting evidence that the mysterious tribe had existed.

A year later, the discovery of the mummy, along with the other relics, caught the interest of the University of California at Berkeley and the Nevada State Historical Society and they sent an archaeologist named Llewellyn L. Loud to investigate the cave. He managed to salvage a number of other artifacts from the mining operation. His excavations were followed in 1924 by M.R. Harrington, from the Museum of the American Indian in New York. He too collected artifacts, but found no other bones. He also asked that the original mummy be reburied so that the Indian workers on the site would stop complaining about the disrespectful treatment of the remains.

His requests were ignored and over the next few years, more red-haired remains were found in the Lovelock area. After measuring the bones and fragments of bodies, Reid and others were able to determine that the bodies belonged to people who had stood from six to nine or even ten feet-tall.

Among what turned out to be over 4,500 artifacts uncovered in the Lovelock Cave were 60 human bodies, many of them mummified, and a wide variety of artifacts that have been considered some of the oldest found in North America. Some of the relics included rock, bone and wood sculptures of animals, realistic duck decoys, coiled basketry, woven textiles, an assortment of bone, stone, horn and leather objects of various uses, articles of clothing and more. Many of the artifacts were found in storage pits and caches, as if they had been left by the original occupants for generations to come. Groupings of the tall bodies were also ritualistically buried in different areas of the cave.

Grouped together, the skeletons and the artifacts were considered so unique that many have called them a part of the "Lovelock Culture". The stone, wood and bone cultures show the Lovelock artists to be unsurpassed for the time period, utilizing a degree of realism that was not found in subsequent cultures. Unfortunately though, findings of tall, white, Nordic types in Nevada did not sit well with mainstream archaeologists or Paiute historians, who had their land and their claims to consider. After the initial excitement over the skeletons subsided, most of the remains were stolen, lost or destroyed. And since the bones did not fit the local Indian profile with regard to stature and hair color, most Native American historians simply hoped the furor over the red-haired giants would die out. Unfortunately for them, there were more discoveries of Nordic skeletons across the region.

One of the most important discoveries to support the Si-te-cahs stories was the Spirit Cave mummy, which was found buried and preserved in the same manner as the Lovelock mummies. Local Paiute Indians strongly objected to a scientific investigation of the Spirit Cave mummy and it was eventually forgotten. In 1931, more remains were found when a rancher unearthed a mystery skeleton in the area. In this case, as with the Spirit Cave Mummy, the skeleton was exceptionally tall, much taller than any of the native people of the Great Basin.

Today, a few of the remains, including a skull, some bones and a few artifacts, are still located at the Humboldt Museum in Winnemucca, Nevada. There are also artifacts from Lovelock at the Nevada State Historical Society in Reno too, but no bones. There is no mention there of giant people, but the fact that the red-haired Indians did exist is no longer disputed.

The Lovelock Cave is located on a hillside about 20 miles southeast of Lovelock, Nevada, just off Interstate 80. There is a small display on the Si-te-cahs in the Lovelock Museum today but does not mention that they may not have been Native Americans.

DEVIL'S HOLE CAVE
Self, Arkansas

As you can see, there have been stories and legends surrounding the mysteries of what lies beneath the earth for centuries. Not all of the stories involve mysterious artifacts and strange skeletons though. A few of these weird tales range from the odd to the downright spooky.

For example, in places like Tacoma, Washington and Hannibal, Missouri, there have been stories told of what might best be called "sinkholes". They are depressions in the ground, or pits, which simply cannot be filled. There are stories of such holes here, and in other places, that people use to throw in extra dirt from gardens and yards and have been doing so for generations. The situation seems harmless and in fact, can be pretty useful, but only until you begin to question the reality of such sinkholes. Where is the dirt actually going? Why does the pit only sink for far, even though it is filled over and over again? Why doesn't the sinkhole continue sinking until there is a deep shaft into the earth?

In some cases, these "sinkholes" become the source of a local legend or a curse. In many cases, the story goes that a man was hanged on the spot and his executioners were forced to dig a hole when the weight of his body stretched the limb of the hanging tree too close to the earth. The story normally continues with the addition that the hole has not filled since, not matter how much dirt has been tossed into it.

Pretty strange stuff --- but not as strange as others.

In Tacoma, Washington, a man named Johnson discovered a hole in his yard that was about four feet in diameter, with the top three feet bricked in. He didn't notice the hole until he moved into the house and his dog found the opening. He apparently dropped a rope into the hole about fifty feet but failed to reach the bottom. Assuming that it was an abandoned well, he loaded it with old tires and the hole actually seemed to be getting close to being filled. Johnson asked around the neighborhood about the hole and was told that the previous owners of the house had dumped a load of marble into it and a short time later "an explosion blew everything out". The former residents moved away soon after. By the summer of 1974, the tire level in the hole began dropping, as if the hole was digesting them, and soon the top of the pile disappeared from sight. Neither Johnson, nor anyone else was inclined to get into the hole to see where the tires had gone.

For years, I also heard about a hole near Hannibal, Missouri that was locally rumored to be bottomless. According to the stories, a number of cattle and animals had been lost in the hole and had never been found. It was located in the woods outside of town and became a place to be shunned and avoided by nearby residents. And while I have never been able to find any records that insist this hole actually exists, the story is a strange one.

The fellow who owned the land on which the hole was located decided to check the place out for himself one day and he tied a rope around a nearby fence post and slid down into the blackness. The story relates that some friends discovered him shortly after his adventure in the pit and his hair had turned completely white and he was wildly insane. Whatever he had encountered down in the cave had broken his sanity!

This is strange --- but it gets even stranger.

In the northern part of Arkansas is Boone County and within the county is a small village called Self. It's a remote place and is not very accessible anymore, but it is home to a story that is both elusive and fascinating. Similar to the story from Missouri, it deals with a strange and largely unexplored cavern called the

Devil's Hole Cave. One day, an indeterminate number of years ago, the owner of the land where the cave is located decided to explore the cavern. He climbed down a rope about 200 feet to a ledge where the shaft narrows to a point that can only be crawled through. He suddenly heard a vicious hissing from the darkness, perhaps like a large lizard would do, and he made a hasty retreat.

Some time later, he and some men from town dropped a flatiron tied to a rope to the same place in the cave. They heard a hissing sound and the rope was pulled hard. When they pulled it back up, they found the flatiron had been badly bent and scored with scratches and teeth marks. They next tried a stone and the rope was pulled taut again. They pulled it back up to find the stone was gone and that the rope was neatly severed. Not surprisingly, no one wanted to dare and climb down to see what was in the cave.

Occasionally, local stories apparently come from the cave, but the "gow-row" as the natives supposedly call it, seems to prefer staying down in the darkness. The story dates back to around 1900 and many believe the monster may be some sort of giant lizard but nobody knows for sure what it is or even if it is still alive. Arkansas spelunkers have informed me that they have visited this cave on several occasions and while much of it remains untouched, they have yet to encounter the "gow-row" though!

The town of Self is not easy to find but if you look at an Arkansas map and find the town of Harrison, you will see State Highway 7. About eight miles east of Harrison on Highway 7 is a place where the railroad tracks intersect the highway. The town of Bergman is about 1/4 mile east of this intersection. These tracks go northwest through Wooden Hills, Myrtle and Self. The town of Self is about 15 miles up these tracks to the northwest. You can drive to Self by going up Highway 65 north of Harrison about 12-15 miles or about 3 miles past the town of Prosperity (this town is very small like Self). There will be a small dirt or gravel road called Dubuque Road and you can follow it to Self.

Caution is advised when entering the Devil's Hole Cave. It is a wild cave and one of over 2,000 such caves documented in Arkansas. It can be very dangerous -- whether the gow-row exists or not!

THE PIASA CAVE
Near Alton & Grafton, Illinois

One final mystery cave is also associated with a possibly mythical creature but this monster continues to have an impact on the people who live in the Mississippi River Valley, along the Great River Road of Illinois. As many visitors leave the city of Alton and drive north along the River Road, they are often surprised to see a rock painting on the side of a bluff that portrays a pretty vicious-looking winged creature. Years ago, this rock painting was actually a petroglyph that showed two such creatures. These monsters, like the modern rendering of the paintings, were called the "Piasa" by the Illiniwek Indians. The original painting existed near this location for hundreds of years and was first described in the journals of Pere Marquette in 1673 as he was exploring the Mississippi River. The original site of the painting is now long gone, but Marquette described the creatures portrayed there in this manner:

> As we were descending the river we saw high rocks with hideous monsters painted on them and upon which the bravest Indian dare not look. They are as large as a calf, with head and horns like a goat, their eyes are red, beard like a tiger's and face like a man's. Their tails are so long that they pass over their bodies and between their legs, under their bodies, ending like a fish tail. They are painted red, green and black and so well drawn that I could not believe they were drawn by the Indians, for what purpose they were drawn seems to me a mystery.

Father Hennepin, another early explorer of the west, published a book in 1698 called *A New Discovery of a Vast Country in America* and he also wrote about seeing the paintings of the Piasa, which incidentally, were first incised and cut into the bluff and then painted over. In 1820, Captain Gideon Spencer came up the Mississippi and saw the paintings on the bluffs. He asked the Indians what it was and they told him that it was a "Storm Bird" or a "Thunder Bird" and that it had been placed there long ago. The Indians would fire their guns at it and some would offer it tobacco by smoking their pipes and blowing smoke in the direction of the image.

The petroglyphs were located immediately below where the first state prison was located in Alton. The paintings were partially destroyed in the 1840's when quarrying was done on the bluff by convicts from the prison.

The painting was later described by a Professor William McAdams, an Illinois State Geologist, who created an illustration of the bird in the 1880's. It is from his drawing that all of the modern-day renditions of the Piasa Bird come. McAdams also seems to be the person responsible for creating the mythology of a single bird-like creature, instead of two monsters, as the Indians originally passed along the story. Even in McAdam's day, the original painting no longer existed. A quarry had purchased the property and they had blasted away the wall on which it could be found some time around 1847. The drawing that McAdams created was based on the testimony of five men who recalled seeing the painting before it was destroyed. It was later featured in the *Literary Digest* and it is believed to be the most accurate drawing of the Piasa.

Some have criticized McAdams and have claimed that he created the mythology that the Piasa was a bird instead of simply a Native American monster. The evidence they cite is that the Piasa had never been written about or drawn with wings prior to McAdam's version in *Literary Digest*. However, there may be an explanation for this. One similar painting that was done of the Piasa at roughly this same time was done by a man named Ladd, a former mayor of White Hall, Illinois. According to Ladd, he based his picture on a recollection of the original image that had been given to him by "Squire Russell of Bluffdale, who had been nearer to the Piasa than any person now living." He spoke to the man who told him this:

I used to climb the rocks to look at it when I was a boy. I have been within sixty feet of it. I once pointed it out from the deck of an English steamer to a lady and she looked at it through a field glass. No wings showed that day for the weather was dry. The colors were always affected by dampness, and it stood out distinctly after rain. Father Marquette evidently saw the Piasa on a dry day for he pictured it without wings.

Who created the original painting? No one will ever know for sure, but it must have existed for some time as part of the culture of the local Native Americans. It was said that on a flat ledge below the painting were hundreds of arrow heads and spear points. It is believed that the Indians who passed the Piasa on the river would "attack" the creature by firing an arrow at it. It apparently became a custom when floating past the future site of Alton.

The Piasa Bird is considered one of the most enduring legends of the region -- a tall tale, an Indian myth that is sufficient to entertain children. But what if it isn't? What if there is more to the "legend" than meets the eye?

The legend of the Piasa Bird dates back to long before the white man came to region. It has been traced to a band of Illiniwek Indians who lived along the Mississippi in the vicinity north of present-day Alton. This tribe, led by a chief named Owatoga, hunted and fished the valley and the river and lived a contented life until the "great beast" came.

One morning, Owatoga's son, Utim, and a friend were fishing when they heard a terrible scream. They looked and saw a huge bird rising from the edge of the river. The legend states that the bird was of such dimensions that it could carry away a full-grown deer in its talons, and that once it obtained a taste for human flesh, it would eat nothing else. The creature the two men saw had a young man gripped in its claws and it carried him away and out of sight. Quickly, the two young men returned to their village and found their people very frightened. They waited all day for the young man to escape from the bird and return, but he did not.

After that, nearly every morning, the great bird would appear in the sky and carry away a member of the tribe, either a man, woman or a child. Those who were carried off were never seen again. The people began to call the bird the "Piasa", which meant "the bird which devours men". Owatoga realized that they were powerless against this beast and he retreated to his lodge to fast and to pray for guidance. He emerged the next day with a plan that had been revealed to him in a vision.

According to his vision, Owatoga was to take six of his finest braves and climb to the top of one of the highest bluffs. The young men were to carry with them only their bows and a quiver of poisoned arrows. They were to hide themselves while Owatoga stood on the edge of the bluff and waited for the Piasa to appear. When the monster came, the chief was to throw himself down on the rocks and hold on while the bird attempted to carry him away. As it did so, the braves would appear with their bows and slay the beast.

Of course, all of the men in the tribe offered to help kill the Piasa, but Owatoga chose only young, unmarried men, his own son among them. The arrows were sharpened and poisoned and the group climbed to the top of the bluff. The six young men hid themselves beneath a rock ledge and Owatoga stepped out to the edge of the cliff. He folded his arms and waited for the creature to appear. Suddenly, the sky darkened overhead and the bird's massive wings were heard. The Piasa swooped down toward Owatoga. Just as the tip of the creature's sharp talon sunk into this shoulder, Owatoga threw himself flat upon the rocks. His hands curled around the roots of a tree and he clung desperately to them. The Piasa roared in frustration and its wings beat furiously, trying to lift the Indian from the rocks.

The wings unfolded once more and as it exposed itself, the young men burst from their hiding place and fired their arrows at the beast. The arrows found their mark but the Piasa continued to fight, trying over and over to lift Owatoga from the rocks. Then, with a howl of agony, the creature released him and collapsed backward, crashing over the edge of the bluff. It spiraled down out of sight and plunged beneath the waters of the Mississippi. The terrible creature was never seen again.

Despite his wounds, Owatoga recovered from his battle and joined in the celebration over the death of the Piasa. They ate, danced and celebrated into the night and the next day, they painted a colorful tribute to the Piasa bird on the stone face of the bluff where it had been destroyed. From that time on, any Indian who went up or down the river fired an arrow at the image of the Piasa Bird in memory of their deliverance from the monster.

When the white men settled this region and heard the tales of the Piasa, they found no evidence (at first) to suggest that this creature really existed. But the Indians who still lived here at that time certainly believed it had. As mentioned previously, they took great pleasure in loosing arrows at the creature as they passed on the river and later would fire their rifles at it also.

In July 1836, a Professor John Russell discovered something very unusual concerning the legend of the Piasa Bird. Russell was a professor at Shurtleff College in Alton and had interest enough in the local legend to do a little exploring and research into the story of the creature. His adventures were later recounted in a magazine article in 1848 and in *Records of Ancient Races in the Mississippi Valley* by William McAdams in 1887. Here is how his story appears, written in his own words:

Near the close of March of the present year, I was induced to visit the bluffs below the mouth of the Illinois River, above that of the Piasa. My curiosity was principally directed to the examination of a cave, connected with the above tradition as one of those to which the bird had carried his human victims.

Preceded by an intelligent guide, who carried a spade, I set out on my excursion. The cave was extremely difficult of access, and at one point in our progress I stood at an elevation of one hundred fifty feet on the perpendicular face of the bluff, with barely room to sustain one foot. The unbroken wall towered above me, while below me was the river.

After a long and perilous climb, we reached the cave, which was about fifty feet above the surface of the river....The roof of the cavern was vaulted, and the top was hardly less than twenty feet high. The shape of the cavern was irregular; but, so far as I could judge, the bottom would average twenty by thirty feet.

The floor of the cavern throughout its whole extent was one mass of human bones. Skulls and other bones were mingled in the utmost confusion. To what depth they extended I was unable to decide; but we dug to a depth of 3 or 4 feet in every part of the cavern, and still we found only bones. The remains of thousands must have been deposited here. How, and by whom, and for what purpose, it is impossible to conjecture.

Was this cave really the lair of the Piasa Bird? Did this bird, always thought to be merely a mythological creature, actually exist? Did the monster really carry off and slay a large number of the Native Americans who once lived in this region? Could such a giant bird actually exist?

As a simple answer to a number of complex questions -- no one really knows. The mystery of the Piasa Bird remains unsolved and while many have gone in search of this elusive cave over the years, none have yet been able to find it. This is not as strange as you might think though. There are many remote areas in this immediate region, overgrown by forests, lost among the bluffs and simply forgotten. Homes, buildings, churches and cemeteries have all just been abandoned by time and so it's very possible that the same thing could happen with natural formations like caves, hundreds of which are scattered through the bluffs along the river. I have talked to witnesses who have entered caves with Indian drawings on the wall, untouched for generations, and even talked to a man who recalls seeing an ancient rendition of the Piasa above the Illinois River beyond Grafton, Illinois. This petroglyph has proven to be as elusive as the bone cave of the Piasa Bird. But the search goes on ...

Alton, Illinois is located just across the Mississippi River and northeast of St. Louis. Nearby is the confluence of the Mississippi, Missouri and the Illinois Rivers. The modern rendition of the Piasa Bird can be found just outside of town along the Great River Road, traveling upriver toward Grafton. The location of the Piasa Mystery Cave remains unknown.

II. HAUNTED TUNNELS

Many years ago, when Americans began building transportation routes across the country, they often learned that it was sometimes easier to simply go through a mountain then to go over or around it. Because of this, many highway and railroad tunnels were constructed, often at great expense both financially -- and with loss of life. For this reason, it's no surprise that a number of these tunnels are reportedly haunted. It was not uncommon for many men to die as the tunnels were constructed and for even more of them to die while inspecting and maintaining these passages over the years. Tunnels are dark, wet, dangerous places that are often the scene of great tragedy -- the perfect conditions for supernatural legends to emerge and for paranormal encounters to take place.

GHOSTS OF THE BLOODY PIT
Hauntings at Massachusetts' Hoosac Tunnel

The rugged lands of western Massachusetts are somewhat dominated by the beautiful and remote Berkshire Hills. They are part of a land that has been haunted for centuries and ghost stories are commonplace here. Many tales are told of spirits in the forest, calling voices that have no source and of those who have wandered into the woods, never to return again. Of all of these stories though, perhaps the most chilling is the tale of the Hoosac Tunnel near North Adams in the Deerfield Valley.

The tunnel was one of the greatest undertakings of the region. Work was started on it in 1851 but it was not finished for almost 25 years. During that period, hundreds of miners, using mostly black powder, shovels, picks and their own hands, fought against the unyielding rock of Hoosac Mountain. By the time the tunnel was finally finished, more than 200 men had died in what came to be known as the "Bloody Pit". They died in fires, explosions, tunnel collapses and in one case, by the hand of another. It would be the cold-blooded murder that occurred in 1865 that would give the tunnel its reputation for being haunted.

It was during that year that the explosive known as nitroglycerin was introduced to America. The construction crew of the Hoosac Tunnel would have the honor of being among the first crews to use it. On the afternoon of March 20,

1865, three explosive experts named Ned Brinkman, Billy Nash and Ringo Kelley decided to use nitro to continue their work on the tunnel. They placed a charge and then ran back toward a safety bunker that would shield them from the effects of the blast. Brinkman and Nash never made it there however. For some reason, Ringo Kelley set off the charge before the other men could make it to shelter. The two men were buried alive under tons of rock.

Soon after the accident, Kelley vanished without a trace, leading many to believe that the "accident" with the nitro may not have been an accident after all. He was not seen again until March 30, 1866 -- when his body was discovered two miles inside of the tunnel. It was found at almost the exact spot where Brinkman and Nash had been killed. The authorities quickly deduced that Kelley had been strangled to death. Deputy Sheriff Charles F. Gibson estimated that he had been murdered between midnight and 3:30 that morning. The death was thoroughly investigated but no suspects were ever found and the crime went unsolved.

And while the authorities determined that no killer could be found, the construction workers had their own ideas about who had killed Ringo Kelley. According to the rumors and whispers, they believed that Kelley had been killed by the vengeful spirits of Brinkman and Nash. They came to feel that the tunnel was cursed and many of them refused to enter it again. Some of the crew members walked off the job and did not return. The dark and brooding place, with the deep shadows and dripping water, became known as a shunned one. It was best avoided most believed, slowing the construction of the tunnel down even more.

In 1868, the construction site was toured by Paul Travers, a mechanical engineer and a respected cavalry officer during the Civil War. He had received a letter from a Mr. Dunn of the construction company, who had asked him to come and examine the tunnel. Apparently, the workers "complained constantly of hearing a man's voice cry out in agony" and needless to say, refused to enter the half-completed tunnel after sundown. Dunn was convinced that the strange sounds were nothing more than winds sweeping off the mountainside but despite his assurances, work had slowed down so drastically that he had contacted Paul Travers to investigate the matter.

Travers and Dunn went out to the site on September 8 and the former military officer did not soon forget when he encountered there. He later wrote a letter to his sister and told her about the weird experience:

> Dunn and I entered the tunnel at exactly 9:00 p.m. We traveled about two miles into the shaft and then we stopped to listen. As we stood there in the cold silence, we both heard what truly sounded like a man groaning out in pain. As you know, I have heard this same sound many times during the war. Yet, when we turned up the wicks on our lamps, there were no other human beings in the shaft except Mr. Dunn and

myself. I'll admit I haven't been this frightened since Shiloh. Mr. Dunn agreed that it wasn't the wind we heard. Perhaps Nash and Brinkman.... I wonder?

A month after Travers' investigation, on October 17, the worst disaster to occur in the tunnel's history took place. A gas explosion blew apart the water pumping station on the surface and 13 men were killed when debris filled the central tunnel where they had been working. A reporter for the *North Adams Transcript* wrote that a worker named Mallery was lowered in a bucket into the shaft. He was told to look for any sign of survivors. He was brought back to the surface a few minutes later, nearly unconscious from the fumes inside. "No hope...." he managed to gasp out to the rescue team.

Without the pumping station, the 538-foot shaft filled with water. The bodies of some of the dead crew members grotesquely began to surface. More than a year after the disaster, the last of them were found. The missing men and the macabre discovery of the bodies created stories and legends in the surrounding area.

Glenn Drohan, the correspondent who had first written about the accident for the *Transcript* wrote:

During the time the miners were missing, villagers told strange tales of vague shapes and muffled wails near the water-filled pit. Workmen claimed to see the lost miners carrying picks and shovels through a shroud of mist and snow on the mountaintop. The ghostly apparitions would appear briefly, and then vanish, leaving no footprints in the snow, giving no answer to the miner's calls.

As soon as the last of the bodies were found and given a decent burial though, Drohan stated, the bizarre visitations ceased. These dead men had apparently found rest but some of the victims of the "Bloody Pit" had not. Even after the apparitions stopped appearing, the eerie moaning in the tunnel continued and the men remained terrified.

Based on the account of a Dr. Clifford J. Owen, the haunting also began to take on other characteristics as well. Owens came to the tunnel on a night in June 1872 and was accompanied by James R. McKinstrey, a drilling operations superintendent. There is no information to suggest why the two men came to the tunnel on the last night of June 25, but one might guess that it was in search of the ghosts who allegedly haunted the shaft. If this was the purpose of their trip, then the journey was apparently a successful one!

The two men traveled about two miles into the tunnel and then halted to rest. There was no light in the shaft, save for their dim lamps, and Owens later described the tunnel as being "as cold and as dark as a tomb." The two of them stood there talking for a few minutes and then they heard a strange and mournful sound. It sounded to Owens like someone in great pain.

He then goes on to write:

The next thing I saw was a dim light coming along the tunnel in a westerly direction. At first, I believed that it was probably a workman with a lantern. Yet, as the light grew closer, it took on a strange blue color and appeared to change in shape into the form of a human being with no head."

The light moved closer to the two men and was so close that they could almost touch it. It remained motionless, as though watching them then hovered off toward the east end of the tunnel and vanished. Owens and McKinstrey were understandably stunned and Owens later wrote that while he was "above all a realist" and that he was not "prone to repeating gossip and wild tales that defy a reasonable explanation" he was unable to "deny what James McKinstrey and I witnessed with our own eyes.

Strangeness continued at the Hoosac Tunnel both shortly before and after it opened to admit trains to pass through it. On October 16, 1874 a local hunter named Frank Webster vanished near Hoosac Mountain. Three days later, he was found by a search party, stumbling along the banks of the Deerfield River. He was in a state of shock, mumbling incoherently and falling down. He explained to his rescuers that strange voices had ordered him into the Hoosac Tunnel and once he was inside, he saw ghostly figures wandering around. He also said that invisible hands had snatched his hunting rifle away from him and that he had been beaten with it. He couldn't remember leaving the tunnel. Members of the search party recalled that Webster did not have his rifle when he was found and the cuts and abrasions on his head and body did seem to bear evidence of a beating.

Later that same year, with the tunnel headings completed, workmen removed rocks from the tunnel and began grading the line and laying track. On February 9, 1875, the first train went through the tunnel, pulling three flatcars and a boxcar. A group of 125 people had come along for the ride. According to the news stories about the event, North Adams had just become the "Western Gateway" to the rest of New England. But this was not enough to stop the strange stories from being told.

In the fall of 1875, a fire tender on the Boston & Maine rail line worker named Harlan Mulvaney was taking a wagon load of wood into the tunnel. He had gone just a short distance into the shaft when he suddenly turned his team around, whipped the horses and drove them madly out of the tunnel. A few days later, workers found the team and the wagon in the forest about three miles away from the tunnel. Harlan Mulvaney was never seen or heard from again!

The stories continued for years, creating believers from those who worked there, passed through or spent much time about the tunnel. One former railroad employee, Joseph Impoco, worked the Boston & Maine for years. He firmly believed that the tunnel was haunted but he was not afraid of the place. In fact, he credited the resident ghosts with saving his life on two separate occasions. On one afternoon, he was shipping away ice from the tracks when he heard a distinct voice telling him to "run, Joe, run!"

He looked back and saw a train bearing down on him! "Sure enough, there was No. 60 coming at me. Boy, did I jump back fast!" He looked around for whoever had called out his name, but there was no one else nearby. Later, he would recall that he had distinctly heard the voice before the train had appeared. He also added that he had seen a man pass by, waving and swinging a torch, but he hadn't paid attention to anything but the shout. The voice, wherever it had come from, had saved his life.

Six weeks after the incident, Impoco was again working on the tracks. This time, he was using a heavy iron crow bar to free some freight cars that had been frozen on the tracks. He was prying at one of the steel wheels when he heard the loud, familiar voice again call out to him. "Joe! Joe! Drop it, Joe!" the voice called frantically. Impoco immediately released the bar and it was instantly jolted and thrown against the tunnel wall by more than 11,000 volts of electricity! The charge came from a short-circuited overhead power line. The unseen friend had saved Joe's life again.

A short time later, Impoco left his job and began working out of the area. Every year though, he would return to the Hoosac Tunnel and pay a sort of "homage" to the ghost who saved his life. He was certain that if he failed to do this one year, some tragedy would befall him. In 1977, Impoco's wife was ill and rather than go to visit the tunnel, he stayed home with her. In October of that year, she died. Joe believed that her death was connected to his failure to journey to the Hoosac Tunnel.

Throughout the 1970's and the 1980's, the tunnel began to be investigated by ghost hunters and paranormal groups who had heard of the long history of hauntings. In 1976, a researcher from Agawam, Massachusetts claimed to come face-to-face with one of the local denizens. He described the figure of a man in old-fashioned work clothing, backlit against a brilliant white light. Could it have been the same ghost seen by Owens and McKinstrey in 1872?

A professor and part-time ghost hunter named Ali Allmaker had what she felt was a close encounter in the tunnel. She wrote that she was accompanied to the tunnel by a railroad official in 1984 and while there, had the uncomfortable sensation of someone standing close to her. She also stated that several students from North Adams State College visited the tunnel one night and left a tape recorder running in the shaft. They left it there and when they returned and listened to the tape, they heard what seemed to be muffled human voices on the tape.

The stories about the "Bloody Pit" still continue to be told today. Locals in the area still claim that strange winds, ghostly apparitions and eerie voices are experienced around and in the daunting tunnel. Visitors who journey to this site today however risk becoming one of the resident ghosts themselves. The Boston & Maine Railroad still runs nearly a dozen freight trains through the tunnel each day, making this a trip that is definitely on the dangerous side! If you're interested in the historical aspects of the tunnel though, you can visit a museum that is dedicated to the site in the Western Gateway Heritage State Park.

But if you are interested in the ghosts, I recommend that you tread lightly here. The spirits of the past are still reported to linger and dark shadows press tightly on every side. Perhaps the Mohawk Indians were right. They named this place Hoosac Mountain, which in their language means "forbidden". Did they know something about this place that the builders of the tunnel did not?

The Hoosac Tunnel is located in Franklin County in northwestern Massachusetts. The tunnel is 22 miles west of Greenfield off Highway 2 and just northeast of the town of Florida. The tunnel is a very unsafe place to visit, thanks to its length and the heavy train traffic that uses it.

THE COWEE TUNNEL
Near Dillsboro, North Carolina

In the middle 1850's, the Western North Carolina Railroad began making its way westward from Salisbury, North Carolina toward Asheville, which it reached more than 25 years later. The progress of the railroad was slowed by the years of the Civil War, Reconstruction and by complications created by trying to build a rail line over the western mountains of the state.

The Western North Carolina pushed on past Asheville and continued west until it reached the present site of Dillsboro in the early 1880's. Plans were made to continue on to Bryson City but a hairpin turn in the Tuckasegee River stood in the way and so the railroad decided to bypass the turn with a tunnel. As workers were hard to find for such dangerous work, the state provided most of the labor using convicts from the prisons. The prisoners were moved back and forth along the line and were housed in camps near where the line was being built.

The new tunnel, called the Cowee Tunnel, was located across the river from the convict encampment and each day, the men were chained into work gangs and then ferried across the river to the work site on an old flatboat. One winter day in 1883, the river was running fast and as a gang of 20 men was being ferried across, the boat capsized and plunged the men into the freezing water. Still chained together with heavy ankle irons, they struggled in the water for only a few moments before sinking into the dark depths. Only one of the men managed to survive. The other 19 were buried on a hillside above the river.

After such a terrifying and traumatic death, is it any wonder that their ghosts are believed to remain behind here?

Eventually, the Western North Carolina Railroad was swallowed up by Norfolk Southern, which saw the decline of the great railroads as automobile and truck traffic increased in later years. By 1988, the company planned to abandon about 67 miles of track between Dillsboro and Murphy, including the stretch where the Cowee Tunnel is located. Recognizing the opportunity for tourism, the state purchased 53 miles of the line and leased it to the Great Smoky Mountains Railroad, a group committed to the historic preservation of the railways. They began organizing not only a transportation line for area communities but also an excursion line to for tourists. The route from Dillsboro to Bryson City passes through the Cowee Tunnel and also passes the site of the staged train wreck from the 1993 Harrison Ford film *The Fugitive*.

The breathtaking scenery vanishes into darkness though as the train enters the historic and infamous tunnel. It is here, according to the legends, that the ghosts of the dead convicts are said to manifest. According to the stories, as well as tourists and maintenance crews on the railroad, the cries of the men echo here in the tunnel -- still calling out from a distant time.

The Cowee Tunnel is located along the Great Smoky Mountain Railroad line. The main office for the railroad is located in Dillsboro and excursion trips can be booked through the office. No one is allowed in the tunnel outside of the excursion trains.

BIG TUNNEL
Between Fort Ritner & Tunnelton, Indiana

Indiana's Big Tunnel seems to be haunted by a bewildering array of ghosts. The renowned Big Tunnel is located along the former Ohio & Mississippi line between Fort Ritner and Tunnelton, Indiana. Once the route to St. Louis, the line curves through what is likely the roughest and most remote section of the state. The railroad was started in 1856 and followed close along the White River, taking advantage of the river valley to pass through the steep hills and ridges in the area. The railroad made the decision to tunnel through over a mile of solid rock to finish the line, saving about eight miles of track. The resulting tunnel was a 1750 foot-long, man made cave that was appropriately dubbed the Big Tunnel. The passageway is not only long but it also curves through the middle stretch, making it impossible to peer into one end of the tunnel and see light from the other.

Thanks to its eerie atmosphere, the tunnel has become a favorite spot for teenagers to visit, which is mentioned by author Linda Degh in her book *Indiana Folklore*. She writes:

The entrance dwarfs its visitors. Its total blackness makes the night seem light by comparison. The teenagers -- sometimes with hands joined --

walk into the tunnel and feel their way along the right wall... The air is chill and damp; the darkness is so complete that vision seems to fail; the walls amplify even the slightest sound of dripping water as it echoes in the Tunnel.

These same teenagers have unfortunately left their marks behind on the tunnel walls of today with slogans and crude pictures and have littered the area with bottles and cans. This has not stopped the stories from being spread though (and perhaps has encouraged them) about those who sometimes feel an unseen hand settling on their shoulder in the darkest spots of the tunnel.

But it was not always such a forbidding place. The first train to pass through the Big Tunnel left Fort Ritner with great ceremony on October 6, 1856 and included a flat car carrying several young ladies in fine, white dresses. It was a memorable inaugural run but was not without incident, as the train engine stalled in the depths of the tunnel and had to be pulled out by mules. It was necessary for the passengers to make their way out on foot and the soot from the engine stack had ruined their fine clothing. This did not dampen their enthusiasm however and locals reportedly crowded the entrance for many days after to watch the trains pass through.

The most popular legend of the Big Tunnel is that of a ghostly railroad watchman who was killed by a train in the tunnel. Other stories insist that he was murdered in the passageway, often claiming that his lifeless body was hung on a metal hook, or spike, in the center of the tunnel. To touch that hook, according to the breathless teenagers who venture here, is said to bring bad luck.

The murdered watchman is said to appear as a misty form or a shadowy figure who manifests in the distance. Often, he is only identified by the sound of a low moaning cry. Others report seeing the gleam of an old kerosene lantern as it moves along the tunnel tracks and then vanishes. Some versions of the legend say that the ghost only appears on rainy nights.

Most longtime residents of the area say that the ghost is that of a man named Henry Dixon, who was said to have been murdered in the tunnel by some local men in the early 1900's. The murder was a revenge killing, committed a few days after Dixon stopped the men from raping a young girl in the tunnel.

It is interesting to see how history actually mirrors the legend in this case. From 1857 until 1908, the tunnel really was patrolled by a watchman. At that time, the walls of the tunnel were bare rock and the railroad soon learned that passage of a train through the narrow tunnel could shake portions of the rock loose, causing them to fall down on the tracks. Watchmen were hired to patrol the tunnel line, walking the rails after each train passed through to make sure that no rocks had fallen from the walls or the ceiling. He would then signal the next approaching train to let them know if the way was clear or not. After the tunnel was enlarged and lined with brick in 1908, the watchmen were discharged because they were no longer needed.

At just about this same time, as the brick lining was nearly finished, a man named Henry Dixon really was found murdered in the tunnel. He was not a watchman however but a local man who had been killed. His body has apparently been placed on the tracks in hopes that an oncoming train would erase the evidence of the crime. Apparently it did, for it has been reported that almost everyone who lived in the area knew who killed Henry Dixon -- but no one could prove it. The crime was never solved, leading many to believe that this may be why his ghost still walks.

But this is not the only haunt to explain the mysterious happenings in the Big Tunnel.

Other legends here tell of mass murders (which incidentally have no basis in truth) and involve murdered prison convicts. The legend has it that a rebuilding project took place here at one time, using prison labor. They allegedly tried to escape and were shot and killed, then buried beneath the tunnel floor. The stories go on to say that the convict's screams are still heard as you walk through the tunnel today. Other mass murder legends also tell of Confederate soldiers or robbers who were also killed in or close to the tunnel. Their ghosts are alleged to walk here as well.

But regardless of who haunts the tunnel, the legends and first hand accounts maintain that someone does --- insuring that few dark passageways of this nature are as haunted as the Big Tunnel.

Tunnelton and Fort Ritner are located in south Central Indiana, between Bedford and Seymour. Just west of the Hoosier National Forest, this is a rural area and near several state forest, caves and recreational areas. The Big Tunnel is located about three miles southeast of Tunnelton on River Road. And while not as many trains pass through the tunnel today as in years past -- it is just as long and dark as it was when it was built back in 1856.

THE MOONVILLE TUNNEL
Near Lake Hope State Park, Ohio

From the McArthur, Ohio *Democrat* Newspaper (March 31, 1889):

"A brakesman on the Marietta & Cincinnati Railroad fell from the cars near Cincinnati Furnace, on last Tuesday March 29, 1859 and was fatally injured, when the wheels passing over and grinding to a shapeless mass the greater part of one of his legs. He was taken on the train to Hamden and Doctors Wolf and Rannells sent for to perform amputation, but the prostration of the vital energies was too great to attempt it. The man is probably dead ere this. The accident resulted from a too free use of liquor."

Southeastern Ohio is a place of many haunts and numerous ghostly legends, from the spirit-infested graveyards of Athens to the long-ago legends of the Koons family of Athens County and their renowned "Spirit Room". Not far from Athens, and just over the line in Vinton, County is a place that has been lost to history. It was once called Moonville, a village that came into existence thanks to the rich coal deposits of the region and the building of the Marietta & Cincinnati Railroad.

Moonville was never much of a town and probably boasted no more than 50 or 60 residents during its heyday in the 1870's. The early residents worked mostly for the Hope Furnace, where weapons and artillery were made during the Civil War, and then later turned almost exclusively to coal mining. Only a handful of buildings ever stood in town, surrounded by the homes of the miners and their families, and included a school house, a rail depot, a general store, a post office, a sawmill along Raccoon Creek and several saloons that could be reached by walking along the railroad tracks. In 1883, the railroad was taken over by the Baltimore & Ohio line and was abandoned by CSX in 1986. Moonville never even lasted that long -- the small town died out in the 1930's. The last occupant left Moonville in 1947 and by the 1960's; almost all of the buildings were gone. Today, only the foundation of the school house and the old Moonville Cemetery remain to show that it ever existed at all.

Just east of town, beyond the large trestle over Raccoon Creek, was the Moonville Tunnel. It was a short passage through a ridge of limestone that had a brick portal on each end that had been remodeled by the B & O Railroad's chief engineer J.M. Graham in 1903. The tunnel is only about 50 yards long and has a slight curve to it. To save money during the original construction of the line, the tunnel was very narrow and offered very little space on either side of any passing train. Thanks to the high speed at which the trains passed through the tunnel, anyone caught inside could easily be killed.

Also dangerous was the trestle that stood between the tunnel and the site of Moonville. The trestle was just wide enough for a train to cross and anyone caught walking across it when a train was approaching had the choice of either being struck by the train or leaping to what would almost be a certain death in the shallow water below. Most panicked and were tragically killed and at least five people lost their lives between 1850 and 1920 to either the tunnel or the trestle. Ironically, the last person killed was a young girl who was struck by a train in 1986, just two months before CSX abandoned the line.

There have been many stories told about ghosts at Moonville, including that of a brakeman who swings a lantern to signal trains and that of a woman who walks along the tracks at night. The stories say that she was killed while crossing over the trestle one night on the way to visit her lover. As there were several people killed in this manner, she could have been one of these. Or she could have been a woman who was walking home along the tracks from the town of Mineral (about 10 miles away) when she was killed by an oncoming train. Regardless of who she was, her ghost has been reported many times over the years near the Moonville Tunnel.

A few years after CSX abandoned the rail line, the tracks were pulled and a roadbed was left that has long been used by hikers. According to one account, two hikers were camping along the roadbed at night when they saw something white pass by the front of their tent. They looked out to see who was there and saw the figure of a woman in period clothing drift by. She made no sound and was clearly not solid. When one of the hikers shouted to her, she turned for a moment in their direction but continued walking. A few moments later, she reached a bend in the path and vanished from sight. The hikers quickly packed up their gear and went off in another direction.

More famous than the spectral woman though is the phantom brakeman. This is a story that actually does have a basis in fact (see the newspaper article at the beginning of this section) but has been changed many times in the telling and re-telling of the story over the years. There really was a railroad worker who was killed in this area years before -- and his ghost was subsequently reported and documented -- however, many variations of the eerie tale exist.

Some say the brakeman, who stopped trains by signaling them with a lantern, was having an affair with the wife of an engineer and that he was killed in revenge while the train was stopped one night. The cuckolded engineer asked the brakeman to check something between the cars and then moved the train forward, cutting off the luckless man's head. Another version has it that the railroad man was drunk one night and decided to ride the train while hanging on the side of a boxcar. He was decapitated while passing through the Moonville Tunnel. In both cases, the man's head was never found, which would explain why his lantern is still being seen --- he is searching for his missing head.

As most readers are likely aware, decapitation stories are often part of the local lore when it comes to explaining instances of ghost lights or phantom lanterns. In those cases, like this one, they have little to do with the truth.

There are other stories as well and perhaps the most popular is the story that claims the ghost is that of a man who was struck and killed by a train while trying to summon help for the people of Moonville. This version of the story recalls a time when an epidemic swept through Moonville and caused so many people to become sick that the residents began to run out of supplies, medicine and food. The man decided to go for help by walking up the rail line and was accidentally stuck and killed by a train. According to the legend, this marked the end of Moonville -- but unfortunately, this story is not true either.

The closest version to the true story that can be found has it that a group of miners and railroad men were drinking and playing cards in a house near the tracks one night and one of the men decided to leave the game and walk along the tracks. He was quite drunk and did not notice that a train was approaching until he got into the tunnel. When he heard the roaring sounds of the engine closing in on him, he began to frantically swing his lantern, hoping that the train would stop. Unfortunately, though he was hit and killed. He was buried in the Moonville Cemetery and his ghost has been seen ever since.

And while this is the closest story to the death that actually occurred here, it is still not entirely accurate. According to the newspaper account, a brakeman did die but only because he was drunk and fell of the train somewhere in the vicinity. The only clue that we have as to the exact location is that it was along this particular rail line and somewhere close to the Hope Furnace. As the phantom and his light have been appearing at Moonville for nearly a century and a half, this seems to be the most likely spot for his death.

Older accounts seem to agree with this. A report appeared in the Chillicothe, Ohio *Gazette* on February 17, 1895:

> *The ghost of Moonville, after an absence of one year, has returned and is again at its old pranks, haunting B & O S-W freight trains and their crews. It appeared Monday night in front of fast freight No. 99 west bound, just eat of the cut which is one half mile the other side of Moonville at the point where Engineer Lawhead lost his life and Engineer Walters was injured. The ghost, attired in a pure white robe, carried a lantern. It had a flowing white beard, its eyes glistened like balls of fire and surrounding it was a halo of twinkling stars. When the train stopped, the ghost stepped off the track and disappeared into the rocks nearby.*

Sightings continued long after Moonville vanished from history and still continue today. A number of people have claimed to see a dark figure with a light, lingering at the entrance to the tunnel and others say that he appears after they have passed through and have turned to look behind them. In one account, a boy who was playing near the tunnel when the railroad was still in operation was actually saved by the ghost. As he was walking into the tunnel entrance, the ghost materialized in front of him and let out an unearthly cry. The boy turned to run and just then, saw the lights of a train coming around the bend ahead of him. If he had walked into the tunnel, he would have been trapped in the middle as the train reached it. The ghost vanished and the boy did not return to Moonville.

A report from 1979 told of six teenagers who ventured out to the site of Moonville one night for some drinking and partying. As they got near the tunnel, one of them noticed a light that was following behind them. Their concern, thanks to the fact that they had been making a lot of noise and that a few of the drinkers were underage, was that the light was being carried by a sheriff's deputy who had been called out to the scene by someone living by. Two members of the group went back to speak with the officer while the others hurried on to the car. They did not hurry fast enough though -- for moments later, the two who had gone to talk to the deputy ran quickly past the others and outdistanced them back to the car!

When they asked what was wrong, the two insisted that no one had been carrying the light. The driver, who had not been drinking, was curious about this and he and another of the group went back to see what they were talking about. As they got closer, they saw that the light was not a flashlight at all, but rather a lantern. It was glowing but did not seem to be giving off any light. As they got closer though, they could make out the dim outline of the lantern itself. Suddenly, the light stopped moving away from them and began to slowly swing back and forth in place. They could now see that it was not being held by any human hands! Needless to say, both of the young men ran quickly in the other direction and never looked back.

Today, the Moonville Tunnel still stands silent and empty -- during the daytime at least -- and visitors still come here in search of forgotten history and of course, in search of ghosts. It is an eerie place and one where time seems to stand still. Should you get a chance to visit here, keep your eyes peeled for not only mysterious lights but for open mine shafts as well. The land around the old town site can be treacherous --- and perhaps, based on past accounts, eerily unnerving as well.

The former site of Moonville is best reached from Route 33, which runs between Columbus and Athens. Along this route is the small town of Nelsonville. Here. You will find Route 278, which runs south. There are signs here leading to Lake Hope State Park. Stay on Route 278 and follow it past Lake Hope. The first road on the left is Wheelabout Road. Turn onto this road and stay on it until it turns into a gravel drive. It will pass through the woods and will eventually come to a one-lane bridge. Immediately after the bridge, the former train bed will cross the road. Park here and follow the roadbed to the left. You will have to cross Raccoon Creek and the tunnel is just on the other side of it. My best advice is to find a map of the area to help with the trip -- this is a remote area and the site is not easy to find.

BIG BEND TUNNEL
Near Hinton, West Virginia

Of all of the haunted tunnels and mysterious passageways that plague the hills and mountains of America, only one of them is haunted by an actual legend. His name was John Henry, the renowned "Steel Driving Man", and according to the story he took part in a duel to the death with a steam drill during the heyday of the railroad. The legend states that this contest took place in the old Chesapeake & Ohio Railroad tunnel under Big Bend Mountain. It was here that John Henry worked and died -- and where his ghost still remains.

The tunnel was built after the C & O decided to construct a rail line from Covington, Virginia to the Ohio River at Guyandotte, West Virginia. Work was started in 1870 and completed three years later and unbelievably, given the rough terrain of the region, ahead of schedule. One of the biggest obstacles along the route was Big Bend Mountain. The designers of the rail line had followed river valleys for most of the route but Big Bend Mountain forced the Greenbrier River to make a ten-mile obstacle around its base. For this reason, the C & O decided to tunnel through the mountain. One of the men hired to work on this tunnel was a large and powerful man named John Henry.

Railroad work in general, and digging tunnels in particular, was difficult, back-breaking work and since this region was a remote wilderness in 1870, much of the labor had to be brought in from other areas. Thanks to the fact that the work was hard and dangerous, and the pay low, the easiest source of labor for the railroad was from the large number of recently freed slaves, who had trouble getting any sort of decent work. Huge numbers of freedmen were brought in to build the tunnel -- and many of them died here.

The Big Bend Tunnel claimed many lives, perhaps as many as one out of ten who worked here. The tunnel was being driven through wet, red shale, which tended to collapse when it dried. In addition, blasting accidents, wall collapses and just plain overwork took a toll as well.

The attitude toward the black workers who were brought in was harsh, much as the attitude toward the Chinese and Irish immigrants would be as the railroads were built in the western states. Often when a black worker was killed in an accident, his death would not be reported for fear of alarming the other workers. The bodies of those who died were treated poorly too. Many of them were simply buried beneath the rubble at the eastern end of the tunnel or taken to Richmond Penitentiary and buried in a common grave. Working conditions were bad here for everyone but the black laborers had it worse than the rest.

Then, according to the legend, along came John Henry. And while there are many questions as to who exactly John Henry was, or even if he existed at all, the stories say that he was a massive black man who stood over six feet-tall and weighed well over 200 pounds. Some say that he was an ex-slave, some day that he came from Jamaica and others insist that he showed up to work one day with no history at all. The Chesapeake & Ohio Railroad has no record to say that a man named John Henry ever worked for them but they do say that employment records from this period were lost in a fire many years ago.

There are many who insist that John Henry was nothing more than a folk story, like Paul Bunyan or Pecos Bill, and that he merely served as a fable about man versus a machine. What makes John Henry different though is that the feats that he was alleged to have carried out were actually possible, unlike Paul Bunyan, who created the Mississippi River by dragging his ax and made the lakes of Minnesota with heavy boot prints. John Henry is more like the legend of Johnny Appleseed, a real, albeit somewhat mysterious person, who entered the realm of legend many years ago. To make matters more convincing, there were those who claimed to have actually known John Henry, to worked and to have talked with him. He was a real person, these men said, who did indeed do battle with a steam drill.

For those not aware of the story, John Henry was a driver. In those days, tunnels were created out of the mountain using explosives and drivers would hammer steel bits into the rock for the placement of the charges. Men called turners would loosen the bits and turn them, while other men would collect the dull bits and sharpen them again, keeping a fresh supply of bits on hand. Good drivers were held in high esteem by the workers, not matter what their color. They would often hold contests to see who could drive the bits the farthest and who could pound the greatest number of them in the shortest amount of time.

John Henry was considered to be the greatest driver that ever lived and was held in great regard by the other men. It was said that he could swing two large hammers on separate bits at the same time. The stories recalled that he would keep a steady rhythm going all of the time and would often sing in time with the ringing of steel on steel.

On day, the railroad decided to test a steam-powered drill at the tunnel construction site. The supervisors believed that the drill could do the work of several drivers, making the men obsolete. The workers were alarmed and angry and so they arranged a contest between John Henry and his two hammers and the steam drill. The duel last for 35 minutes and at the end (according to one version of the story), John Henry managed to drive his steel bit 15 feet into the mountain, while the steam drill only managed to drive one down just nine. Sadly though, John Henry was so exhausted by his victory that he laid down his hammer -- and he died. Or did he? Some say that Henry died of a stroke caused by his exertions, that he was killed in a tunnel explosion or that he died from a fever after working himself to death.

But no matter what the circumstance, the final result was that John Henry died shortly after his spectacular contest. Soon after, workers began to refuse to go into the tunnel because they claimed they could hear the musical banging of John's hammers in the darkness. A foreman insisted that the sound was nothing more than water dripping from the ceiling but no one believed him. Eventually though, they all returned to work -- but the stories persisted.

A documented account from 1876 stated that a bricklayer named Alfred Owens was working in the Big Bend Tunnel one day, trying to prevent dry slate from falling on the tracks. He was hard at work when he was startled by the sound of a hammer clanging on steel. Owens looked up quickly towards the tunnel entrance and saw a huge, shadowy figure swinging a hammer in each hand. In a panic, the bricklayer scrambled to get away from the specter and as he did so, he tumbled to the floor of the tunnel. When he looked up, the looming figure was gone.

Over the years, the belief that John Henry's ghost still haunts the old Big Bend Tunnel has remained strong, especially among the black families in the area. In 1932, a new tunnel with larger clearances was dug through the mountain next to the original and traffic through the old tunnel died out considerably. It was finally replaced altogether, and its rails removed, in 1974. Strange stories persisted though and while the floor of the number 3 shaft was being covered with concrete, workers claimed to discover an old hammer and a drill bit on the tunnel floor. Believing that they belonged to John Henry, the men refused to disturb them. They remain in place today, secure under the concrete floor.

And the tales continue even now. Whether he is the legendary John Henry or not, a steel driving ghost is said to walk through the shadows of the old tunnel. For those who visit here, it is not hard to believe the place is haunted. Deep in the murkiness and the gloom, even the most hardened skeptic would not be too surprised to hear the rhythmic clang of steel. The Big Bend Tunnel was once a place of tragedy, despair and death --- and a place where the dead still walk.

Big Bend Mountain is a little distance west of Talcott, West Virginia, in the southeast corner of the state. There is statue of John Henry that stands in Talcott. To reach the tunnel, turn onto CR-17 in Talcott and then turn onto a gravel road that parallels Route 3. The two tunnels are visible ahead. Trains still use the newer tunnel, so do not enter it. The original tunnel, on the right, is in dangerous disrepair and should only be entered with great caution unless posted.

III. HAUNTED MINES & MINING CAMPS

There have been a number of different ores and precious metals mined in America over the years and numerous strange occurrences have occurred in the mines that were created to see them -- as you will see in the pages to follow. Underground mining has always been one of the most dangerous professions in history and has been plagued with a staggering loss of life. And is it any wonder?

Almost all industrial work was dangerous in years past but none of it was as dangerous as mining. By the 1860's, some anthracite coal mines in Pennsylvania had reached depths of more than 1,500 feet, using techniques that are now considered unbelievably primitive. The problems came with the sinking of such shafts, largely due to the fact that there were few Americans with the expertise needed for deep mining. There were no professional engineers at that time and so coal mine owners depended on skilled miners from England, Scotland and Wales for assistance. These men had a practical knowledge of mining and helped to construct the deep mines. Even with this knowledge though, there remained a number of problems with working so deeply underground, including methods to drain water out of the mine and also to a system to ventilate the mine and provide fresh air for the miners. A particular problem to coal mines was the methane gas that sometimes accompanied the coal and could (and often did) catch fire and explode.

These problems, along with falling rock, dangerous equipment, cave-ins, runaway mine cars and general accidents, posed a horrible threat to miners. Fires that broke out in the deep recesses would consume the available oxygen in the mine and even men who were not close to the fire could be suffocated and killed. This is exactly what happened at the Avondale Mine disaster in 1869, the greatest early industrial accident in history.

The Avondale Mine was located on the banks of the Susquehanna River, four miles from Plymouth, in the heart of the anthracite coal regions of Pennsylvania. The disaster occurred on the morning of September 6, 1869, the first day after a lengthy labor strike had come to an end. The mine opened early that morning and 110 men and young boys had gone into the shaft, determined to make up for the losses caused by the strike. Unknown to the men, a fire has started during the early morning hours when the ventilation fans had been turned on. A fire in the furnace caused some of the surrounding wooden braces to go up in flames and the fire quickly spread.

The blaze was discovered around 9:00 A.M. by the stable boss of the mine, who had gone down into the pit to bring a load of hay for the hauling mules. He immediately gave an alarm but moments later, a cloud of smoke, followed by a wall of flames, rose through the upcast compartment of the mine. The flames set fire to the engine house and the equipment at the top of the shaft, sending everyone into a panic and driving the engineer from his post. Because of the smoke and the intense heat at the mouth of the mine, there was no way to get to the miners trapped inside.

Dispatches were sent to all the neighboring cities and in a short time the fire departments of Wilkes-Barre, Scranton, Kingston, and adjoining towns, were on their way to the scene. The news of the accident spread quickly and thousands of people rushed to the burning mine, hoping to rescue the miners, but they were powerless against the searing heat.

The flames swept up and engulfed the immense wooden structures that covered and surrounded the mine shaft, sending flames hundreds of feet into the air. The great clouds of smoke from the fire could be seen for miles around. As the wooden buildings burned, the pulley wheels, chains and all matter of steel material that was spread through the engine house collapsed down into the mine, following by burning timbers and flaming debris.

As the fire engines began to arrive, they pumped a feeble stream of water onto the inferno but it did little to slow the spread of the flames. The fire continued to devour the buildings around the mine, raging on for several hours. By almost nightfall, the fire had been subdued and a band of 50 volunteers, made up of other miners, superintendents and firemen, offered to go down into the mine. They vowed to rescue the trapped miners --- or die trying to do so. The set off on their quest, but with the shaft choked for nearly 40 feet with fallen debris, darkness had come before they could gain entry into the mine itself.

A dog and a lamp were first let down as far as possible. They pulled them both back up and found that the dog was still alive and the lamp was still burning. An hour later, a miner was lowered down the shaft and he returned in a few minutes, nearly exhausted. It took a large group of men to move all of the charred timbers and ruined equipment out of the way so that passage could be gained by the rest. They opened a landing at the bottom and they advanced about 60 yards into the main gallery of the mine. Their boots echoed hollowly in the silent chamber, for no sounds came from within.

They soon made an unsettling discovery. The stables were now filled with dead animals. The mules that had been used for hauling in the mine were now lifeless on the floors of the stalls.

Just beyond the stables was the main door into the mine. Under normal conditions, the door would remain open and would direct forward a ventilating current of air. Now, it had been sealed shut. The rescue party, now starting to fall ill from the smoke and gases in the mine, began pounding on the door with a club and shouting as loud as they could to the men still trapped on the other side. They received no response and now, nearly overcome; they returned to the bottom of the shaft and were drawn back up to the surface.

A second rescue party had already been assembled and they went down into the mine, only to return a short time later, unable to withstand the gases. A large ventilating fan was put together at the surface and a canvas hose was dropped down into the shaft to provide fresh air. A third team was sent down and they penetrated deeper into the mine. They found that the ventilation furnace was still burning and that gases from the original fire were being ventilated into the rest of the mine. This fire had to be put out before the men could venture any deeper and so water was sent down from the surface to try and put the fire out. Unbelievably though, the hoses were too short and only a small amount of water could be applied to the blaze. Efforts continued throughout the night and by morning, the furnace fire had finally started to die out on its own accord.

During the second day, several attempts were made to reach the trapped miners but the accumulated gases prevented any extended search. By the early morning hours of the third day, the air had greatly improved and the another team entered the depths of the mine. Within two hours, they came upon two corpses, who could not be recognized because of their blackened and burned features. They were the only two bodies that were found to be burned, leading the search party to believe that they had been separated from the rest of the miners when the fire broke out.

A message was sent to the surface stating that two casualties had been discovered and several more bands of explorers descended into the mine to assist with the search. A few hours later, a search party that had entered the eastern tunnels of the mine discovered the entire work force of the mine, all huddled behind an embankment that had been erected to seal off the deadly gases from the fire.

All 108 of them were dead.

Fathers and sons were found clasped in one another's arms. Some of the dead were kneeling, as if in prayer, while others lay on the ground with their faces downwards, as though trying to extract a mouthful of fresh air from the floor of the mine. Some of the men sat holding hands with one another, afraid to face death alone, while others appeared to have fallen while still walking. Death had not come from the fire --- at least in that they had not been burned to death --- but from the sudden loss of oxygen caused by the fire. With no ventilation, and no alternate air course, the fresh oxygen in the mine had been sucked out and consumed by the flames. The gas from the fire had seeped into the mine where the fresh air had once been and killed everyone who came into contact with it.

Two hours after this grim discovery, sixty of the bodies had been taken to the surface and the last of the unfortunates followed a short time later.

Is it any wonder that old mines become haunted?

THE HANDPRINT
Carbon County Jail, Pennsylvania

Although not actually a haunted mine, there is one eerie story that is intimately associated with the history of coal mining in America and it begged for inclusion here.

As mentioned previously, coal mining was a brutal and often dangerous way of making a living. In the middle 1800's, the mines of eastern Pennsylvania were owned and managed by English and Welsh Protestants and labored in by mostly Irish Catholics. The two factions had hated one another for centuries and the conditions that existed between the lives of the mine owners and the laborers in American fostered the ill will between them. Working in the mines was physically hard but in addition to that, the Irishmen were forced to work long hours, faced frequent accidents and were taken advantage of by being paid in a scrip that was redeemable only at the company store. In addition, the owners required the mine workers to pay for their gear and supplies. Any men objecting to the low pay and hazardous conditions were fired. There was a desperate need for reform.

Beginning in 1842, there were unsuccessful attempts to unionize the miners. These attempts often led to riots, violence and sabotage and the union organizers became a secret society known as the "Molly Maguires". No one can say where the name of the society came from. Some say that "Molly Maguire" may have been the wife of a miner who died and this does seem possible. It should be noted that one of the "benefits" provided for the widow of a worker killed in a mine was that her husband's body would be delivered to her -- or rather unceremoniously dumped on the front porch of their company-owned house. She would be expected to move out of the house immediately after. One such widow might have been named Molly Maguire and those men who swore to protect her from the cruelty of the mine owners took her name for their secret society.

Others do not believe that the name was obtained for such a benevolent reason. Some historians believed the Molly Maguires may have been transported from Ireland under the guise of The Ancient Order of the Hibernians to continue their informal war against England in the United States. To what extent the Molly Maguires were unionists fighting against unfair treatment of miners, or whether they were Irish terrorists, will probably never be known. Regardless, blood flowed freely in eastern Pennsylvania until the Molly Maguires were destroyed and the unions were finally established.

The dismantling of the Molly Maguires began in 1869 when the Pinkerton Detective Agency was brought in to try and uncover the men behind the society.

Agency head Alan Pinkerton decided to plant one of his detectives, James McParlan, within the group to dig up information that could be used in criminal proceedings. He spent 44 months undercover and due largely to his efforts, 20 of their number were eventually charged and hanged. Whether the men were guilty or not, their trials were grossly unfair. Not only was all of the evidence collected and presented by the Pinkerton Agency, the representatives of the mine owners, but the judge maintained a pronounced bias against the Irish. The juries included only Protestants, excluded all Irish Catholics and even managed to include some non-English speaking German immigrants, who had a notorious disdain for their Irish neighbors.

On June 21, 1877, four men who were allegedly associated with the Molly Maguires were executed in the Carbon County Jail after being found guilty of murdering two mine operators.

One of the Molly Maguires found guilty of murder was a man named Alexander Campbell. He admitted being present at the murder of mine superintendent John P. Jones, but he denied actually carrying out the act. Although he was only an accessory to the crime, the jury found him guilty of first degree murder.

Campbell continued to state his innocence, even as he was dragged away to the gallows. As he was pulled from his cell, he made a declaration to his executioners:

> I am innocent, I was nowhere near the scene of the crime." Then, he slapped his hand against the wall of his cell, and continued, "There is proof of my words. That mark of mine will never be wiped out. It will remain forever to shame the county for hanging an innocent man.

And the handprint has remained, though it has been repeatedly scrubbed and painted over by superstitious officers and sheriffs. In 1930, a local sheriff named Biegler got so exasperated with the handprint, and its notoriety, that he had the entire wall knocked out and replaced. The handprint reappeared on the new wall in the same place the very next day. Thirty years later, Sheriff Charles Neast tried to cover it over with green latex paint, but the handprint again managed to come through.

In the early 1990's, a forensic scientists from George Washington University named James Starrs and a police chemist from Hagerstown, Maryland named Jeff Kercheval performed a professional analysis of the phenomenon using infrared photography and high-tech equipment. They found no paints or pigments or oils that would explain why the handprint exists, much less why it persists to this day. "We did everything short of painting over the print or literally taking it off the wall." Starrs later reported. "We measured the handprint and its precise location on the wall, so if it's ever painted over and reappears, we'll know if it appeared in the same location or a different one."

Needless to say, the handprint returned.

The Carbon County Jail closed in 1995 but reopened as a museum on the 120th anniversary of the hangings. The eerie handprint in cell 17 remains the chief attraction.

The Carbon County Jail is located in the present day town of Jim Thorpe, Pennsylvania in the eastern part of the state.

WEST VIRGINIA'S HAUNTED MINES
The Monongah & Grant Town Mines

Coal mining has always been a major source of West Virginia's wealth and as in other places, remains a harsh and dangerous occupation. There have been hundreds of mine accidents in West Virginia, along with a few disasters, and thanks to this, the dark passageways of the coal mines have become likely places to find ghosts. The Grant Town Mine, which is one of the largest coal mines in the United States, has been a source of ghostly tales for many years. But there are other haunted mines in West Virginia as well...

The ghost of a man named Jeremy Walker began haunting the Barrackville Mine after he was killed, along with several other men, in an explosion. The old black man was well-liked by the other men that he worked with and one of the things they always remembered about him was his loud and boisterous laugh and his generous nature. In the days when the coal cars were filled by hand, the men were required to maintain a certain quota each day. Walker was always the first of the men to help others to fill their quotas after his had already been completed. He was sorely missed by the other miners after his life was cut short -- but he was not missed for long.

For eight years after his death, until hand loading was no longer done in the mine, the men on the graveyard shift (which Walker had worked for years) always managed to fill their quotas with no trouble. Whenever one of the miners would go to the foreman and explain that he had been unable to fill his quota, the foreman would go and check the amount loaded and always find the quota to have been filled. The legends say that in the distance, the men would often hear the sound of Walker's laughter as the foreman made his discovery.

As mentioned, mine disasters have produced more than their share of ghost stories and hauntings and the Number 6 and Number 8 mines of the Fairmont Coal Company in Monongah are no exception. On December 6, 1907, an explosion tore apart the main shafts of these two mines and the resulting inferno killed 362 of the 367 men working that day. It became known as the worst mine disaster in West Virginia history. After the tragedy was investigated, officials came to believe the explosion had been caused by coal cars coming loose from their couplings and falling down to the bottom of the shaft. The impact managed to ignite coal dust and combined with natural gases in the mine, caused the whole place to explode.

In addition to the miners killed in the disaster, a number of mules who were used to haul coal inside of the mine were killed as well. The explosion caught 12 of the animals at the junction of two tunnels and the mules were literally ripped apart by the blast. Rather than haul the dead animals to the surface, the clean-up crew drug the bodies into a side tunnel and sealed them up. In time, the mine was re-opened and a new batch of miners took the place of the unfortunate men who were killed. Strangely though, the old mine mules never seemed to realize they were dead.

According to reports, the miners would sometimes hear the sound of hooves trotting down the darkened tunnels behind them. The mules would stomp and snort and the sounds of the animals would pass by the men in the shadows and then eventually, would fade away. Many of the men reported hearing the mules in the mine, but no one ever saw the spectral animals. The echoes of their passing remained the only part of them left behind.

The Monongah mines are no more though. Only an overgrown field at the end of a rutted dirt road still provides any evidence that these mines once existed. They have long been closed off and there is nothing left to see today. But one has to wonder if there is anything left to *hear* at this desolate spot? Could the echo of mule's hooves still be beating deep under the ground? If we were to come here on some dark night and sit and listen as the wind begins to die --- would we hear these mysterious sounds from the past?

There was no other mine in West Virginia (and perhaps in America!) that was as filled with the history of ghostly lore as the Grant Town mine was in years gone by. There were of number of spirited tales, both legends and first-hand accounts, that came to be told about the place and they dated back to the mine's early years of operation. Perhaps the oldest involved a blasting accident that took place one day that claimed the lives of six miners.

Many problems occurred in mines when the drillers encountered what were called "sulphur balls", spots in the coal vein that are harder than iron and impossible to drill through. They normally had to be blasted out of place with explosives, which would send the familiar call of "fire in the hole!" echoing through the mine. The men knew at that point to take quick action and to take cover as best they could. On occasion, accidents occurred during this type of work and often, miners were killed by unforeseen weak spots in the ceiling of the mine that would cause portions of the rock to collapse. This is exactly what happened one day in South Main section of the Grant Town mine. Six men were killed when part of the ceiling collapsed --- but strangely, their bodies were never recovered. A short time after the area was cleaned out, it was shut down by the mine company and while never used again, the men had to pass through it to get to other areas of the mine. They described it as a deathly silent and unsettling area of the shaft.

In those days, the Grant Town Mine used an electric railroad to transport the men underground. One night, a buggyman (the "buggy" was the small locomotive that was used to haul the cars in the mine) was on his way to pick up men for the midnight shift. He had dropped off one load of miners and was on his way back for another. As he was passing through the eerie section of the mine, he spotted two red lanterns, swinging back and forth on each side of the tracks. As this was a signal used by miners who needed a ride, he stopped the buggy beside the lights and opened the doors for them to climb in. He then went on his way to the end of the line, where he planned to pick up more men. As he pulled to a stop, he opened the doors and waited for the two miners that he had picked up to climb out -- but no one did. Puzzled, he went back to check and see what was going on and he found the car to be empty, save for two red lanterns that had been left lying on the floor of the car. Strangest of all, the red lanterns were of a type that had not been used since before the cave-in at the South section.

A few weeks later, two friends named Hack Retton and Stanley Minlovitz were working the midnight shift in the battery shack of the mine. They had little to do, other than wait for the batteries to charge, and so they decided to catch up on their sleep. All they had to do was to keep an eye out for the foreman since a bell would ring once the batteries were charged. Stanley always bunked down near the door to the shed so he could hear if anyone came near. In the very early hours of the morning, Stanley was roused from his sleep by the sound of someone walking around outside. Thinking that it might be a foreman or a section boss, he shook Hack awake and they went to the door. They creaked the old shed open and peered outside. What they saw terrified them both...

As the door swung open, the dim glow from the interior of the shed illuminated the nearby surroundings, providing the only light into the darkness -- until they saw the red glow of six lanterns approaching them. The lights came slowly in their direction, heading towards the South Main section. As the last light flickered past the shed, a quiet voice spoke out from the dark. "Hi Stan", it said, speaking in Polish. Stanley was positive that the voice had belonged to one of the miners who had been killed in the earlier explosion and cave-in.

When the story spread to the other miners, no one would go near the section where the disaster had taken place and they began using other, often longer routes to get to various parts of the mine. The section was finally sealed off by three yards of concrete but even in spite of this, the miners claimed to hear the sounds of muffled cries and moaning coming from deep inside the South Main section.

One of the most enduring legends of the Grant Town Mine involved a woman named Mrs. James, who had lost her first husband in a fire at the mine.

She had been left with two small boys to raise but about six months after she was widowed, she married a man named James, a close friend of her first husband.

Each morning after her second marriage, Mrs. James would get up early and would prepare breakfast for her sons and her husband. Once she had them off to work and school, she would go back to bed for awhile and sleep. Then one day, she was unnerved by a presence in the room with her. She looked up to see the transparent image of her first husband standing down at the end of the bed. She let out a small gasp, blinked twice and when she looked again, the figure was gone. Thinking that she must have been dreaming, or imagining things, she put the strange visitation out of her mind -- until the next day, when it happened again. In fact, for the next month, the man's ghost appeared in the bedroom each day, sometimes standing, sometimes sitting in a chair next to the bed.

Finally, Mrs. James could stand it no longer and became so terrified that she had to be placed under a doctor's care. When she recovered a little, the doctor suggested that she get away from Grant Town for a time. She decided to go and visit her mother for a few weeks and when she returned, she found that her husband had gotten a new house for them to live in, almost a half mile from the old one. She was sure that her past troubles would now be over.

For a time, she was right, and nothing unusual happened. Then one morning, her dead husband appeared once again. He sat down on the end of the bed and looked at her mournfully. The next day, he returned again and this time, Mrs. James demanded of him, "In the name of God, what do you want?" He told her to come with him.

Mrs. James quickly dressed and followed the specter from the house, walking in the direction of the mine. When she arrived there, she saw Mr. James just about to enter the cage and go down into the mine. She called to him and he came running, thinking that something might be wrong or that she had fallen ill again. When he learned what she was doing there, he was torn between being angry and being concerned. His foreman, who was sympathetic to the problem and was also a friend of Mrs. James' first husband, allowed James to leave and take his wife to the doctor.

When they returned to Grant Town later that afternoon, Mr. and Mrs. James saw a large crowd gathered around the mine. They went to see what had happened and discovered that there had been a slate fall in the mine and that 10 men had been killed. The fall had occurred in the section where James was supposed to have been working that day --- his wife's dead first husband had saved his life!

The Grant Town mine no longer exists, save for in memory and lore. Grant Town is located on CR-17 but the local power plant was built over the mine and it lies on the right side of the road in town.

GOLD IN NORTH CAROLINA
Specters of the Reed Mine & the Ghosts of Gold Hill

America's first gold rush took place, not in California, but in the mountains of North Carolina. It began on the land of a man named John Reed, a German immigrant who had been conscripted to fight for the British during the American Revolution. After several tries, he managed to escape from service and ended up in a small German settlement, where he turned his hand to farming. Around 1799, Reed bought about 300 acres of land from the state of North Carolina but shortly after, his plans for farming were all but forgotten when gold was discovered on his property.

One Sunday morning in 1799, John and his wife were attending church services and left their children in the care of their oldest child, Conrad. The small group went to play and look for fish in nearby Little Meadow Creek and as Conrad waded through the water, he glanced down and saw a shiny, yellow rock that was reflecting the sunlight. He picked it up, finding it far heavier than he had imagined, and carried it home to show his father when he returned from church. Reed had never seen such an unusual-looking rock and he was curious enough about it to take it to William Atkinson, the silversmith in the local village of Concord. Atkinson did not recognize the mineral either and he returned it to Reed, telling him that he had no idea what it could be. Reed took it back to his farm and for the next three years, used the rock as a doorstop.

Reed's crops flourished and in 1802, planned a trip to Fayetteville, a trading center on the Cape Fear River. Conrad was making the trip with his father and convinced him to take the shiny doorstop along with them. They took the rock to a jeweler in the city and he immediately recognized it for what it was -- but did not tell Reed. He asked how much Reed would take for the rock and the farmer, not realizing the real worth of it, named what he thought was a big price, $3.50. Needless to say, the jeweler was happy to fork over the money.

A few weeks after Reed returned home, word came from a friend who had been trading in Fayetteville that a jeweler there had sold a small bar of gold for hundreds of dollars. Reed immediately saddled his horse and rode to Fayetteville. The first place he called was the jewelry store and he managed to leave the shop with a couple of hundred dollars of his own. The two men had settled their affair and the jeweler paid the farmer off, likely with hope that he would receive more of the precious metal in the future.

When Reed returned home, he started to do something that he had never imagined doing before -- searching Little Meadow Creek for more of the nuggets. He soon found that it was strewn for nearly a mile with small chunks and rocks of gold. Farming was now forgotten and each day, the family went down to the creek and gathered gold from the bottom of the river and from the gravel and sand along the banks. Reed was literally sitting on top of a gold mine, as the hills under his farm carried veins of white quartz and gold.

When the news spread, local farmers began to dig on their own land and began turning up small pieces and nuggets of gold. Although their finds did not compare to those of Reed, the first American gold rush was underway. News of it was carried throughout North Carolina and to the rest of the country.

Reed expanded his operations and took three other farmers as his partners. After their summer crops were harvested, the partners supplied Reed with equipment and slaves to dig for gold in the creek bed and the surrounding areas. For the next 20 years, Reed and his partners continued their seasonal mining operations along Little Meadow Creek and by 1824, they had netted more than $100,000 in gold.

The operation turned to underground gold mining in 1831 and Reed amassed even more wealth. Little about the man changed though. He never learned to read or write and except for the fact that he hired many more servants and built a larger home, his simple lifestyle remained the same. Sadly though, in 1835, a family argument resulted in a court order that closed the mine for the next 10 years. Reed never saw it reopened for he died in 1845, still an incredibly wealthy man. After his death, the Reed mine was sold at public auction and in the years that followed, changed hands many times and was closed for a time during the Civil War. The last large nugget was found here in 1896 and it was eventually abandoned in 1912. Many years later, the mine would be designated a national historic site and would be taken over by the state of North Carolina.

With such an interesting and checkered history, it's no surprise that this place boasts a ghost or two.

William Mills was a Welsh immigrant who came to work at the Reed Mine in the early 1840's. He brought his wife, Eleanor, with him from Europe to work the Carolina gold rush and they settled in among the small shacks and tents surrounding the area. Eleanor was disenchanted by the dismal surroundings of the area, by the cold weather and poor food and she constantly complained to her husband each day as he returned home from work. They had a number of violent arguments but Mills loved the woman, despite her mean spirit and her insistence to not understand their situation. If only he could manage to make a fortune of his own, they could return to Wales and live in fine style. He vowed to keep his temper with her but it had become nearly impossible.

One night, during another fierce and terrible argument, Eleanor tripped on the hem or her dress and pitched forward, striking her head on a bench. She crumpled to the floor, her face a bloody mess, and she died. Mills rushed to her side and tried to revive her, washing her face and bundling her up close to the fire. When he realized that she was actually dead, he lay down beside her body and cried himself to sleep.

At some point late in the night, he awakened to find the room cold and so he added more logs to the fire. He was almost asleep when he heard a familiar voice croak out his name -- it was Eleanor's voice -- and as she so often did, she begged him to leave North Carolina and to take her back to Wales. Startled and thinking that perhaps his wife was alive after all, he turned her over and looked for a sign of life in her eyes. But her mouth sagged open and her lips had turned blue -- Eleanor was most assuredly dead. But then who had spoken to him?

Convinced that the voice had simply been his imagination, Mills had other, more troubling thoughts. Even though Eleanor's death had been an accident, there were many who knew the two of them often fought. What if someone accused him of having murdered her? He decided to get rid of the body and if anyone asked, he would tell them that she had gone home as she so desperately wanted to do. Mills looked for some bindings to tie her arms and legs together so that he could carry her corpse more easily.

A few minutes later, he wrapped the ropes around her and prepared to carry her out into the night. Before he could do so though, he heard her spectral voice again -- and this time, it was not the work of his imagination. Once again, she begged Mills to take her home but added that if he did not, she vowed to stay with him forever. Mills broke into a cold sweat and he quickly wrapped his wife in an old blanket and stumbled out into the night. He made a direct path for the Reed Mine. He would throw Eleanor's body down into the Engine Shaft, the deepest tunnel in the mine and one that had been recently abandoned. No one would ever discover her there, he believed. As he reached the top of the shaft, he pushed her body up and over the edge and she tumbled down into the darkness. As she plunged into the shadows though, Mills heard the sound of an eerie moaning wail -- and then silence.

In the weeks that followed, Mills made excuses for his wife's absence. He first explained that she was sick and then that she had gone to Charleston to visit relatives that had just arrived from England. Finally, he bemoaned the fact that she had left him and had returned back home to Wales. Although saddened on the outside, Mills secretly rejoiced and relished his quiet, solitary life without Eleanor's complaining and nagging. His days passed in peace --- until one night when she came back. Mills was jolted out of his sleep by the strident and piercing voice of his wife, demanding that he find her body and remove her from the cold, dark depths of the mine. He soon turned to drinking heavily in the local saloons, searching for whatever solace he could find.

It was soon after that talk began that the Reed Mine was haunted. The stories were first told by a peddler who had camped near the Engine Shaft one night and who had heard the voice of a woman shrieking inside. Soon, miners in the area began repeating the story and adding their own macabre encounters to the tales. Shortly after, Mills vanished from the area. Some believed that he had gone on to other diggings in Georgia and others surmised that his wife's abandonment had bothered him more than he had admitted. In any event, he was never seen again.

Many years later, when the sound of the picks was stilled at the Reed Mine, the story of the phantom in the tunnels was still being told. The woods around the old Engine shaft were cut down for timber but workers made sure that they left the area before dusk for they had heard the sounds of a woman's cries in the night and none wanted to repeat the experience.

Even today, long after the mine has gone from a working operation to a historic site, the tales of Eleanor Mills are still told. It has been said that on nights when the wind whips through the oaks and the hickory trees, a shrill voice is also carried on the wind -- a voice that calls out for William and begs to be taken home.

The first recorded discovery of vein deposits of gold in North Carolina occurred in 1825 on the farm of Matthew Barringer. Like Reed, Barringer was a German farmer who owned a few hundred acres of land in the same vicinity. He had removed a considerable amount of gold from the creek on his farm for several years and then one day, noticed that beyond a certain point in the creek, no gold could be found. At the point where the gold seemed to stop, he saw a white quartz vein running into the hill. As he had found some quartz with gold embedded in it, he came to conclusion that the gold found in the creek bed must have come from this section of rock. He decided to pursue it into the hill and found a succession of gold areas unlike anything that he had seen before. There was great excitement in the area and within a few weeks, the farmer was leasing out prospects to more than 50 gold hunters.

More mining properties were developed near Charlotte including the Capp's Hill, McComb and Rudisil mines. The local farmers and prospectors began leaving the creeks and streambeds and began heading into the hills, searching for a source of the gold. Not long after, four shafts with depths of up to 90 feet were opened at the Reed Mine. Tracts of land were being leased out by the farmers and property owners and although often poorly operated, were quickly turning a profit. Soon, larger commercial mines began to open and gold mining, like its coal counterpart, became a dangerous, and sometimes deadly, profession.

Perhaps the most deadly mine during this period was the McIntosh Mine. As readers have likely deduced from earlier pages in the book, accidents and disasters have never been enough to close down a mine on a permanent basis. However, the McIntosh Mine is one of the only mines in this region that legend maintains was closed down permanently by a ghost.

For years, the McIntosh Mine was regarded as being one of the wealthiest mines in the region. It was owned by a man who had a reputation for being tight with a dollar and this was reflected in the low pay that he offered his workers and also in the unsafe conditions of the mine. When a large deposit of gold was discovered running deeper underground that any of the veins found in the past, McIntosh was finally forced to offer his men large sums of money and bonuses to get them to sink a deeper shaft. Of course, he made up for the money spent by spending less on mine supports and equipment. He told his foremen that he had purchased the finest tools and the best timbers for use in the mine, but he had not. The tools were cut rate and cheap and the timber supports were filled with knots and far from the fine oak that he promised.

As the new shaft sank deeper into the ground, the vein began to pay off in fabulous amounts of gold. The men worked around the clock and nothing out of the ordinary was reported until one day the wife of one of the mine's most experienced miners, Joe McGee, came to the mine and asked if anyone had seen her husband? The men were surprised and then realized that Joe had not been around for nearly three days. Several of his friends went down into the mine and spent several hours searching and calling Joe's name -- but no sign of him was found. They searched fruitlessly for hours and then went back to the surface to report to Joe's wife and the rest of his friends.

The next day, she went to the office of owner McIntosh and told him that Joe was lost somewhere in the mine. She begged for him to send a search party down to look through the lesser worked tunnels of the mine. Four of Joe's friends accompanied her but McIntosh dismissed them from the office, rudely telling her that Joe had just run off and would likely return when he was ready. A week later, she went to see McIntosh again, this time to make the claim for the $2,000 that the owner had promised to the wives of men killed in the mine. He brushed off her request, this time implying that perhaps Joe had simply left her and her baby after becoming bored with married life. By now, she was getting low on food and firewood and while the other miners were giving her whatever they could spare, her situation was growing dire. Finally, she returned to the mine office again but this time McIntosh sent out a message that he did not have time to see her.

Late that night, Joe's closest friend, Shaun O'Hennessy, was awakened in the middle of the night by the sound of a terrible rattling at the front door. Without thinking, he ran into the front room and threw the door wide open. There, standing on the steps was Joe McGee -- but looking nothing like Joe ever had. His face was white and gaunt, his clothing covered with dirt and filth and his eyes, which were sunk deep into his head, seemed to give off a red glow. Joe was surely dead, Shaun realized, for here stood his ghost.

He begged his friend to help get his wife the money that she was owed by McIntosh and explained that he could do so by discovering Joe's body in the mine. He had been killed by a cave-in on the mine's second level -- the result of the shoddy timbers that McIntosh had purchased as tunnel supports. He insisted that Shaun seek out his body that night and then he vanished.

Shaking with fear, Shaun quickly dressed and started to the mine. He was not going to go down there alone though and he woke up four of his friends along the way. With lighted lamps, they descended into the mine, looking for the place where the spectral figure had directed them to. As they neared the final turn in the tunnel, the fearsome figure appeared out of the darkness ahead of them. He spoke to them and told them the mine was unsafe and that McIntosh had lied about the safety measures he claimed were in place. Then, he pointed out the place for them to dig.

The miners began to dig into a pile of loose rubble and debris and within a few minutes had uncovered Joe's lifeless body. His ghost, they soon realized, had vanished. They carried Joe's body up into the elevator and home. Shaun went down to the mine office the next day and told McIntosh that Joe McGee had come home and wanted to see him. Startled, the mine owner went with him and walked over to the McGee house. A group of sullen miners stood around outside and several women stood talking on the porch as the mine owner walked up to the door. McIntosh followed Shaun inside and at one end of the room saw a long pine box that held the corpse of Joe McGee. His wife sat next to it in a rocking chair, holding her baby and crying softly. He grimly told her that she could pick up her money that afternoon in the mine office.

The following morning, the mine stood empty and quiet. The men refused to come back to work. Finally, by late afternoon, McIntosh called a meeting of all of the miners at which he promised them more money and a safer mine. He explained that he had not meant to be disrespectful to Joe McGee's wife and apologized for not giving her the money sooner. The men listened silently and then left.

The next morning, the mine was still silent. McIntosh learned that all of his men, except for the few who had left the area, had been hired on at other mines. Word had spread quickly that the McIntosh Mine was not only dangerous -- but haunted as well --- and the men refused to work there, despite the fact that there was still plenty of gold under the ground. McIntosh visited the men and tried to convince them to come back to work for him but they refused. He attempted to hire new men, offering high wages, but he could convince no one to enter the mine again. According to the legend, McIntosh later went insane at the thought of having a fortune in his hands and no way to get to it. As many have said, McIntosh was not the first man to lose his mind over gold.

About 25 miles outside of Charlotte was an area known as Gold Hill, a small village that was made up of the homes of the men who worked the mines and the stores and saloons that served them. It was a wealthy and thriving community for many years and one of the leading, and richest, residents was a man of questionable character named Walter George Newman. A Virginia man who had been born around 1860, Newman came to Gold Hill and began buying up property and mines. He built a large mansion across the road from the mining office and then summoned his wife from Virginia to take up residence with him. He drove one of the finest teams of horses in the region and kept a number of carriages. Later, he would be the first person to own an automobile in Gold Hill and while generous to his wife and daughters, he could be dangerous, unpredictable and prone to violence.

He had first heard about the riches to be gained from the strike at Gold Hill from his brother, Joseph, a mining engineer who had worked the North Carolina mines since the 1880's. Walter tried to buy out his brother's claims but Joseph refused his offer. The pair were drinking in a local saloon one night when Walter, in a particularly vicious mood, began shouting at his brother and making all sorts of threats toward him.

A few weeks later, all of Gold Hill was awakened in the middle of the night by a terrific explosion. Joseph Newman and his home had been destroyed. Investigators learned that a charge of dynamite had been placed under his bed as he slept but Walter insisted that his brother had committed suicide. No one had the power or courage to dispute this and while most suspected murder, Walter walked away unscathed and inherited his brother's estate at the same time.

In 1898, Newman began buying up more property and in a year's time owned the Union Mining Company holdings, the old Honeycutt Gold Mine, the Earnhardt, the Helig and the Randolph Mine -- all of the major mining properties of Gold Hill. By this time, many of the gold mines had begun to play out and Newman turned his energies into the production of copper. Newman secured the backing of some Boston businessmen and began to transform his property at Gold Hill to accommodate new facilities and a larger work force. Soon though, he found himself overextended and less than a year later, a cash shortage forced him to turn over the control of the Union Copper Mining Company to managers from Colorado. Two of his companies failed at this same time.

The new managers managed to make the mine profitable again for a time but soon slipped even deeper into financial problems. The mines were run alternately by a receivership, the Colorado managers and Newman himself. He battled with the banks, the managers, the stock holders and the company officers, writing angry letters and sending threatening messages.

By 1910, he was the owner again and immediately put another 100 men to work. By September however, the mine had failed and was sold in a foreclosure proceeding. Determined though, Newman refused to give up and tried to raise money to open the mines again. He soon exhausted his sources on Wall Street and even turned to friendly senators in Washington, which prompted an investigation by New York newspapers. His final exploit at Gold Hill was a comedy of errors. He arrived in town just ahead of a carload of potential investors but his finances were in such a state that the investors had to pay their own passage by train. Newman borrowed money from unemployed miners to buy paint and whitewash, rounding up workers to spruce up the village --- and also to put on their coveralls and to pretend to be going to work in the silent mines. Newman's scam worked and the investors eagerly contributed $12,000 to help him develop the copper mine further.

But after the visitors left, angry miners, who wanted not only the money that they had given Newman for paint but back wages as well, converged on the mine office and cornered Newman on the second floor balcony. He tried to pacify the crowd, but without success. Finally, perhaps fearing for his life, he tossed a large handful of money into the air and allowed it to fall down onto the men below. In the confusion, he slipped out the back door and boarded his private train while the miners bickered over what turned out to be Gold Hill's last payroll.

Newman later drifted away from the area and abandoned his family, wandering around the country for a time before finally ending up in New York. He died in his hotel room in 1918 --- on the same day that his wife was granted a divorce petition. He was only 58 years old but had lived what many would consider to be the equivalent of more than one lifetime.

The fascinating history of Gold Hill has spawned at least two ghost stories -- and one of them involves the grisly murder of Joseph Newman. In January 1954, two witnesses reported a strange and frightening apparition near the old Randolph Mine. The apparition appeared to be pieces of a body, floating in the air. A disembodied head, arms, legs and feet seemed to be suspended somehow and were said to be glowing with some sort of unearthly light. Suddenly, the terrifying sight began moving toward them and then, with a sound like a cracking whip, the ghost vanished.

According to accounts, the head belonged to Joseph Newman, the brother of wealthy mine owner, Walter George Newman. Newman had died several years before in a terrible explosion that had destroyed both he and his home. The explosion had been deemed mysterious by the locals and by the authorities, who were unable to prove foul play. The locals suspected differently though and as mentioned, Walter became the subject of both fear and derision in Gold Hill. After Walter died in 1918, his legend took another turn as his ghost was said to be haunting the mine and walking the streets of Gold Hill at night --- perhaps still wondering how his dreams had all fallen apart.

Another spirit, also believed to haunt the old Randolph Mine, was that of Aaron Klein, who was murdered in the mine in 1842. Klein, who was Jewish, was often tormented with anti-Semitic pranks and cruel jokes during his time at the mine, but one night, a fellow worker, who was jealous of Klein's affections for a young woman in town, killed him. He lured the man into the mine and then pushed him down an 850-foot deep shaft. Klein's body was never found, but shortly after he disappeared, a shimmering yellow light began to be reported near the mouth of the mine. Dozens of people reporting seeing the light, but assuming that there was a logical explanation for it, were never really frightened by it.

However one man, Stanley Cukla, was bothered by the appearance of the light. He had been the man who had murdered Klein in the mine and he began to obsess over the strange manifestation. Cukla began to act very oddly and was overheard mumbling about ghosts and Aaron Klein, who the other miners just assumed had left town. Cukla was also sometimes seen at night, digging through the rubble at the bottom of the mine pit. He was last seen doing this the night before his body was found there, lifeless and smashed beyond recognition. No explanation was ever found for what had killed him.

Could it have been the ghost of Aaron Klein, seeking revenge?

The Reed Mine is now a National Historic Site, located northeast of Charlotte. Take Highway 24/27 east out of Charlotte to Highway 200 North. This road leads eight miles to the mine. The McIntosh Mine was located on a hill near the Reed Mine, also in Mecklenburg County.

Gold Hill remains a small community that is still in existence today. It is located just outside of the town of Concord, which is about 25 miles northeast of Charlotte.

THE MILFORD MINE
Crow Wing County, Minnesota

While Minnesota is scattered with mines that are alleged to be haunted by former workers who were killed there, or returned to haunt the place after their death, there are few places that were said to be as haunted as the Milford Mine in Crow Wing County. Even though the ghost of the place was seen only one time -- it was witnessed by several dozen men who were convinced that they had seen the ghost of a dead fellow worker.

The disaster happened on February 5, 1924 at the Milford Manganese Mine. The mine was over 200 feet deep and at the bottom of the shaft worked a man named Clinton Harris. His job was to operate an electric hoist that dumped ore from the ore cars into a bucket that was raised to the surface. When it was emptied, it came back down and he repeated the process. Harris was called a "skip-tender" as the bucket was often referred to as a "skip". On February 5, Harris was unfortunately filling in for another skip-tender who had called in sick.

That afternoon, miners blasted a cut near Foley's Pond, which abutted a portion of the mine. A hurricane of wind rushed through the mine, knocking men down and putting out the electric lights. The lights flickered off, came back on again and then went out for good, plunging the mine into blackness.

Moments later, the deafening roar of water filled the mine --- the blasting had caused the earth to collapse next to the pond and the tunnels rapidly began to flood. Miners scrambled for the surface, falling and wading through water that grew deeper by the minute. Some of the miners were slammed into the walls by the force of the water and killed instantly, their bones and bodies crushed against the stone. Others, knocked down by the terrible wind, simply drowned beneath the murky water. Of the 50 men who were working during the shift, only seven of them survived.

Clinton Harris, the skip-tender who was working at the bottom of the shaft, died there. He apparently could have escaped but chose to remain, pulling on the warning whistle that would alert miners on the upper levels of the coming danger. For over four hours, long after mud and water sealed off the shaft, the warning bell continued to sound. It is unknown whether his body was caught in the rope, or if he had tied himself to it, but eventually someone in the engine room disconnected the bell and silenced the melancholy sound from the now flooded mine.

The survivors who escaped from the water made it to the surface and then collapsed, soaked and exhausted, on the frozen ground. Moments later, men from the mine office rushed over with blankets to help them. They quickly began taking a roll of the men who had survived --- and discovering those who were still trapped in the darkness and water below. One of the young men who survived, Frank Hvratin, had a father who perished in the mine.

Word of the disaster spread rapidly through nearby Crosby, where the village siren blew for hours, summoning families to the mine. People watched as the water in Foley's Pond sank lower and lower, flooding into the mine, and clusters of young widows walked arm in arm throughout the village all night. Others silently gathered at the entrance to the mine, now with the horrible realization that the men who had not immediately come out of the mine would not be coming out at all.

By midnight, mine clearing operations were underway. In the sub-zero temperatures of northern Minnesota, men took turns operating the water pumps that sucked out over 12,000 gallons of mud and water each minute. They hoped against all hope that someone could have survived but Crow Wing County mine inspectors began to doubt if any of the bodies would even be found, let alone any surviving miners.

Finally, it was realized that as long as Foley's Pond held water, the mine could not be drained, so the tasks changed and nearly twelve days were spent emptying the pond. It took another three months to drain the mine. Then, the mud that clogged the passages and shafts had to be shoveled out by hand before the bodies could be found. This grim and filthy task took another nine months to complete. Eventually all 50 of the bodies of the missing miners were retrieved, making the Milford Disaster the worst on Minnesota's Iron Range.

Despite the horror and the memories, many miners signed on to go underground again when the mine reopened. Manganese was in great demand by the steel industry and jobs were promised to any man who would go back into the Milford Mine. Of course, it should also be remembered that for many of these men, mining was the only job they had ever known.

But the Milford Mine held horrors that few of them had counted on --- not only was the shaft filled with the stench of decay and decomposed flesh, but a ghost as well. At the base of the shaft, the first workers down caught a glimpse of a figure in the darkness, fluttering away from their approach and sinking back into the shadows. The men pursued it with their lights and their lamps revealed a hideous-looking ghost specter. And while semi-transparent, he was easily recognized as being the form of Clinton Harris, the heroic and doomed skip-tender. He now looked starved and decayed, as if his flesh had been removed, leaving only molded skin and bones. His deeply sunken eyes were black and vacant sockets and they peered upward along the ladder that he was clinging to. A phantom whistle cord was still knotted about his waist.

The miners bumped and jostled each other in their haste to retreat from this ominous figure, but that haste soon turned to panic --- as the warning whistle, which no longer existed, began to scream through the dark shafts, sounding a warning that no man should enter the mine again. The terrified men scrambled back up to the surface and after that day, not a single one of them ever came back to the Milford Mine.

The Milford Mine was located in Crow Wing County in north central Minnesota, and near the town of Crosby. The survivors of the disaster have all passed away but the story of the mine and the ghost of Clinton Harris are still told today.

THE HAUNTED OPHIR MINE
Virginia City, Nevada

There is no town within the state of Nevada that is considered to be as haunted as Virginia City. With its long history of violence and strange events, the cemeteries here boast a larger population than the city itself. Virginia City, which became the first real industrial city in the west, began in the late 1850's. Gold was discovered at the head of Six-Mile Canyon in 1859 by two miners named Pat McLaughlin and Peter O'Reilly. A fellow miner, Henry Comstock, stumbled upon their find and claimed it was on his property. The gullible pair believed him and assured Comstock a place in history when the giant lode was named in his honor. Prospectors who had lost out during California's gold rush, as well as other would-be prospectors from all over the country, came scurrying into the region for another chance at wealth. And the legends of the Comstock Lode were born.

Following the discovery of gold in the canyon, an outcropping of gold was also found embedded in underground quartz veins. The ill-fated Grosch brothers, Hosea and Ethan Allan, were the first to understand the importance of this discovery and how to sink shafts in a search for it. Unfortunately though, both of them tragically died within three months of one another --- long before they could enjoy the fabulous wealth they had uncovered.

In January 1859, a miner named James Finney, who was nicknamed "Old Virginny" thanks to his birthplace, dubbed the name of the settlement that had started to spring up around the mines and claims during a drunken celebration. He dropped a bottle of whiskey on the ground and christened the newly-founded tent-and-dugout town "Old Virginny Town," in honor of himself.

Ironically, the greatest wealth of the region came not from the gold that was discovered but from the sticky blue-gray mud that stuck to everything, including the picks and shovels of the miners. The men unceremoniously pitched it aside in disgust but when the mud was actually assayed, it proved to be silver ore that was worth as much as $2,000 a ton! Gold, along with the high quality silver ore, was recovered in large enough quantities to catch the eye of President Abraham Lincoln a few years later. He needed the gold and silver to keep the Union solvent during the Civil War and so in October 1864, Nevada officially became a state, even though it did not contain enough people to constitutionally authorize statehood.

The resulting boom turned "Virginny Town" into Virginia City and it became the most important settlement between Denver and San Francisco. Thousands of people flooded into town and grubby prospectors were turned into instant millionaires who built mansions, imported furniture and food from Europe and built the Virginia & Truckee Railroad, which ran from Reno to Carson City and beyond. The investments made in mining on the Comstock during this period literally built San Francisco as men like Leland Stanford, George Hearst, John Mackay and many others made their fortunes in Comstock mining.

The area also attracted men who would go on to become legends of other sorts as well. When he grew tired of mining in Aurora, a man named Samuel Clemens came to Virginia City and began a writing career for the *Territorial Enterprise*. He found his niche and settled in, making himself at home writing tall tales that would arouse the curiosity of those who lived in more civilized parts of the country. Clemens, who would go on to fame as Mark Twain, penned *Roughing It* based on the people and his adventures in Virginia City.

During its heyday, Virginia City was a boisterous boomtown with something going on both above and below the ground both day and night. More than 30,000 residents overflowed the town and there were visiting celebrities, opium dens, newspapers, competing fire companies, fraternal organizations, at least five police precincts, a thriving red-light district and dozens of prosperous businesses. The International Hotel that opened in town was a towering six stories high and boasted the first elevator in the west, then dubbed a "rising room".

Today, many of the mansions that were built as monuments to the opulent life on the Comstock still stand, remarkably preserved. The Virginia & Truckee Railroad runs again between Virginia City and Gold Hill. The largest national Historic District in the country is maintained in its original glory here, lining the old streets of the city with buildings from the town's greatest days. While many things have changed here, such as the glory days of mining coming to an end, other things have remained the same --- spirits of the past still walk the streets and haunt the hills of Virginia City.

Life on the Comstock was perilous under the best conditions. Unexpected deaths happened nearly everyday as violence erupted in gunfights and saloon brawls, fires broke out, diseases ran rampant and of course, lives were claimed in mining accidents. The miners died in what could be called the cruelest ways possible -- in horrible fires, mine floods, cave-ins, by falling debris and by being mangled in the dangerous mine equipment. All of these things combined to help fill the city's graveyards, but not all of those whose bodies ended up beneath the earth in the cemetery were quite ready to be there.

Stories have been told for decades of moans and cries that echo from the tunnels and shafts of the now abandoned mines. The lust for wealth was sometimes so strong that even death was not enough to tear a man away from the legendary Comstock Lode. In fact, even the man for which the fabulous strike was named for refuses to rest here in peace.

The surface mining on the land claimed by Henry Comstock at the head of Six Mile Canyon eventually played out and Comstock lost millions when developers bought out the site and then sank shafts underground to reap greater benefits than Comstock himself could have imagined. Bitter and angry, he died a few years later, convinced that he had been cheated out of land that he had gotten through his own questionable methods. The Ophir Mine, which became one of the richest on the Comstock, was carved out of the earth below the region's original claim.

In the years that followed, so many men died in the mine that most of the workers considered the diggings to be haunted. Strange sounds were often heard in the passages and crosscuts of the mine and in the large caverns where ore had been blasted away and hauled to the surface. The men worked in an almost constant state of fear but the most frightening event in the mine occurred in 1874.

One night, in the winter of that year, residents of Virginia City observed a glowing light that rose up out of the entrance to the Ophir and gained a height of almost 60 feet. Witnesses say that it gave off such a glow that it lit up the surrounding hillside before vanishing back into the mine again. Townspeople and firemen rushed to the mine, fearing that it was burning and that the timbers inside could collapse and seal off the shaft. When they arrived though, they found no flames or smoke. The only sign of a disturbance was the same glowing light that had been witnessed all over town. By this time, it was down at the bottom of the shaft, as though someone had an impossibly bright lantern that they were using to work by. As they peered down at the light, they began to hear the familiar sound of a metal pick striking against the rock below. The men argued about who would be down in a deserted section of the mine in the middle of the night, but no one wanted to go down and see. Slowly, both the light and the sound faded away. These strange events were only the beginning of a flurry of activity that occurred at the mine over the next several weeks.

The weirdness continued the following morning when the first shift arrived for work at the mine. The engineer who worked the elevator into the shaft received a signal to bring the cage down to the 700-foot level and he pressed down on the levers to lower it. The cage descended and then he received another signal to take it down to the level below the first, then to raise it back to the surface. The elevator clanked and clattered back up to the top of the shaft but when it arrived, it was empty. Strangely, no one had worked at the 700-foot level for many years, since the mine was now much deeper. He was puzzled as to what had happened and he mentioned it to his fellow workers later in the day. Several of them told him that while they were taking the cage down to deeper portion of the mine, they had heard a man's voice, as well as the clanging of metal on stone, while passing this level of the mine. Another man spoke of hearing a bizarre laugh as he moved down past the level in the darkness.

Over the next few weeks, the strange reports continued. Workers who were being lowered down into the mine claimed to hear laughter, to hear tools being hammered against the stone and to see moving lights within the shadows of the now avoided level. Despite the curious events, the superstitious miners refused to set foot on the level -- until finally a young man agreed to see if he could find out what was going on.

Filled with bravado, he entered the cage and began to descend down into the mine. When he reached the 700-foot level, he stepped off into the darkness of the dreaded area, casting the light from his lantern ahead of him. As he had suspected, the area was abandoned and empty and covered with dust from years without use. The area had not been worked in quite some time and the young miner was puzzled about what the other men were claiming to hear. Finally, he walked deeper into the closest tunnel and then traveled on through passage after passage until he at last feared that he might become lost. There was no one down here, he thought, and certainly nothing supernatural at work. He dismissed the other men's stories with a laugh and then turned to make his way back to the main shaft and the cage that would take him back up to the surface.

As he began to turn back though, he heard a faint sound in the distance -- coming from deeper in the tunnel. He recognized it as the clink of a miner's pick as it worked its way into rock. The young man raised his lantern and peered into the shadows but he saw nothing. Cautiously, he began to walk back in the direction he had originally been going and as he rounded a bend in the tunnel, he saw a dim light begin to appear. The sound of the pickax began to grow louder. At last, he entered a cavern that had been created by blasting years before and was greeted with the incredible and horrific sight of an old man who was himself the source of the light that he had seen.

As the specter turned in his direction, the miner recognized the face of Henry Comstock himself, the man who first discovered gold in the region. Although seemingly solid in form, the old man was obviously no longer among the living. In fact, the miner gasped in shock and disgust when the ghost turned his face to him. Wrinkled and rotted flesh clung sharply to the man's skull and his hair had pulled away from his scalp in decayed clumps. His once fine clothing was now tattered and hung loosely from his form. The man's eyes were yellow and orange in color and seemed to shimmer with a blue light that was at once both hypnotic and terrifying.

The young miner panicked as the ghost lurched toward him and he turned to run. He only made it a few steps before he stumbled over something and went sprawling onto the floor of the tunnel. Before he could get up and run, the specter was looming above him, his skeletal hands clutched in anger. He snarled and snapped at the young man and began to scream at him -- insisting that the mine belonged to him and that only he had the right to the gold that had been stolen from him. He took another step and the miner began to scream. He scrambled to his feet and dashed down the mine passage, his ears still filled with the threats and insane ramblings of the horrifying ghost.

The miner did not stop running until he reached the elevator and according to the accounts of the men who pulled him up out of the mine, he was never the same again. He quit working at the Ophir Mine that day and he left Virginia City soon after. The ghastly specter that he described in his stammering statement to the other men had unnerved him completely.

From that point on, none of the miners ever entered the 700-foot level of the mine again but even so, the stories of the strange events did not cease. The laughter and the weird sounds continued to be heard and occasionally, the ghostly happenings entered other parts of the mine too. Occasionally, the ghost would go down the tunnels and would extinguish the lights along the passageways, plunging the miners into darkness. As lights went out on level after level, the men could hear the ring of laughter as Henry Comstock had his revenge on the men he believed had stolen his mine away from him.

Virginia City is located in the mountains of Nevada, between Carson City and Reno. There are many hauntings here in the city, including the mine. The old Ophir Mine was located south of D. Street between Six Mile Canyon Road in the north part of town.

HAUNTED MINES IN COLORADO

The Rocky Mountain region of the American West is filled with a wide variety of legends and lore and some of the most horrific tales of the area involve the ghosts that can be found in the mines. One has to wonder what causes these spirits to remain? Is it because of the sudden deaths that so many suffered in the dark passages under the earth? Or perhaps something far stranger?

We have already determined in pages past that mines are eerie places, even under the best of circumstances. The total absence of light, the dangerous conditions and the weird surroundings are almost enough to create the stories -- but once we add in the strange tales of things that happen in them, we can understand why hauntings become easy to believe in.

Many of the men who worked the mines of the Old West emigrated from Europe and the British Isles, bringing the folklore and legends of their mines with them. These men had no illusion about the fact that any mine could be endowed with supernatural characteristics. Strange creatures called "Tommyknockers" arrived in America with the immigrant miners (or at least the stories of them did) and these mischievous spirits were believed responsible for the eerie sights and sounds underground.

The Tommyknockers, and other assorted weird creatures, joined the supernatural beings already fully ensconced in the mines -- the ghosts, which had been present since the first mining accident or disaster took place. Since the creation of each mining ghost implied the loss of at least one miner, it's strange that the ghosts did not multiply at a phenomenal rate given the number of accidents that took place. Regardless though, there were a number of mines in Colorado that were haunted by the ghosts of dead miners -- and often, even stranger things.

Stories of ghosts in Colorado mines were not difficult to track down. For instance, records told of the ghost of a miner named Stephen Pierce, who was murdered at the Mammoth Mine in October 1877. He was often reported lurking about the entrance to the mine and was later credited with protecting the lives of some of the miners who worked here.

And he was not the only one. Two miners who drowned in the Bates Mine at Black Hawk, Colorado in 1885 later were reported assisting workers as they escaped from the mine after an explosion. The spirits of the two men allegedly supported wall and ceiling timbers, keeping them from collapsing, as the workers ran outside.

But not all of the ghosts were as interactive. The ghost of a miner who was killed at the Star Mine in Leadville, Colorado simply re-enacted his death by suffocation over and over again for years. The haunting did not stop (or at least was no longer witnessed) until the shaft was eventually closed.

Some specters could be downright terrifying to the men who worked beneath the earth. In the spring of 1879, an especially fearsome ghost -- that of a woman -- began appearing in the New Discovery Mine in Leadville. As most miners are very superstitious about the presence of a woman in a mine, believing that it brings bad luck, they were horrified by this phantom. A number of the miners actually quit working in the mine, took their final pay and went off to look for work elsewhere. A few of the miners who stayed behind actually tried to capture the ghost. They chased after her, through the dark passageways, until she faded away and vanished. The ghost seemed to enjoy the attention gained from these pursuits as the more often she was chased, the more often she appeared. As the men finally gave up, realizing the spirit would never be caught, she appeared less and left often and eventually vanished for good. Who she may have been and what purpose she had in the mine remains a mystery.

The Moyer Mine, which was also located in Leadville, boasted hauntings of its own and for the most part, the trapped spirits seemed to be those of miners who had suffered a grim fate in mining accidents and who remained behind. The spirits, although unsettling, were more helpful than they were troublesome and were often credited for scaring miners away from areas where disaster was eminent. One death that occurred in the mine should have never happened -- but the victim refused to heed the warning of one of the resident ghosts.

One of the owners of the mine was a man named Gallagher, who did not believe in ghosts and was irritated that the men constantly talked of spirits in the place. Concerned that such talk would ruin his investment, he became determined to prove that spirits did not exist and he went into the mine one day to confront the men about their fostering of myths and rumors. Gallagher got much more than he bargained for however, when he walked down one of the mine tunnels and came face to face with a ghost. Anxious to prove that such things could not exist, Gallagher proceeded to walk right through the spirit --- and right over the edge of a chasm. He fell hundreds of feet and died instantly when he struck the bottom of the shaft.

According to legend, Gallagher's ghost never left the mine after this and it seemed as if he was doomed to wander the passageways as one of the spirits that he professed to not believe in. Unlike the other haunts, who apparently tried their best to protect the miners from injury, Gallagher's ghost was said to be a malicious one -- luring men to their deaths and causing accidents and cave-ins. More than one miner abruptly quit working at the Moyer Mine after encountering his presence and escaping with his life.

One of the enduring stories is about that of a night watchman who was employed by the mining company to watch over the place after the shifts had ended for the day. One night, as he was walking his patrol, he came face to face with Gallagher's malevolent ghost and suffered such terror that he was never the same afterward. He was discovered, babbling and shaking with fear, the following morning and he spent the remainder of his life in and out of mental hospitals. He died a few years later, never fully recovering his sanity.

Men stopped agreeing to work the mine a short time after this and eventually the Moyer Mine, like others in the haunted west with similar problems, closed down.

The hauntings of mines in Colorado take many strange twists and turns and at least one mine, located in Silverton, was not so much inhabited by ghosts -- but its location was pointed out by the spirits instead.

In the summer of 1875, a Scotsman named Edward Ennis came to Silverton. He arrived in the settlement, which was already a booming silver camp, with what he claimed were exact directions to a mother-lode of gold in the hills. These directions, he explained to anyone with an interest, were given to him by spirits. Ennis was an avid Spiritualist and according to a medium whose séance he had attended, he could find gold in Silverton. The spirits had been so specific that they had even provided him with detailed directions and hastily drawn maps. Strangely, although Ennis had never been to the region before, the maps he brought with him were eerily accurate.

When he arrived in Colorado, Ennis already had a fortune from his years in the shipping business and so he began spending huge amounts of money. He was so sure that his supernatural instructions were correct that he began buying out the owners of mining property in the area where he believed that gold would be found at higher than fair market value. As soon as he owned the land the spirits told him to purchase, he began to dig. Months and then years passed with no success, but Ennis never wavered. He was sure that he would someday strike it big and he was so convinced that his riches would come from gold that he disregarded the numerous veins of silver that he uncovered in his search.

As the search wore on, Ennis began to receive spirit communications of his own. They instructed him to dig in certain locations or to excavate to the right or the left of the shafts that had already been sunk. One message informed him of an impending flood in the mine and Ennis heeded the warning. A few days later, a wall crumbled and thousands of gallons of water flooded into the mine. Fortunately, since Ennis had listened to the warning, he was able to get all of his workers out of the mine and to safety.

The mystery remains though that if Ennis' maps and spirit warnings were so accurate, then why was he not successful in his search for gold? That question remains unanswered but Ennis' faith in his own success never faltered. As time went on though, his resources and his fortune dwindled and finally, the bank that was funding the mine went bankrupt, leading to Ennis' own financial disaster. The Scotsman died a short time later, believing, even on his deathbed, that his repository of gold remained in Silverton, just out of reach.

The mysterious Spiritualist was largely forgotten by the people of Silverton by the time another Scottish immigrant arrived in town six years after Ennis' death. Her name was Mary Murrel, or "Highland Mary" as she was often called. Like Ennis, she possessed her own fortune and came to Silverton believing that the ultimate gold seam was hidden somewhere in the region. Murrel had heard stories of Silverton and of a strange fellow Scotsman who had envisioned gold in the area -- and had been directed to it by the spirits. Perhaps out of curiosity, she bought out Ennis's claims and directed his mine shaft to be blasted back open again. The crew then began tunneling at just the point where Ennis' financial decline had forced him to end his shaft. There, just 1200 feet from the end of the tunnel was a literal "lake of gold" that contained millions of dollars in gold, as well as silver, zinc and copper.

All of the investors in the mine, as well as Mary Murrel, became rich beyond their wildest dreams and those who remembered the weird claims of Edward Ennis now realized that he --- and of course the spirits --- had been right after all. And then, as if a phantom herself, Highland Mary vanished not long after the riches in the mine had been depleted. She was never heard from again.

THE MAMIE R MINE

Cripple Creek, Colorado

Cripple Creek is a town that should likely never have existed. In the 1890's, there were perhaps a number of men in town, beaten and broken by the brutal conditions of the mines, who wished that it had not come to be. The town was eventually founded largely due to the belief of one man that a rich lode of gold lay beneath Mt. Pisgah, particularly in the ground near a cabin he had in what he called Poverty Gulch.

The man's name was Bob Womack and he had come to Colorado years before, having been brought here by his father around 1861. Sam Womack had traveled to the region from Kentucky to keep his son of out of being conscripted into service in the Civil War -- and also in hopes that he would strike it rich. He and his sons began working and learning as much as about mining as they could. They worked a claim of their own but it never paid off and thanks to Sam's failing health, the Womack's turned to cattle ranching instead. Unfortunately, the piece of ground later turned out to have a rich vein of silver running through it and the area, which later became Georgetown, yielded a bonanza that was worth about a half million dollars.

The Womack's had not left the area penniless though. Their prospecting had managed to bring in enough money to buy a cattle ranch in the wild area south of Pike's Peak near Mt. Pisgah. Bob Womack though, was not cut out to be a cattle rancher or anything else for that matter. He was really suited for drinking himself into one stupor after another, which is what he proceeded to do. In between his drunken benders, he had lucid periods in which he promoted a fanatical relief that gold lay beneath the mountain -- and beneath his cabin in particular. Oddly, there was no logical basis for this belief. The terrain didn't have the right kind of rock and the geological formations were all wrong, leading most in Colorado Springs to believe that Womack's stories of gold were nothing more than the ramblings of a drunk. Even when Womack turned up a gold nugget in 1878 that was worth more than $200, there was still no one to believe him, even with this piece of evidence. This was party due to his odd behavior, his drinking and also thanks to painful memories of a hoax that had been perpetrated by one "Chicken Bill" and called the "Mt. Pisgah Hoax". This "discovery" of gold had been nothing more than salted ore that resulted in a frantic rush on the location. Thousands came and many were wiped out when it was announced that the whole thing had been a scam.

Despite the local feelings for Womack, he did manage to find one investor for his mine operation, a dentist named Grannis, who was a newcomer to the Colorado Springs area. Grannis had looked over the geology of Mt. Pisgah with an open mind and realized that Womack could be right. The area was the center of an ancient volcano and had the type of conformation that should show vertical plugs, or gold-bearing veins. He gave Womack $500 to get started and what the man did not use to buy whiskey, he spent on some digging equipment. Amazingly, he uncovered the top of a rich vein that was concealed under a few feet of earth in a cow pasture. But Womack's reputation still bedeviled him. Even though his partner and some of his workers took the ore samples into Colorado Springs, no one wanted anything to do with them, knowing that they had come from Womack's claim.

About this time, James Pourtales of Colorado Springs, a German count and a man of social prestige, decided to invest some money in the mine. He brought in a vast fortune, buying up land and starting new claims. Word spread and soon other miners began to descend on the area, starting shafts and purchasing claims that were starting to pay off. Shacks, tents and ramshackle building began to appear to house the miners and to supply them with food, tools, supplies, women and of course, whiskey.

Horace Bennett and Julius Meyers were partners who had bought up a good deal of Cripple Creek land before the gold rush began. According to the story, the area had gained its name thanks to an early settler who had been building a house with a friend and the other man's gun had gone off, wounding the settler in the foot. He dubbed the area "Cripple Creek" after the weeks that he spent hobbling around as his accidental wound healed. In 1891, Bennett and Meyers decided to lay out a town, bringing some order to the chaos that was beginning to appear. They made a pile of cash selling off building lots and Cripple Creek replaced the name of Poverty Gulch on November 8. When the plan for the town was transferred to the new site, the designers were dismayed to find that the map didn't lay flat on actual ground, which was all up and down and in every direction. The main east-west streets were, of course, named Bennett and Meyers and the crossing north-south streets were numbered. Bennett Avenue was the main thoroughfare from the beginning and was filled with all manner of businesses from saloons to brothels.

Later on, the houses of ill repute moved to Meyers Avenue and the street became lined with more than 70 saloons, large brothels and numerous individual cribs. These were placed strictly in order of preference, starting with the young white girls at the upper level and ending with the cheaper, older women and minority groups at the bottom of the hill. Near these establishments were many cheap rooming houses and dance halls and one of these was the Central Dance Palace, where the first big fire in Cripple Creek started in 1896. A gambler and his woman, Jeannie Larue, lived above the dance hall and during a violent argument, overturned a gas stove. In moments, the whistle of the Mocking Bird Mine was shrieking one blast after another, spreading the word that a major fire was burning. Scores of volunteer firemen showed up to fight the blaze and while it was quickly brought under control, a more severe fire broke out just a few days later and almost destroyed the town. Most of the residents were left homeless, hungry and cold but nearby towns, who were bitter rivals in most times, came to their aid with food, blankets and tents for their neighbors. This fire marked the end of flimsy wooden structures in town and most of the buildings that replaced those that were destroyed were built from brick, turning Cripple Creek into a real town.

Cripple Creek prospered through the 1890's and into the new century and a number of railroads came to town during this period. But not everything was bright during this time. The years 1894 and 1903 saw dark and violent periods that were brought on by labor disputes -- some of the worst ever suffered by any mining communities. There were a number of murders, incidents of sabotage and even bombings, including that of a railway station in Independence, which killed a number of men and injured many others. This act broke the labor union as public reaction brought in soldiers and law enforcement officials to stifle the violence and to arrest the agitators. As many as 112 men were deported to Kansas and New Mexico.

By July 1904, peace finally came to the region but now other troubles had taken the place of labor strife. Water was becoming a menace in the mines of Cripple Creek and other nearby towns. Shafts were being flooded, equipment destroyed and operations were being forced out of business. In addition, many of the older mines were petering out and it was becoming apparent that the gold of Cripple Creek was starting to run out.

Bob Womack, the man who accidentally started it all, died penniless in Colorado Springs in August 1909. In spite of his heavy drinking, he reached the age of 66 but spent most of his later years in poor health and poverty. Cripple Creek made many millionaires but as time went on, one mine after another shut down. The last mine, the Carlton Mill and Mine, closed down in 1961.

Today, Cripple Creek remains a wonderful piece of Colorado history. Much of the town has been remarkably preserved and offers history buffs and tourists the chance to see what the region looked like in times past and even to tour the interior of some of the remaining mines. The fascinating city is a time capsule of the decades past and while much has changed over the years, some parts of Cripple Creek remain the same --- like some of the former residents, who are still lingering here where they found their greatest glory and perhaps their final moments of horror.

There are a number of haunted spots in Cripple Creek, including the renowned Fairley Bros. & Lampman Building, a block-square structure on the corner of Third Street and Bennett Avenue. The resident ghost is called Maggie and she is a direct link to Cripple Creek's mining past. She is seen wearing period clothing and is a young woman, perhaps in her 20's, who wears her long, brunette hair pinned on top of her head in the style of the 1890's. Contractors, employees and visitors have seen and heard this specter walking through the second-floor corridor of the building or have encountered her as she dances in the building's third-floor ballroom.

Two other hauntings in Cripple Creek are more closely connected to the mines and the most famous is that of a former mine itself. The Dunn Building, which is located a short distance outside of town, is said to house at least two ghosts. This building was once a funeral parlor but when her husband died, Mrs. T.F. Dunn turned it into a boarding house. Her presence is still experienced in the 11 original rooms and her footsteps are sometimes heard walking about as she tries to clean them. Her spirit has long been accepted as a part of the building but she is not the most disturbing presence in the house. According to the stories, this ghost is thought to be that of a miner who was killed in an explosion at one of the local mines. Late one night as the undertaker, Mr. Dunn, was preparing the body, the "dead" miner began to moan in pain. Not wanting to stop the preparations that he had already made, and believing the man would die anyway, the mortician injected morphine into the man's veins to quiet him down and stop his heart. Dunn then continued his work and prepared the man for his funeral. It is believed that the restless ghost of the miner still haunts the house today.

But the most chilling haunting in Cripple Creek remains the most famous and involves the ghosts of men who haunted the mysterious Mamie R Mine.

It was no surprise to the men who worked the Mamie R Mine when they learned that ghosts and spirits were being reported here. Most of the men already believed the place was cursed and inhabited by Tommyknockers, those strange creatures who lived in the depths of the mine. They were said to knock and rap on the walls and tunnels, playing tricks and frightening the miners. Often they caused beams to give away, explosives to go off prematurely and were blamed for many of the accidents in this mine and others. Rationally speaking, the Tommyknockers were likely nothing more than a way for the superstitious miners to explain the accidents and the weird sounds and happenings that occurred below the earth. To be able to blame a mishap on a mischievous spirit was almost more comforting than to accept the idea that the work a man was doing could easily lead to his death.

The ghosts who haunted the mine were believed to be the victims of some of the accidents caused by the Tommyknockers. The mine earned a gruesome reputation during its few years of operation but the pay was good and the work solid and aside from a few accidents, which happened in every mine, the men were content to remain here. They worked hard and the stories that were told normally involved the tapping of the Tommyknockers in deep portions of the mine. Usually, as the spirits mimicked the work being done by the miners, rapping sounds from a particular section could mean the discovery of a new vein of gold, which attracted the spirits. The men followed the sounds and were always careful not to whistle, a sound that irritated the Tommyknockers, and could cause accidents to occur. For this reason, it was always considered bad luck to whistle in a mine.

On a sunny afternoon in the summer of 1894, spirits were likely the last thing on anyone's mind when the crew at the top of the shaft received a signal from below to lower the mine bucket and bring a miner to the surface. The lift operator responded and after waiting the usual time, he reversed the lever and brought the bucket back up again. When it reached the top of the shaft though, the lift operator and some of the other crew members were surprised to find the bucket empty. More puzzled than worried about the incident, the men went about their work and forgot all about it. The empty bucket would never have been mentioned again -- if not for the events that followed.

A few days later, as the afternoon was turning into the evening, a signal came from down in the mine to lower the bucket. The operator pushed the lever forward and the lift slowly lowered down into the darkness. The lines twitched as a weight settled into the bucket and he brought it back up again, expecting nothing out of the ordinary. In the back of his mind though, he remembered the odd incident from a few days before and he peered into the shadows as the bucket came up higher, straining to see if anyone was inside.

When the bucket reached the top of the shaft, the crew saw that it carried a horrific load --- a bloody and fatally injured miner who looked to be barely alive. He was covered in gore and his clothing was blackened and charred. One of his arms had been torn from his body and was nowhere to be seen. The men assumed that he was dead until they saw his chest heave once as he tried to pull air into his lungs. One of the crew members was immediately sent for help and the other workers hurried into the bucket to bring the man to safety. As they bent to help him though, their hands passed right through his body as though nothing was there. Almost as one, the men let out a frightened gasp and scurried out of the bucket, retreating to what they hoped was a safe distance.

A few moments later, the men watched in shock as the spectral miner struggled to his feet, climbed out of the bucket and stumbled away from it. He only made it a few steps before he disappeared. The crew stood in silence for a moment and after a brief discussion, decided to call down to the other portion of their crew, who worked at the bottom of the shaft. They asked the men to come up and after the bucket was lowered to them, they rode to the surface. The surface crew explained what had happened to the others and it was only then that the lift operators learned that something similar had happened a few days before when the empty bucket had come to the top. The men below had encountered the badly injured specter and as it struggled into the lift, the signal was sounded on its own and as the bucket began to rise, the ghost simply vanished. The men below were so unnerved by this that they made a pact not to tell anyone what they had seen. Believing that it would be an isolated incident, they planned to honor the pact -- until someone else had the same experience they did.

The grim scene was played out again and again in the weeks to come. The crew never had a choice as to whether or not to lower the bucket as they never knew if it was a miner who needed to come to the surface or the gruesome spirit. Eventually, they worked out a signal with the men below to alert them as to whether or not the calls for the lift were genuine or ghostly. Unfortunately though, on late nights, when the shift below was only a skeleton crew, there was no one to provide a warning and life operators brought the specter to the surface time and time again. Soon, it was nearly impossible to find men who would work the late shift on lift duty.

By later that year, it also became harder and harder to find men to work in the mine at all. Rumors were running rampant about ghosts and spirits and soon it began to be whispered that the mine was cursed. Accidents began to happen more and more often and men were being maimed and killed in cave-ins and equipment mishaps. One afternoon, an explosive charge went off while still in the hands of one of the miners and his legs were blown off his body. Finally, on Christmas Day 1894, the mine flooded and filled the main shaft with water. The lift bucket was used to try and bail the water out and as it was being lowered for the thirteenth time, the cable came loose from its pulley and the bucket plunged back into the mine. As it came down, the cable looped around the operator's neck and as his men watched in horror, he was beheaded.

After that, the Mamie R Mine was closed down for good and was never re-opened. If not for the ghost stories, the mine would likely not be remembered at all today. In fact, Colorado Bureau of Mines has no record of the mine ever operating in Cripple Creek but most believe this can be explained by the fact that it closed down in 1894. Most of the records from that time burned in the huge Cripple Creek fire in 1896 -- wiping out the written records of the Mamie R Mine for all time.

The Mamie R Mine was located in Cripple Creek, Colorado, which is southwest of Colorado Springs. The mine was located on Raven Hill in Cripple Creek.

UTAH'S HAUNTED MINES & MINING CAMPS
Deadly Disasters, Ghost Towns, Women in White, Lost Treasure & More

Utah is one of the most beautiful states in the Union and also one of the strangest and most haunted. Between the Indian spirits, the lives of pioneers lost and the unusual lore of the Mormons, it has come to be regarded as a place where hauntings are easy to find -- but not often talked about. In this land of mountains, wondrous deserts and mysterious ghost towns, haunted mines are simply realized as a part of the wonderful landscape.

About 13 years ago, I had the chance to spend an extended period of time in Utah, working in the book business. During the time I was there, I became fascinated with the region and spent almost all of my free time hiking, exploring ghost towns, half-heartedly looking for lost treasure and of course -- tracking down legends of ghosts and haunted places. It turned out to be a great experience for me and many of the adventures that I went on are chronicled in this book for the first time. On occasion, they were not for the faint of heart.

When the Mormon settlers first arrived in Utah in 1847 and took up residence around the Great Salt Lake, it was quickly realized many of the things necessary for carving a life out of the wilderness were missing. There was little timber for lumber or fuel and it was also soon apparent that coal would be needed. There was none close to the valley and so the pioneers directed their search toward the cliffs and mesas that would come to be known as Carbon County.

By 1849, extensive coal deposits were found in the canyons of the region but were too far from Salt Lake City to be mined economically. In 1854, Brigham Young offered a reward of $1,000 for the discovery of a coal vein within 40 miles of the city. While a number of mines were started in the vicinity, none were close enough to gain the reward. After the railroad was completed in 1869 though, the distance did not matter quite so much and almost overnight, towns like Nolen, New Peerless and Coal City became booming mining camps. Almost all of the coal mines were within the borders of Carbon County.

Today, nearly all of the coal camps are ghost towns, hidden away in brush-choked canyons and along seldom-visited plateaus. They are silent and now forgotten but a few of them have fascinating stories to tell. One of these ghost towns, Latuda, was located several miles up Spring Canyon in Carbon County and over the years, it has gained a fascinating story of a woman in white whose life was destroyed by the coal mines.

The town was settled in 1917 but actually saw its first residents three years earlier when an ambitious coal developer named Frank Latuda opened the Liberty Fuel Company high along a rugged canyon wall. Although the location seemed almost inaccessible, he operated tiny wooden coal cars inside of the mine and delivered his product by tramway to the railroad below. Latuda continued this operation until 1917, when a new mine was opened on the canyon floor. Several mining innovations, including a mechanical loader and an air-sand cleaning plant, were first used at this Utah mine.

In 1918, about 20 homes were constructed around the mine and the new town was christened Liberty, in honor of the company. The water for the settlement had to be supplied by the nearby town of Helper, although bitter water for the mine was pumped from a small spring up a side canyon. In spite of the remote conditions and undrinkable local water, the community slowly grew. The mine office was built in 1920 and 35 more houses were constructed in 1922. The top floor of the office was used as a hotel for visiting executives and a doctor's office occupied another section. The first school sessions were also held here until 1923, when a separate building was constructed. Around this time, the post office demanded a new name for the town, as they were already overrun by other towns called Liberty. After a vote, the residents decided to use mine developer Frank Latuda's name instead.

The town prospered in the years that followed and the mine employed an average of about 100 workers. Stores and shops opened to serve the needs of the miners and their families and the community grew to about 400 people. In 1927, disaster struck and in one afternoon, several avalanches thundered down the steep canyon walls, killed a number of people and wiped out a row of homes. The terrible event was not enough to kill off the town though. The residents rallied around one another and pressed on for nearly 30 more years.

In 1954, after some four to five million tons of coal had been produced, the mine shut down most of its operation. Only 20 families stayed on during the late 1950's and early 1960's, some of them still working the mine. Mining stopped completely in 1966 and the last of the families moved away over the next year. By 1967, the town of Latuda consisted of nothing more than a few houses, the abandoned mine and the silent Liberty Fuel office building, which still stands today.

Several years ago, I visited the decaying town of Latuda while traveling in Utah and was delighted to find that some remnants of the place remained. Scattered around this portion of the canyon, I found the ruins of a number of homes, although all had long been picked over by souvenir hunters and explorers. Strangely though, the Liberty mine office building was in still in very good condition, save for a portion of the building that had been destroyed by a troubled teenager in 1972. The stone building was two levels high and had a wide, two-level porch that ran the length of the building. Inside, I found carpeting still on the floor and grillwork and a counter still remaining in the payroll office. I had heard that an old safe was still located in one corner of the office, still locked and hiding its treasures, but it had vanished by the time that I arrived in town. My explorations led me to the remains of the old mine, which still looms above the crumbling settlement, but entrance to the shaft was so dangerous that I decided not to try it alone.

Besides that, the old mine was not what had brought me to Latuda -- the reason for my visit had been the ghost who was rumored to haunt the place. I was told that the town and mine were haunted by a "White Lady" who had been known for years to wander about the ruins of the town. According to an old timer that I talked with, sightings of the woman even pre-dated the demise of the town in the 1950's. The problem was that no one seemed to know who this woman was or why she haunted this place. Most versions of the story seem to agree that she was the wife of a man who was employed at the mine but beyond that, the legends vary. Some believe that she was home on that fateful day in 1927 and was killed by one of the rockslides that wreaked havoc on the town -- or that her child was left home alone while she went to the general store and the toddler was killed by the avalanche. The woman committed suicide soon after.

The most common version of the tale seems to be that her husband died in a mining accident and she was never fairly compensated for his death, which is why her ghost always ends her rambling near the mine office. The widow was now left with a small child to raise and it is at this point that the legend takes yet another series of different routes. Some say that her life ended in a mental institution after she killed her child in a twisted attempt to spare her from a lifetime of suffering. Others say that she hanged herself from the upper balcony of the mine office. Regardless of how she died though, the lady in white has returned to Latuda after death. She walks the now abandoned streets of the town, my sources assured me, oblivious to the fact that everything in town has changed. Other explorers and hikers have reported seeing the woman, wearing a white, outdated dress, as she walks through town in the direction of the mine office -- only to vanish just before she reaches it.

With a notebook filled with accounts, a battered book on Utah ghost towns and a sleeping bag, I camped out along the old road in Latuda on a chilly night in October, waiting and watching for the lady in white to stroll past. I have to confess though -- I never saw her. But even so, having the experience of looking for her in such a scenic and historic region, it was well worth the time that I spent.

The following morning, on my way out of town and in pursuit of another abandoned mine and ghostly tale, I stopped to talk with a longtime resident of the area who was driving toward Latuda in a Jeep that had seen better days. He grinned when he saw me and asked if I had been looking for treasure -- or the ghost. Apparently, these two distractions had brought many up the road to the old town. I laughed and explained that I had been hoping to see the Lady in White. I hadn't had any luck though, I told him.

"I saw her once," he replied, "must've been back around 1985. I've been prospecting, fiddling around really, in these canyons since I retired. I camped back here one night and while I'd heard all the stories, I never expected to see her. But around midnight, there she was. She walked past my fire like I wasn't there at all. I was too surprised to do anything but watch her go. Before long, she was just gone -- I didn't see her anymore."

I told him how I had heard about the story and had come hoping that she wasn't just a legend but he interrupted me quickly.

"Oh no," he assured me, rubbing at his rough, white beard. "She's no legend. She's the real thing. Don't know who she is, but they've been talking about seeing the lady out here for years."

Then he laughed and looked at me with as he shook his head. "Don't suppose I believed it either 'til I saw her --- seeing really is believing sometimes."

THE HAUNTED WINTER QUARTERS MINE
Near Scofield, Utah

Sometimes, hunting for ghost stories can not only be a lot of work -- but a lot of driving as well. There was no direct route to get from Latuda to the site of the old Winter Quarters Mine, so I had to take Highway 6 to the north and swing around through Colton on Route 96 to get to Scofield. When I got there, I still had to travel by way of a rutted dirt road, over a fence and along an abandoned railroad grade to the ruins of Winter Quarters. Once again, it was a tale of ghosts and hauntings that brought me here.

The area, once known as Pleasant Valley, was a welcoming place in the 1870's. There were a number of settlers who lived in the area, most of whom grazed cattle on the lush grass here. Coal was discovered in the dark canyon beyond the valley in 1875 and two years later, a small mine was opened on the western slopes of the canyon and the coal was transported out along narrow roads. The winter of 1877 came early and was very severe, stranding the miners in the coal pit and keeping them snowbound until the following February. The ordeal led the miners to name their forced camp "Winter Quarters" and this became one of the first commercial coal mines in the state.

The new town became a thriving one and one of the most impressive cities in Utah. It is hard to imagine, from the ruins that remain, just how important this town once was. The business district was said to be more than a mile long and boasted dozens of substantial stone buildings, many of them as fine as any in Salt Lake City. As the mine and the community grew, new and more efficient methods were sought to move the coal from the mines and so the Utah & Pleasant Valley Railroad was constructed, running from Springville to Winter Quarters and Scofield. It connected with the Denver & Rio Grande line in Colton, which was about 20 miles away. Its businesses included Covington's Hotel, Higney's Store and five saloons. The town actually burned and was rebuilt three times but Colton's future as a bustling city was tied directly to that of Winter Quarters. Unknown to both of them, the future was not very bright.

In 1882, the Utah Fuel Company took over the mine and town and it soon became a subsidiary of the Denver & Rio Grande Railroad. The region continued to thrive until 1900, when there were several hundred men in the mines and residents that numbered as high as 1,800. The mine was considered to be the safest in the region and according to reports, was free from the gases that plagued so many other coal operations. But that was not enough to save it from disaster....

On May 1, 1900, an errant spark touched off the fine haze of coal dust deep underground and the Winter Quarters #4 mine exploded with fury. Exactly 100 of the men were killed in an instant and another 99 died from the poisonous afterdamp, making this one of the worst coal mine disasters in history. That one moment of time left 105 widows and 270 fatherless children behind. Men from all over the area descended on the city and began to pull the mutilated bodies of the victims -- and a few survivors -- from the debris. The town's boarding houses, churches, hotels, school and barns were cleared out to receive and identify the victims. As imagined, trying to cope with the disaster stretched the town's resources to the limit. Mistakes were made when the bodies were identified and many of the men were buried under the wrong names. Grave markers were made up in such a hurry that many of the men's names were misspelled on them. When word spread, every available casket in Utah was sent to Winter Quarters. This did not prove to be enough to hold the dead though and another carload had to be sent in from Denver. Almost 150 of the slain miners were buried in the cemetery in nearby Scofield and two special funeral trains carried the rest of the victims to burial grounds in Utah and in other states.

The terrible tragedy cast a pall of sorrow over the entire town and the deaths of the miners seemed to signal the slow death of Winter Quarters. The gloom never lifted, although the mine remained in operation until 1928. The coal became suitable only for inexpensive locomotive fuel though until finally the transportation costs doomed the mine. By 1930, many houses had been moved to Scofield and Winter Quarters was abandoned. Only caved in cellars and broken foundations remain today.

To reach the site of Winter Quarters, you have to pass through Scofield, which is only a shadow of the boomtown that it was decades ago. It is not a ghost town, but it's not far from being one. When I traveled this way, I was told that I might also want to see another former coal camp at Hale, which is just north of Scofield. Its site was marked by the remains of a few shacks at the edge of a hillside. Some of the mines here at Hale were located downstream from the Scofield Reservoir, while the lake covers the upper part of it. I was told that if I planned to camp overnight, I might consider the lakeshore near the site of Hale rather than the shadowy canyon at Winter Quarters. "The ghosts of the dead miners," I was told by a man that I met, "are not likely to make good company".

But of course, that was exactly the company that I was looking for!

I knew that there had been stories told about ghosts at Winter Quarters for years. In fact, less than a year after the disaster that claimed so many lives, an article appeared in the *Utah Advocate* newspaper in January 17, 1901. It read:

The superstitious miners, who are foreigners, have come to the conclusion that the property is haunted, inhabited by a ghost. Several of them have heard strange and unusual noises, and those favored with a keener vision than their fellow workmen have actually seen a headless man walking about the mine and according to their statements have accosted the ghost and addressed it or he.

At other times the headless man would get aboard the coal cars to which mules and horses are worked and ride with the driver to the mouth of the tunnel when he would mysteriously vanish and again reappear in the mine. Many supposedly intelligent men have claimed this and some twenty-five or forty have thrown up their jobs in consequence.

These same people and others have seen mysterious lights in the graveyard on the side of the hill where many victims of the explosion of May are buried.. Efforts to ferret out the cause have been fruitless though close observations have been made by reputable citizens of the camp. These lights are always followed by a death, so it is alleged by others than the miners who might be disciples of the supernatural. Tombstones where the light appeared have been blanketed but the light remains clear to the vision of those who watch from town.

I found Scofield easily enough and then had to ask for directions to the dirt road that would take me out of town. About a half mile along, I had to leave the car and cross an old barbed wire fence and walk another half mile or so along the railroad bed to reach to reach the town site. There wasn't much left by the time I arrived, although there were sections of the walls that made up the former Wasatch store, which was once the center of town. Antique photos show stacks of coffins outside the store in the days following the 1900 disaster. I walked through what was left of the town and started up toward the mine site.

However, I soon found that I was not alone. The ghost town remains very popular with treasure hunters due to the fact that so many of the men who were killed at Winter Quarters were bachelors. It is thought that many of them had what were called "post hole banks" dug into the ground near their cabins and so the money they had secreted away was never recovered. When the town was abandoned, who knows how many other caches may have been left behind, unknown, hidden and forgotten?

This is what I was told by two young men who had hiked into the site with metal detectors. They told me that they had been coming out to Winter Quarters for a couple of years and just a month before had found a metal box that contained old silver coins. In the past, they had also turned up odd coins, a few tools, a pocketknife, a hand mirror and even a rusted straight razor. I explained to them what I was doing around the town site and asked them if they had ever heard or seen anything strange in the area.

One of the young men, Mike, looked at his friend and I could tell they were both a little uneasy about the question. If anything, they seemed to be unsettled by it. "Actually, yes," Mike finally spoke up. "We were camping out here one night last spring and heard some pretty weird sounds coming from the direction of the mine."

"Weird sounds -- like what?" I asked them.

Mike's companion, Josh, spoke up. "I woke up in the middle of the night and went outside the tent to go to the bathroom and I heard voices coming from the canyon. At first, I just thought that maybe someone else was camping out here but..."

"We never saw anybody and we were out here all day," Mike interrupted.

Josh added. "And we didn't see any fires either. I woke up Mike and well, you just never know who might be out here. Then it started to get a little stranger. The only way that I can describe the sounds is that it was like people moaning and crying."

"It sounded like a big group of people, moving around, talking -- real weird," said Mike. "I know there was some sort of accident out here or something, I don't know -- maybe that had something to do with it."

His friend agreed. "I have to say that I never really gave much thought to ghosts and stuff, but I don't know what else this could be. I guess if you decide to camp out here, I don't suggest that you do it up the canyon anywhere."

I talked to Josh and Mike for awhile and then wandered off on my own, contemplating the fact that this had been my second warning about camping in the canyon beyond the town site. I had heard that the cemetery where the miners were buried in Scofield might be haunted (see the newspaper article from the *Utah Advocate*) but now the ghostly sites seemed to include the area around the mine as well. I became determined to spend the night in what turned out to be a rather frigid canyon. I had hoped that my search for these ghosts might turn out to more successful than my hunt for the Lady in White in Latuda -- and this time it was.

To say that it was cold out there that night would be an understatement. The tent that I had brought with me offered little shelter from the wind that came blowing through the canyon and even huddled close to the fire, my sleeping bag offered little comfort from the cold. At one point, I turned quickly to see what the strange noise behind me was and then realized that it was my teeth chattering! I stayed up most of the night and while largely uneventful, I do believe that I heard the weird sounds that had been described to me by the treasure hunters.

By this time, it was well after midnight and the sounds that I heard came from the darkness near the old mine site. The best way for me to describe it is to say that it was an odd crying sound, almost like an animal in pain. I wondered for a moment if it might actually be a wounded coyote or something that was out beyond the light from the fire but then I dismissed this. The sound was further away than that and then it seemed to be joined by another voice, then another, until there was a chorus of them. If I am completely honest with the reader, I would have to say that perhaps my imagination was at work (or perhaps not?) but it sounded to me like a group of woman crying and moaning. I envisioned the dozens of women who must have come to the mine on the day of the explosion, weeping for the dead and searching desperately for their husbands as the victims were pulled from the depths. The sound faded and dipped and then came back strong again.

Was it the wind? I don't think it was -- but whatever it was, I have never forgotten that sound and for more than a year afterward, I would awaken at night having dreamed about it. It was not the most chilling experience that I would ever have searching for ghosts (that would occur years later in an abandoned tuberculosis asylum in Kentucky) but it was one of the most unnerving. To this day, I cannot give you a rational explanation that would explain the eerie keening that I heard that night.

And yes, I did search for an explanation. I gathered my courage and armed with only a flashlight, I set off in search of a source for the sound. As I started up the hill toward the mine site though, the sound abruptly ceased. It did not return that night, leaving me to ponder the mystery of what lingers at Winter Quarters, even after all of these years.

CURSED MINES OF UTAH
Brigham Young's Mine & The Curse of the Lost Josephine

My search for the unusual in Utah turned up a variety of strange stories in regards to the mines and mining camps of the region. Some of these stories, most of which dated back a number of years, involved cursed mines that had been lost to history -- but were still closely guarded by the supernatural.

One such mine was dubbed "Brigham Young's Cursed Mine" and it was located near the ghost town of Lake Point, which was located at the north end of the Oquirruh Mountains and about a mile from the Great Salt Lake. When the place was first settled in 1854, it was an outgrowth of E.T. City, a small settlement named in honor of Ezra Taft Benson, a Mormon church leader. Lake Point never really grew until Dr. Jeter Clinton decided to build a resort here. Since E.T. City was not faring well, thanks to the salty soil that prohibited farming, the residents packed up and moved to Lake Point. Soon after came the advent of steamships on the Great Salt Lake and since mine owners discovered that they could cheaply ship ore across the lake to Corinne, where mills and smelters were located, Lake Point became Utah's first seaport, almost overnight.

Silver ore was hauled by wagon to Lake Point and then loaded onto steamships to make the journey across the lake. *The City of Corrine* and the *Kate Connor* were two of the largest freighters and the *Kate Connor* also carried as many as 300 passengers as well. This helped Lake Point to prosper even more and business was so good at Dr. Clinton's resort that he also built the Clinton Hotel, which hosted as many as 50,000 guests per year.

In August 1873, the Salt Lake, Pioche and Sevier Valley Railroad came to town but it was hardly a boon to the economy, offering higher shipping rates rather than lower ones. As shipping ore by wagon was already expensive, mine owners retaliated against the railroad prices by building mills closer to their mines. This sent Lake Point's main source of income into a decline. Soon, the long piers that stretched out into the lake began to decay and collapse and the once proud ships that used them came to even more inglorious ends. The huge *City of Corrine* was renamed the *Garfield*, in hopes that it could be used for excursion cruises. Unfortunately though, it burned near Black Rock, leaving a charred skeleton on the sand here for years. The luxurious *Kate Connor* was sold to a livestock company and they used it to transport sheep and cattle the lake's islands.

Lake Point was now dead and soon, was only a memory. The lakeshore reverted back to grasslands and before long, cattle could be seen grazing where buildings once stood and businesses thrived. Today, the ruins of several stone buildings, Lake Point's forgotten woolen mills, can be found crumbling far from the lakefront, where the receding waters of the lake have left them.

The story of the curse came about a number of years before the demise of Lake Point. During the 1860's, John Croslin, a convert to the Mormon church, was hunting for stray sheep in a canyon above Rowberry's Sawmill, which was located at Twin Springs, just southwest of town. As he was searching for the sheep, he came upon a jagged outcropping that was heavily criss-crossed with gold veins. In deference to Brigham Young's admonition against mining, he did not tell anyone where the ledge was and instead, went directly to the Mormon leader with the information. Instead of giving the man a special dispensation to develop a mine, he told Croslin that he wanted no mines whatsoever in the vicinity of Salt Lake City. "If you Elders want to go gold mining, go and be damned," he reportedly told Croslin. "I would not give a picayune to save you from damnation!" He then added that a curse would befall Croslin or anyone else who worked the gold ledge. Croslin returned to Lake Point, well aware of the value of the site --- but fearful of the prophet's warning.

As it turned out, his fears may have been justified.

Rumors spread around Lake Point about Croslin's find and his friends and family members pressed him hard to get him to reveal the site of the gold ledge. He was true to his promise not to work the site but he did admit that he knew where it was, claiming that he could stand in the doorway of Rowberry's Sawmill and look into the canyon where the gold could be found. When he was accused of lying, he stated that he passed by the ledge every time that he followed his sheep into the canyon. "It is still there!" he insisted.

A few years later, Croslin's brother-in-law showed up in Lake Point and began selling pieces of raw gold. People began to suspect that perhaps Croslin had revealed the location of the ledge to him. They searched the canyons beyond the sawmill, looking for some sign of diggings, but turned up nothing. The search continued though and one day, a man's body was discovered at the edge of the foothills. Some said that he had been killed by Indians but there wasn't a mark on his body. Clutched in his hands though were several rough nuggets of gold. Not surprisingly, Croslin claimed that Brigham Young's curse had killed him.

And if Croslin did reveal the location of the mine to brother-in-law, then it might explain what happened soon after -- he was killed in an accident at a local mill. After his death, two young men, who claimed to be his nephews, said that they had a map Croslin had made. They may have indeed found the location of the mine that had been started for they got into a fight, perhaps over the division of gold, and one killed the other. The killer was banished from Utah with a warning never to return. These dire events were accepted by many as further effects from the curse.

Just months after the death of Croslin, Bill Hickman appeared in Lake Point and persuaded Croslin's widow to show him where the gold diggings were located. At that time, Federal marshals were on his trail for murder for Hickman had been accused of being a leading figure in the "Utah War", which, among other things, was a last-stand effort by Mormons to quell an attempt by U.S. Army troops to march to Utah and remove Brigham Young from the office of governor. Hickman was accused of killing as many as 54 men on direct orders from Brigham Young but later had a falling out with the prophet over his work for the military. Desperate for money, he agreed to take part in a book that detailed the secret workings of the church and especially the work of the Danites, the Mormon's so-called "angels of death". Much about Hickman's life has been questioned in recent history, as well as his connections to the Croslin mine, but according to the legend, Croslin's widow was shunned because of her brief association with him. Many credit this, as well as Hickman's death in Wyoming, as just another part of the curse.

Until the death of Brigham Young in 1877, no one dared search for the cursed mine and according to author George A. Thompson, no one has looked for it since.

The Lost Josephine Mine is one of the most famous and best authenticated lost mines in Utah. The history of the mine is twisted around stories of death, murder, ghosts and ancient Native American curses -- and remains out there, somewhere, still hidden in the mysterious and remote Henry Mountains.

The Lost Josephine Mine is forever tied to the ghost town of Eagle City, one of the least known of all of Utah's mining camps. The settlement was perched high in the Bromide Basin, near the head of Crescent Creek and in a rugged area of the Henry Mountains. They were the last major mountain range to be discovered in the United States and portions of the mountains remain unexplored today. John C. Fremont called them the "Unknown Mountains" and this remains a good name for them, for few know what secrets these mountains still hold.

The first gold that was discovered in the Henry Mountains was found by John Angrove but he was murdered for his find shortly afterward. Some say that this ghost still haunts the mountains but if it does, the specter never bothered Jack Sumner and Jack Butler, who found gold in 1889 at a spot that became the Bromide Mine. Other mines opened over the course of the next few years and mills were built along Crescent Creek to work the gold ore. These crude mills were unable to recover the high grade copper and silver in the ore and much of it was lost in the tailings that washed down the creek.

Eagle City came into being at the fork of the canyon two miles below Bromide Basin and soon boasted a store, a hotel, a doctor's office and a saloon. Legend had it that Butch Cassidy and his Wild Bunch often stopped at Eagle City and that Jack Moore, a lesser known outlaw, sometimes dealt faro in the saloon.

As the mines near Eagle City were sunk deeper and deeper into the mountains, water began seeping into the shafts. A 3,000 foot drain tunnel was planned to empty the shafts but a lack of financing stopped it before it was driven halfway. To make matters worse, the Bromide Mill burned to the ground in 1911. With the leading mill gone, most of the shafts flooded and with the Great War taking away many of the best young men, the miners left Eagle City and soon the camp was abandoned.

Only one man remained, a hermit and prospector named Frank Lawler, and he stayed in Eagle City for the next 60 years. During this time, Lawler had plenty of time to think about the local legend of the Lost Josephine Mine, the richest and most famous of all of the lost Spanish mines. He never doubted that it was hidden somewhere in the Henry Mountains and he and Ed Wolverton, another lonely mountain resident, found plenty of evidence of Spanish miners. Lawler uncovered the entrance to an old Spanish tunnel buried beneath the gravel next to Crescent Creek, while Wolverton found many Spanish markings, the ruins of a mill, slag piles and waste dumps that were so old they had pine trees growing on them. The two of them never found the Lost Josephine but if you believe the tales -- it's still out there!

While some have dismissed the idea that the mine exists at all, numerous references to it can be found in Catholic Church records, Spanish land grants, royal records of gold shipped to Spain and in old journals. It was known by several names over its long history but official records in Madrid, detailing shipments of gold from the New World, simply refer to it as the Josephine Mine. It was claimed to be one of the richest mines in the Spanish empire.

But while these records claim the mine is real, they never reveal where the Josephine was located or when it was first worked. Some clues have been found though. Along an old pack trail that leads from the Henry Mountains to the Colorado River, one faded inscription has been found scratched into a sandstone wall reads "1642 Ano Dom" and between the Colorado and Bear's Ears Pass on the Old Spanish Trail is the name and date "De Julio 1661". Near the north end of the mountain range is an old burial ground that marks a battle between Spanish soldiers and Indians. The dead were buried by Jesuit priests, who erected a cross and left the date 1777 and an illegible name behind. There are few clues that can be dated between 1680, when most of the Spanish mines on the northern frontier were lost because of an Indian slave revolt, and 1765, when Father Rivera's expedition reopened the area.

During his expedition in 1853, the previously mentioned explorer John C. Fremont followed ancient steps that had been cut into the stone cliffs at the Spanish Bottoms on the Colorado River. He noted in his journals that, near the Henry Mountains, his men found "the very old bones of a pack mule, and on either side of them a pile of gold ore, from packs long since rotted away." Later explorers also found sites where miners had been killed by Indians and the pack animals left on the desert floor, leaving only scattered bones and little piles of gold ore.

But all of the clues have yet to be gathered in a way that could lead an intrepid prospector to the Lost Josephine. And if the day should ever come when they do, that prospector would be wise to consider the final tale of the mine. According to Navajo Indian legend, an old medicine man actually placed a curse on the Josephine when the Indians finally drove the Spanish from the mountains. The curses states that:

> To him who reopens the mine will come great calamity. His blood will turn to water and even in his youth, he will be as an old man. His squaws and papooses will die and the earth will bring forth only poison weeds instead of corn.

It certainly makes one think twice before journeying off into the Henry Mountains in search of lost Spanish gold, doesn't it?

THE MINE OF LOST SOULS
Near Vernal, Utah

Of all of the lost and haunted mines that I heard about in Utah, I was most intrigued by the name of one mine in particular -- the Mine of Lost Souls. Apparently, the mine had been dubbed with this name by an old woman who had witnessed the murder of a group of miners here. She began calling it this because she believed the spirits of the miners returned to haunt the place. After hearing about the legend, I recruited a friend of mine (and often a reluctant guide) to take me out to this rather remote region and to help me find the now deserted town of Bullionville, near where the mine was located. I assumed that the mine would be easy to find, for my battered ghost town book offered detailed directions to the town, but I would soon learn that I was only the latest in a long line of people who had searched for the mine near Bullionville without success.

The early history of the mine can be found in the records of a town called Bullionville. It came about back in June 1880, when the Carbonate Mining District was organized by a group of miners who gathered at the Vortex Café in Vernal. A month later, the town of Bullionville was laid out near the head of Brush Creek, 27 miles north of Vernal. Although it was a mining camp, the town became a hideout for outlaws for a time, or at least a place to get food, drink and women. A place called Brown's Hole was only a few miles away and it was often used by men on the run from the law.

As exploration in the area commenced, the mine owners were dismayed to find very little gold, but large amounts of undesirable copper. Very little was accomplished until 1887, when L.P. Dyer, a cowboy and prospector, discovered more good copper ore and opened the Ace, the Antietam and other mines at the Kane Hollow Fork of Brush Creek. In 1894 and 1897, additional gold strikes were made near Gilbert's Peak and Marsh Peak and the town finally began to prosper. Some of Bullionville's ore was hauled away to Park City but most of it was taken by teams over Carter Road, which had been built through the Uinta Mountains to Wyoming. Ore would be stockpiled in the summer and then hauled out in the winter, since sleds pulled much easier through the several feet of snow than wagons traveled in warm weather.

Although several of the mines here contained high grade copper ore, most of the diggings were shallow, so when the gold strikes in the Uintas played out and the Dyer mines closed, Bullionville folded up as though it had never existed at all. A handful of men remained for a few years but in 1920, the miners left for good. The town was reoccupied for a short time in the early 1930's as a Civilian Conservation Corps camp but they also departed and left the town to be reclaimed by the wilderness.

We found the former camp easily enough, hiking back along overgrown trails to where Bullionville once stood. Since the town was never much more than a mine camp with long cabins and frame buildings, not much of it remains today. There were some tumbled-down walls of a few cabins and some rotted wooden sidewalks when I was there, silently testifying to the fact that anyone ever lived here at all, but this is not why I had come. Although always fascinated by ghost towns, I was here seeking the old Spanish mine that existed long before Bullionville ever did.

According to the stories, the miners of the past century were well aware of a lost mine that was rumored to exist in the area. They knew that hundreds of years before, Spanish pack trains carried heavy loads of silver ore from the Uintas and even found evidence of their passing in rusted tools, lost spurs and even an ornate sword but they never found the mines.

Long ago, before the Indian uprisings that drove the Spaniards from the mountains, a rich silver mine was worked in a canyon whose landmarks were peculiar to that canyon only. The miners were slaughtered by the Indians and their bodies were unceremoniously tossed into the mine shafts. Only a few of them managed to escape with their families and one of these residents was a small girl who, along with a few others, made her way to the Spanish settlements in New Mexico.

Years later, when she was an old woman, she recalled the massacre and the dead miners that she believed now haunted the mine. She called the place the "Mine of Lost Souls" and she warned those she told about it of the vengeful specters that she was sure would be guarding over the place. To try and steal the silver in the mine would be to incur the wrath of these ghosts. In spite of her warnings though, she did remember, and was able to describe, the landmarks located in the canyon where the mine was. There is only one place that matches this description and it is on the Dry Fork of Ashley creek, northwest of Vernal -- which is not as close to Bullionville as the miners believed.

We decided to backtrack after visiting the town site and to try and find the mine, which was described by the old woman. According to her recollections, the mine was located on one side of a high point of land where two streams came together. One of the streams flowed into a swirling sink hole, leaving its bed dry until it resurfaced several miles downstream. There was a natural stone bridge that spanned a side canyon, and not far from the bridge, a cave where some of the miners lived. The mine was not very far from the cave. The woman said that she and her mother had been picking berries near the stone bridge when the Indians attacked and killed the miners. The two of them hid in the forest that night until they found some of the other survivors. Her warnings of ghosts came from the eerie sounds that were heard coming from the mine in the darkness. She was convinced the sounds were the voices of the dead men, calling out for vengeance.

Needles to say, we decided to chance it and set off in search of the mine. Following directions that we had found, we drove from Maeser, which is three miles west of Vernal, toward Dry Fork. After that, the roads got bad. We passed the Red Cloud Loop Road and went about 17 miles past Maeser. At that point, the road forked to each side of a high point of land where two streams come together. The rocky road to the left only went a short distance and then we had to get out and hike about a half mile to where we saw a stone bridge that spanned a side canyon to our right. According to the woman's story, there would be a thick area of brush about a half mile past the bridge, where the hidden mouth of the cave was located -- and she was right. We easily found it, just like the old woman had described.

Even though we were seeking the haunted mine, we decided to check out the cave too. We crawled inside with our lights and I have to admit that I had a hard time believing that anyone would want to live in here. The cave narrowed down to no wider than my shoulders and then dropped off into the blackness. We backed out of the cave and continued on in search of the mine. We walked on for another half mile, where the mine was supposed to be located, and then another half mile past that, where the Dry Fork disappeared into the sinkhole. The stream bed was dry but when I put my ear down to the bed, I could hear the water flowing underneath it.

We decided that we had gone too far and so we went back through the canyon to search again -- but we never found anything. The clues were all there, from the point of land to the two creeks, the stone bridge, the cave and the sink hole. The mine was supposed to be near the cave but we never found it. I later learned that no one else ever has either. Does this mine even exist? Or is it merely a legend from Utah's bloody past? That's one mystery that I can't offer any clues toward solving.

To search for the Mine of Lost Souls on your own, follow the directions in the narrative but be very careful if entering the cave and with your vehicle on the rutted roadways. To visit the site of Bullionville: Take Red Cloud Loop about 23 miles north of Vernal and along the Loop Road is the East Park Reservoir Road that swings north to the steep Kane Hollow Road, which winds another two miles to the west. You should still be able to find a faint trail that leads north off the main track to the town site.

GHOST OF MURDERED MINER'S CACHE
Near Milford, Utah

Hickory was a mining camp that was organized in 1882 at the southwest tip of the Rocky Range, about five miles north of Milford in Beaver County. It was named for the Old Hickory Mine, which assayed a high rate of silver and copper, making it one of the richest in the area. The owners of the Old Hickory installed a stamp mill on the site in 1883 and while it cost them nearly $45,000 to build, it was paid for in less than one season. The stamps pounded out bullion from the Old Hickory Mine and gold ore from John Bradshaw's Cave Mine at Bradshaw City. The following year, the mine was sold at a good profit to investors from Nevada, who then hauled their ore to the Miller Mill for processing. It was located at the site of the present-day library in Milford.

Hickory was never a large camp and its daily doings were often overshadowed by the wild antics that occurred in some of the camps to the south. However, Hickory did have one exciting day, long after it had been abandoned and forgotten, and that moment of death left a mystery cache that has never been found -- as well as a resident ghost.

In the late 1930's, a prospector named Gus Knuts began reworking one of the old mines at Hickory. He was a quiet old recluse who kept to himself and lived in one of the cabins near the mine. Knuts was a savvy, small-scale prospector and around 1940, when the war in Europe had driven mineral prices up, he made several ore shipments at a good profit. Whenever he went into Milford for supplies, which he did as seldom as possible, he always paid for everything with cash. It soon became common knowledge in town that the miner was well off and rumor had it that he had a secret cache buried near his cabin.

On November 18, 1941, after someone mentioned that Knuts had not been into town in several months, the sheriff decided to investigate and found that the miner's cabin had been torn to pieces and that holes had been dug all over his property. The old man's throat had been cut and his body had been dumped into the mine shaft. No one was ever arrested for the crime but no one in Milford became suddenly wealthy either. There was no indication that the cache had ever been found -- which set off a rush to the property by treasure hunters and curiosity-seekers.

But they soon returned to Milford, not with tales of uncovered riches but with stories of a ghost instead. According to their frightened reports, the specter of Gus Knuts was now haunting the property around the mine, driving away the treasure seekers who came looking for his cache. Soon, the land around Hickory was largely abandoned and only a few courageous explorers still wandered out to the site -- only to come away empty-handed. The murdered miner's treasure has yet to be found.

CRAZY JOHN'S CACHE
Great Salt Lake Desert

I was not surprised to learn, while in Utah, that Gus Knuts was not the only reclusive miner who was believed to haunt the site of his closely guarded diggings. I ran across another story that I couldn't pass up, this one involving a ghost town, a strange hermit and his ghost.

During the 1870's, a wild gold camp was carved out of the Great Salt Lake Desert called Clifton. It was a boom town, which boasted scores of homes, businesses and stone buildings, and had been built thanks to the fact that gold had been discovered in the Deep Creek Mountains. The gold had actually been found more than a decade earlier by Major Howard Eagan and employees of the Overland Stage Company but the diggings had not been worked because of Indian troubles. When the mines finally opened though, it was found that Clifton's gold was especially high grade, which made it attractive to not only investors but outlaws as well. Since the ore had to be shipped all of the way to Salt Lake City for processing, thieves stole many of the shipments before they got there. To elude the robbers, the mine owners devised a unique and clever plan.

Several large hollow balls were manufactured by the Eagle Iron Works at Salt Lake City for the mine owners. The inch thick balls weighed as much as 200 pounds and had locked keyways that were flush with the surface of the balls. The keyways could be opened and then filled with nuggets, dust and gold concentrate before being locked. The only key to the locks were at the Salt Lake City bank. The gold laden balls were then loaded onto a wagon for the long trip across the desert. One day, as was expected, a holdup attempt was made and the robbers found the gold filled balls to heavy too move and made too well to break open. They managed to roll them off the wagons and into the sand, which then made them impossible to move at all. The thieves worked feverishly under the desert sun, pounded on them with rocks and even tried to shoot holes in them but they were unable to get inside. Finally, they were forced to flee with the approach of law officers. The balls were then reloaded and arrived soon after in Salt Lake City.

More than 2,500 mining claims were located around Clifton and many of them became rich mines, like the Coleman, the Stonewall and the Young American. The mines produced high grade but most of the ore bodies were shallow, so when rich strikes were made at nearby Gold Hill, the town of Clifton began to fade.

Long after the rest of the town had been deserted, two of Brigham Young's nephews stayed on at the camp. Brigham and Oliver Young managed to keep the town from being completely abandoned; waiting for a new boom that just never came. When they died, Clifton lost its caretakers and the desert took its toll on the structures that remained. A few years ago, a friend reported to me that a few of the stone buildings still remained, as well as a portion of the Young's sturdy old log cabin.

Years after Clifton became a ghost town, an old miner who was remembered as only "Crazy John" lived alone in a clapboard shack between Clifton and Gold Hill. As he grew older, he became dangerously violent. Finally, the county sheriff had to place him in a mental institution. He had been reworking some of the old mines for years and during his more lucid moments, he told staff members at the hospital that he planned to go back to his claim and dig up a large "flask" of gold that he had hidden there.

No one paid any attention to his ramblings but after he died, the sheriff talked to a mine owner at Gold Hill who had an interesting tale to tell. The mine owner said that before "Crazy John" went insane, he went over to visit him and saw the old man pouring what looked like gold dust into a rusted iron ball. When the old prospector saw him approaching, he chased him away from his shack, threatening to shoot him if he ever came back. The mine owner recalled the odd looking iron ball was in a wheelbarrow and a deep track in the sand led off into the brush.

Could the iron ball in the wheelbarrow have been one of the iron balls that were made for the owners of the Clifton mines? If it was, did it contain gold that had been mined in years past or gold from "Crazy John's" own diggings? No one knew but when the story got around, people were intrigued. Predictably, treasure hunting parties were organized and went out to the hermit's claims to search for the buried iron ball. Also predictably, a few of them told of being chased off the land by an "insane man" who raved at them and screamed until they left. No one lived nearby at the time and when "Crazy John" was described to them, each of the witnesses stated that he was the man who had accosted them -- even though he had died some time before.

Time passed and eventually, the lost cache was forgotten and soon it was hard to recall where the hermit had worked or where his cabin had been. Whatever happened to the buried "flask" is unknown but it's probably still out there somewhere, waiting to be found.

And one has to wonder if a lonesome ghost still lingers out there as well?

LOST MINES & TRAGIC SPIRITS OF THE MOUNTAIN MEADOWS REGION
Utah's Dixie National Forest

One of the most horrific events in Utah history occurred in September 1857 at a place called Mountain Meadows, a lush, green pasture with sparkling streams that had long been a favorite resting place for weary travelers along the Old Spanish Trail. It would take an entire book to explain the intricacies of what occurred here but in 1857, the meadows hosted an encampment of 138 men, women and children from Missouri and Arkansas known as the Fancher party. For reasons unknown, the encampment was attacked by a band of Mormon zealots and Indians and after a three-day siege, and a promise of surrender, the Mormons slaughtered 121 members of the party in cold blood. They spared 17 children because they were too young to remember the massacre.

Almost from the time this massacre took place, it has been seen as a blight on the history of Utah. For years, it was denied that it ever took place, then was grudgingly accepted but was (and remains) a carefully avoided subject among those of the Mormon faith. During the time that I was out in Utah, the massacre was again the subject of controversy as my trip was around the time that a historical marker had been situated at the site. Unfortunately, the passive words on the marker laid no blame on anyone, which was being roundly criticized from almost every direction.

To make matter worse, rumors also ran rampant that the meadow where the massacre occurred was haunted and had been so for years. The bodies of the victims had never really been properly buried and whispers had it that their restless spirits still lingered here. This, unfortunately, put me into a difficult position. To start with, stories of ghosts and hauntings are not really welcomed by those who belong to the LDS (Latter Day Saints / Mormon) Church. I was often treading on thin ice with my friends who were Mormon and for me to bring up visiting the Mountain Meadows Massacre site would have caused problems that I didn't want. I really did want to visit the location though and haunted or not, I knew of enough mystery associated with the area, and some of the characters involved with the massacre, to travel there on my own. I also felt that the area was worthy of mention within these pages and since this trip to the southwest corner of the state was the last of my excursions in Utah, I wanted to chronicle it here.

The Mountain Meadows Massacre was closely tied to the history of the small community that was located nearby called Hamblin. The town was located near the east end of the Mountain Meadows in what is now the Dixie National Forest. Although it was small, its name was destined to become known throughout the country in the years following the massacre. Sadly, it was a young town at the time, having been settled in 1856 by a small band of Mormons led by famed explorer Jacob Hamblin. It grew quickly into a number of cabins and a fort and as all of the homes in town were built on the same street, it did offer some protection from the Indians in the area. After a church and a schoolhouse were built at one end of the street and the Hamblin Co-Op store was built at the other, the street was safely closed off.

After the massacre took place, the children who were not killed were taken to Hamblin until they could be given to Mormon families to raise. Although the events were meant to be kept secret, the story soon shocked the nation and people all over the country heard of Mountain Meadows -- and of course, of

Hamblin. Jacob Hamblin, for whom the town was named, had always been a peacemaker and friend to the Indians and to the travelers who passed through the area. He was completely unaware of the tragedy until after it had occurred and then was understandably devastated.

Some said that Mountain Meadows was cursed after this. The springs that once watered the meadow stopped flowing and the grass dried up and was swallowed by the desert. Sagebrush now grew where only grass had been, as though trying to hide the nameless graves. Hamblin tried to survive in spite of it disgrace and for a time, new settlers continued to arrive. A town site was surveyed and enlarged but now its days seemed numbered. Irrigation water came from Meadow Valley Creek but a series of floods in the 1890's cut deeper into the already steep wash until water could no longer be raised up into the fields. People began to leave and before long, Hamblin was a ghost town. And even at that time, rumor had it that the massacre site was haunted -- and now the ghosts of the luckless victims were said to be walking the deserted street of the town too. There is nothing left of it now. Today, a rough dirt road leaves Route 18 and winds its way to the Hamblin cemetery, which is all that remains of the town started by Jacob Hamblin.

It was at the Hamblin Cemetery where I was told to start my search for the Lost Hornblende Mine. This old Spanish mine was believed to be somewhere in the area, only a stone's throw from the haunted massacre site. Over the years, many settlers and prospectors had found signs of Spanish mining operations, including George and Fred Ashdown, settlers at Cedar City. They had discovered one old mine tunnel high in the cliffs not far from Mountain Meadows. It had been dug to a depth of about 200 feet and looked as though it had not been worked in a long time. The Ashdown's dug out the badly cluttered entrance and found a number of old tools. Those made from brass were still intact but those made of iron crumbled as soon as the outside air touched them.

The Ashdown's were sawmill operators and had little interest in the old mine. But they did pick up several pieces of heavy black rock that they found in the mine and later gave the rocks to a prospector friend named Ben Evans. Several years later, in Jaunary 1868, Evans wandered into Austin, Nevada and had the rocks assayed. The ore caused a huge sensation and newspapers reported that the unusual black hornblende ore was rich in galena and silver -- rich enough that a man with even a small portion of the weird ore would be fabulously wealthy. Needles to say, Evans returned to Cedar City but found that the Ashdown's had moved on and that no one else knew where the mine was located.

The lost mine would have undoubtedly have been forgotten if an old gentleman of Spanish descent had not arrived in St. George in the 1920's. He had an ancient-looking map that had been given to him by his father. The old man stayed with a rancher but spent most of his time riding alone in the country around Mountain Meadows. He stayed for several weeks and seemed very bothered by something. Eventually, he decided to leave and as he thanked the rancher for his generosity, he gave him the old map that he had brought with him. He said that he might return one day, but if he did not, perhaps the rancher could solve the mystery of the map. He explained that he was very old and had no one on whom to bequeath the map. The mystery had been passed down in his family for several generations and now he was the last -- and the treasure would likely never be found.

The rancher had no better luck with it. It had been written in Spanish and had all sorts of strange markings on it, showing mountain ranges and streams that the rancher didn't recognize. It appeared to have been torn from a larger map which, if it had been intact, might have made the mystery easier to solve. The Spaniard had told the rancher that the mine was in an outcropping of black hornblende rock that most prospectors would ignore. He also gave him a small piece of rock that had belonged to his grandfather and it was heavily streaked with pure silver. The rancher knew that if he could find the mine he would be a rich man and although he searched for years, he never found it.

Strangely though, about two years after the old Spaniard departed, he had an unusual experience while riding near Mountain Meadows. Alone on a quiet, early morning, he was a bit startled when he heard the sound of a horse snort somewhere high above him on the cliffs. When he looked up, he was surprised to see the old Spaniard on a horse. He waved and called up the man but the gentleman did not respond. The Spaniard's horse stood there for a moment and then the animal and rider turned and vanished from view. The rancher was puzzled but expected to perhaps see the old man at dinner that evening. He was very happy about the man's return, as they had become good friends during his earlier stay, and waited all evening for him to arrive. He never came though and the rancher never heard from the old Spaniard again. Later on, he wondered if perhaps the sighting of the man may have marked his last moments on this earth -- still worrying about the lost mine even as he passed on.

Whether or not the rancher encountered the old man's ghost remains as great a mystery as the location of the mysterious silver mine. The rancher never learned where it was located and what finally became of the ancient map is anyone's guess.

Four miles down the Meadow Valley Creek below Hamblin stood another small town, this one called Holt. In the early days, it rivaled Hamblin as the region's most prosperous community, mostly because it had been built along the creek bottom, directly on the Old Spanish Trail. It was settled by James Holt and his followers in 1874 and soon grew into a thriving village. It was doomed to fail though, mostly because it was plagued by alternate periods of drought and flood. In some seasons, the town of Hamblin would use most of the available water and in other seasons, flash floods would come racing down the canyon and wash out the streets and homes, receding to leave thick red mud behind.

Although the residents tried hard to make Holt a permanent settlement, they just couldn't triumph over the unpredictable river. One by one, they drifted out of Holt and left the town to fend for itself. Years after the last resident departed, I traveled to the site of Holt and found very little still remaining. There are some outlines were houses and buildings once stood and a sign that marked the bottom of the canyon as part of the Old Spanish Trail but that was about all. Of course, the real draw to Holt was not in the canyon but in the red rock hills around it -- and of course in the Lost Holt Mine, which prospectors had been seeking for generations.

According to the legend of the mine, village founder James Holt was searching for stray cattle in the foothills north of Holt when he came upon an outcropping of what he described as "pretty red rock". Holt was interested in prospecting, so he took a few pieces of the rock, remembered where he had found them and later had them assayed. His "pretty red rock" turned out to be filled with gold.

In spite of Brigham Young's strict warning against mining, Holt was determined to develop the find and he began digging. Knowing that he needed help, he decided to take his sons out to the claim to work with him the following day. As they prepared to ride out, Holt saw an old man with a long white beard riding a broken down mule approaching his farm. The stranger came up to the door of the house and asked for food. Although Holt was annoyed by the delay, he invited the old man into his home. The man struggled into a seat at the table and almost as soon as he was seated, he told Holt that he knew about his discovery of gold at the red outcropping. Then in a deep and commanding voice, which Holt claimed to never forget, he warned him: "Forget what you have found, or that you ever saw it, or it will be the ruin of you and your family."

Holt was taken aback by the man's words but he hardly knew what to say. Embarrassed, he instead decided to see to the preparation of the man's food. He turned away to retrieve a plate and when he turned back around, he was stunned to see that the old man was gone. He ran to the open door and looked out to see that the man's mule was gone too. To add to the mystery, there were no tracks of either the old man or the mule in the dust of the roadway. He had simply vanished without a trace -- as if he had never been there at all!

Holt became convinced that the strange man was one of the Three Nephites of Mormon legend and with his warning in mind, Holt never went near the ledge again and he never discussed it with his family or his friends.

The legend of the Three Nephites is well known to those of the Mormon faith and there is likely no story of vanishing strangers as mysterious in American history. Mormonism was founded in upper New York State in the early 1800's. It was started by a man named Joseph Smith, who claimed to be visited by angels who revealed to him some golden plates that were translated into the *Book of Mormon*. The book claims to be the record of the first inhabitants of America, descendants of the Israelites who led a rebellion and were cursed with dark skin. These Lamanites (as they were called) became the American Indians and they warred against the righteous men, who were descended from Nephi, and who were faithful and became Disciples of Christ.

An important part of the Book of Mormon is the story of Christ's ministry in the New World. Three of the disciples that Jesus gathered around him were Nephites and they asked that they be allowed to remain on earth to continue their ministry until Christ returned. According to the *Book of Mormon*, the Three Nephites made many appearances over the years but the legends really took hold after the Mormons settled in Utah.

One recorded story involving the Nephites occurred in April 1852, after a long period of hardship for the Mormons. One day, an old man knocked at the door of a local family and asked if he could eat with them. There was little food but the woman shared what they had, bread, water and onions. When the man finished, he asked what he could pay the woman for the food and she would take nothing. With that the man blessed her and walked out of the house. The woman asked a neighbor, who had been visiting, to look out and see where the man had gone, but he had vanished. After that, the woman's family survived the famine and when he neighbors were starving, she had more than enough to feed them and her family too. She was convinced that she was being repaid for her kindness toward the old man, which legend holds was one of the Three Nephites.

In the summer of 1874, another Utah woman was alone at home and turned around suddenly to find an old man with a white beard standing in her kitchen. He asked her for food and she prepared something for him. As they talked, and the old man ate, the woman mentioned that she had not been feeling well. The old man replied that her illness was caused by her liver, but that it would not be bothering her any longer. After eating, the old man blessed the woman and left. She looked out moments after he went through the door, but the man was gone. She came to believe the man was one of the Three Nephites. Her health problems ceased soon after and her family began to prosper. When the woman died at age 89, her wealth was enough to provide for all of her children's families for life.

And there were many other stories of mysterious men helping out Mormon families, speaking of their work on earth and making predictions of things to come. In the case of James Holt, he saw the Nephite's warning as a reminder of Brigham Young's admonition against mining -- which could have led to his damnation. Being one of the faithful, he naturally heeded the stranger's warning and the Holt Mine was lost for all time.

In the years that followed Holt's death, occasional samples of high quality ore would appear in the hands of local residents and sometimes in the possession of Holt's family members and children. Many in the area knew of Holt's amazing find but no one knew where the mine was actually located.

Before the town died its slow death, mining parties, prospectors and schemers headed into the foothills to look for the "pretty red rock" but none of them ever discovered the secret. Treasure seekers still wander out into this region today, hoping to stumble across it but as author George A. Thompson warned -- "Be sure to watch for an old white-bearded man riding an ancient mule. If he stops to talk to you, you'd better listen closely to what he has to say!"

MONTEZUMA'S TREASURE CAVE
Kane County, Utah -- East of Kanab

My final excursion in Utah started out as a lark. It only happened because of a rumor that I heard about a ghost town that was haunted by Spanish conquistadors and even the Mexican emperor Montezuma! Intrigued to visit the remains of the town, and to perhaps discover the mysterious cave where Mexican treasure was hidden, I traveled east from the Mountain Meadows region, through Kanab, and to the area known as Johnson Canyon.

The town that became known as Johnson started out in 1871 as Spring Canyon Ranch. As more families moved in, it was renamed Johnson after the four Johnson brothers, Joel, Joseph, Benjamin and William. It soon had a fine brick schoolhouse, a post office, a blacksmith shop and two stores. Orchards, vineyards and open fields provided the town's prosperity for some time until several years of drought forced a change from farming to ranching.

Not long after Johnson was settled, John D. Lee established a ranch about 15 miles upstream from the town. Lee named the homestead Skutumpah, which was Native American for "colored water". The location was a good one and soon other families followed Lee to the site. By 1875, a town had grown up around the ranch and its named was changed to Clarkston, in honor of a local prominent family. The drought conditions that affected Johnson at this same time had an even greater impact on Clarkston and many of the residents moved away. At almost the same time, the death knell sounded for John D. Lee, which left the town without a leader.

John D. Lee had been the leader of the massacre that had taken place at Mountain Meadows. After leading the fanatics in the slaughter of the settlers in 1857, Lee became a hunted man. He was eventually arrested at Pawrowan, while he was there visiting one of his wives, and was held at Fort Cameron for trial. A jury found Lee guilty of his crimes on September 20, 1876; 19 years after the massacre took place.

Clarkston was abandoned in disgrace but nearby Johnson continued to thrive for another two decades. In 1874, the United Order of Enoch, a socialistic scheme devised by the Mormons, was established at Johnson. The plan required everyone to contribute to its stores and receive dividends as needed. Not surprisingly, it failed miserably. People put in five years of labor but received nothing in return and as the order began to fail, people began to leave, tiring of trying to eke out a living from the land. Around 1910, Johnson was completely deserted.

Oddly though, the site of Johnson would not remain deserted. Years later, an entire Old West town was built here to be used for television shows, movies and commercials. Some of these programs would include *How the West Was Won, Death Valley Days, Have Gun, Will Travel, Wagon Train, Gunsmoke, Call of the West* and others. The movie set was closed down for almost 18 years and then re-opened in 1994. It is currently open to the public for guided tours but when I came here back in 1990, the site was closed down and I was only able to see it from the roadway. I wondered, after all of the changes, if the ghosts of yesterday still walked the streets of Johnson as they once reportedly did.

The story of the ghosts of the conquistadors (and perhaps that of Montezuma himself) got started around 1914 when an eccentric treasure hunter named Freddie Crystal came to the area and began poking around the slopes of White Mountain in Johnson Canyon. He had a map that he had allegedly copied from an old book that he discovered in a Mexican mission and it seemed to show the hiding place of an Aztec treasure, which Crystal claimed was the treasure of Montezuma.

The story of the treasure was an old one and began in 1519, when Spanish troops led by Cortez marched on the Aztec capital of Tenotchitlan. Without any bloodshed, Cortez took Montezuma captive and began to rule Mexico through the king. However, Cortez had renounced his allegiance to Governor Velasquez of Cuba and in 1520, the conquistador had to return to the Mexican coast to defeat an army that had been sent by Velasquez to remove Cortez from power. While they battled for control of the Mexican coast, Tenotchitlan was under the control of Cortez's general, Pedro de Alvarado. The Aztecs rallied against the Spanish and forced Alvarado and his men out of the city. It was not until 1521 that Cortez was able to retake the city and with that battle, he destroyed what remained of the Aztec Empire.

It was during the brief period of independence in 1520 that Montezuma ordered the city stripped of gold, silver and jewels. Gold ingots were removed from the treasury and seven caravans of 100 porters, each carrying about 60 pounds of gold, marched to the north. They were to return when the Spanish had finally been driven from Mexico for good.

The mystery of what became of this amazing treasure was never solved. There have been many accounts as to where the caravans ended up but most of them point toward the Four Corners of New Mexico, Arizona, Colorado and Utah, an area that some believe was the ancestral home of the Aztecs.

Crystal's map described a place where ancient petroglyphs would point the way to a canyon with four branches, surrounded by four mountains, one on the north, the south, east and west. In the center, there was another mountain and this is where the treasure had been hidden. Everything on the map could be found in Johnson Canyon and White Mountain seemed to fit the description of the treasure mountain exactly.

Since an expedition to look for the treasure would be expensive, Crystal took the map to a wealthy rancher named Oscar Robinson, who agreed to bankroll the search. It was not unusual for a businessman to outfit a prospector under an agreement to share any wealth that was discovered and this is what Robinson did. Freddie Crystal and his string of packhorses trailed off into Johnson Canyon -- and were not seen again for eight years.

By 1922, most people had forgotten about the prospector and his wild tales of Aztec gold but it was very exciting when Crystal came ambling out of the mountains and told the local people that he had found the treasure but needed help to get it out. With assistance from almost every man from the surrounding towns, he headed back into the canyon. A tent town of treasure hunters was established and the town of Kanab was nearly deserted as everyone hurried out to Johnson Canyon to help with the search. Just as the map revealed, ancient steps that had been cut by hand were found leading up the mountain face. Although the opening was cleverly concealed with closely fit stone blocks that had been cemented into place, the treasure hunters found a man-made shaft that entered the mountain. To add to the mystery, the perfectly cut blocks were of stone unknown in the region and apparently the cement had been made from a fine sand that could only be found many miles away in New Mexico.

When the granite wall was eventually removed, a tunnel was found behind it, leading deeper into the mountain. The workers were only able to gain about 60 feet of the passage though and then they ran into another granite wall. In the days that followed, this wall was also removed and more tunnels and shafts were found, leading off in various directions. As the work progressed, they moved another 100 feet or so into the tunnels. Here, they found a several large rooms and within them, deadly concealed booby traps, including huge boulders that had been delicately balanced to fall if triggered by unknown means.

Over the next two years, the search was started and re-started and was slowed by more granite walls, mazes of tunnels and more deadly traps. When no treasure was discovered, the searchers began to get discouraged. When their money ran out, the local ranchers and townspeople were forced to return to their work and homes and the hunt was finally abandoned. Freddie Crystal announced that he was going to return to Mexico to look for more clues but he was never heard from again -- and no one has looked for the Aztec treasure in this mountain since.

So it's still out there, hidden away in some remote or old Spanish mine, just waiting for someone to find it. Many have tried and the Treasure of Montezuma remains one of the greatest unsolved mysteries of the Four Corners region. Someday, I plan to make it back out there again and maybe I will finally get the chance to look for the treasure -- and of course the ghosts of the conquistadors -- and who knows, maybe the spirits will be willing to show me the way?

The mysterious Moonville Tunnel

The abandoned Big Mountain Tunnel, where the ghost of John Henry still drives his steel.

Bill Hickman - alleged Mormon assassin. Was he a victim of the curse on a Utah mine?

The movie set that was constructed at the site of Johnson

The last remains of the of the old Wasatch store at Winter Quarters. These remaining walls were still there when I visited years ago.

The abandoned mine offices at Latuda.

This graveyard is now all that remains of Hamblin

The remains of one of the now forgotten mines that I visited in Utah. This lonely spots are now home to only memories -- and ghosts.

The entrance to the mysterious Bell Witch Cave

A vintage advertisement for Cherokee Cave during its heyday

The entrance to the Lemp Caverns from the brewery

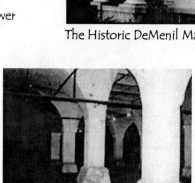

The Historic DeMenil Mansion

(Below) One of the vaulted chambers in the lower sections of the abandoned Lemp Brewery

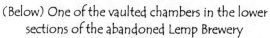

A passage leading down into the lower depths of Cherokee Cave

(Below) The same Historic entrance shown at right but with the modern fittings of concrete steps and safety rails

A historic entrance into Mammoth Cave, Kentucky

"Hercules" -- the train used for excursions to Mammoth Cave

A vintage panoramic view of the old Mammoth Cave Hotel

An antique engraving from one of the dozens of books and travel guides that were printed during the Mammoth Cave's early days.

(Right) Floyd Collins around 1924 -- just one year before his fateful days in Sand Cave

IV. HAUNTED CAVES

As mentioned already in this book, I have tried in vain to explain my fascination with caves -- especially haunted ones -- but I am not sure that I can. There is certainly something undeniably eerie about being in the dark corners of a cave. It is a chill that comes from the damp coolness of the passageways and manages to work its way up your spine in a manner that has you looking over your shoulder and wondering what lurks in the blackness beyond where your light can reach. But darkness and coolness aside, why do we have such macabre associations with the underground? Is there really something lurking around the corners of those shadowed passages?

I'll leave that up to the reader to decide but if you are unsure now, you may not be so hesitant after reading the pages that follow. Over the years, I have visited well over 150 commercial and wild caves and while the vast majority of them were in no way linked to the supernatural, I have been able to find records that state that many of them were -- and these records were in addition to my own personal experiences in some of them.

THE BELL WITCH CAVE
Adams, Tennessee

There is no greater ghost story in the history of American than that of the Bell Witch of Tennessee. It would require an entirely separate book to chronicle the strange haunting that occurred in Robertson County between 1817 and 1821 (and I have written one -- see my book *Season of the Witch* for the complete account) but in short, the family of a local farmer named John Bell was plagued by a mysterious and violent spirit for nearly four years. The haunting involved spectral creatures, disembodied voices, unbelievable violence and even resulted in the death of John Bell --- all at the hands of the infamous Bell Witch.

The haunting began in 1817 when the Bell family began experiencing strange phenomena in their home. First, the house was plagued with knocking and rapping noises and scratching sounds. Blankets were pulled from beds, family members were kicked and scratched and their hair pulled. Particularly tormented was young Elizabeth Bell, who was slapped, pinched, bruised and stuck with pins. At first, John Bell was determined to keep the events secret, but soon confided in a friend, who then formed an investigative committee. John Bell's friends soon learned that the strange force in the house had an eerie intelligence. It soon found a voice and from that day on was seldom silent.

The spirit identified itself as the "witch" of Kate Batts, a neighbor of the Bell's, with whom John had experienced bad business dealings over some purchased slaves. "Kate" as the local people began calling the spirit, made daily appearances in the Bell home, wreaking havoc on everyone there. People all over the area of soon learned of the witch and she made appearances, in sounds and voices, all over Robertson County.

The ghost became so famous that even General Andrew Jackson decided to visit. He too experienced the antics of the witch and his carriage wheels refused to turn until the witch decided to let them.

John Bell fell victim to bouts of strange illness, for which Kate claimed responsibility. While he was sick in bed, the spirit cursed and prodded him, never allowing him to rest. One day, he went to bed and never recovered. He was found senseless in his bed one morning and a strange bottle was found nearby. Bell's breath smelled of the black liquid in the bottle, so a drop of it was placed on the tongue of a cat and the animal dropped dead. John Bell soon followed suit and Kate screamed in triumph. She even made her presence known at his funeral, laughing, cursing and singing as the poor man was buried.

Kate didn't vanish immediately after the death of her proclaimed enemy though. She stayed around, threatening Betsy Bell to not marry the man that she truly loved, Joshua Gardner. The witch would never say why, but she did allow the girl to later marry the local schoolteacher, Richard Powell. Kate soon left the family but promised to return in seven years. She did come back and plagued the family again for two weeks. She soon departed but many believe that she may not have gone far.

Who was the Bell Witch? Was she really a ghost, who claimed to be connected to a living person? Or did the resentment and the hatred of the real Kate Batts create an entity of its own? Or could the haunting have been poltergeist activity linked to Betsy Bell? No one will ever know for sure -- but whoever, or whatever, the Bell Witch was, many believe that she has never left Adams, Tennessee at all.

Near the Red River, on the former Bell farm, is a cave that has been called the "Bell Witch Cave". Thanks to local legend and lore, many people have come to believe that when the spirit of the witch departed from the torment of the Bell family, she went into this cave. Others (myself included) believe that the cave marks the entrance to a doorway through which Kate came into the world, departed, and perhaps even returns today. Who knows? But I can tell you that with the large number of bizarre incidents reported in and around the cave in modern times, notions of the witch returning may not be as odd as you might think.

While the cave has become quite famous in recent years, there is little mention of it in contemporary accounts of the haunting. It is believed that the cave might have been used for the cool storage of food in those days, thanks to the fact that it remains a constant 56 degrees. It was also mentioned in some accounts that Kate's voice was often heard nearby and one day, Betsy Bell and several of her friends had a close encounter with the witch inside of the cave.

The cave itself is located in the center of a large bluff that overlooks the river. The mouth of the cave opens widely but entrance to the cavern itself must be gained through a fairly long tunnel. The cave is not large compared to most commercial caves; however its true length is unknown because of narrow passages that go beyond the 500 or so feet accessible to visitors. Although geologically, this is a dry cave that has been carved from limestone, in wet weather, a stream gushes from the mouth of the cavern and tumbles over a cliff into the river below. This makes the cave nearly impossible to navigate and even shouted conversations become inaudible over the roar of the water.

In dry times, the cave has proven to be quite an attraction to curiosity-seekers and ghost hunters. Once you pass through the entrance passage, the visitor enters a large room that opens into yet another tunnel and an overhead passageway. Another large room can be found at the rear of the explored portion of the cave, but from that point on the tunnels become smaller, narrower and much more dangerous.

The Bell Witch Cave became an attraction thanks largely to a man named Bill Eden, who owned the property for a number of years. Eden was a wealth of information about the cave and about the fact that strange occurrences were continuing to take place on the land that once belonged to John Bell. Although he was mainly a farmer, Eden did make some early improvements to the cave by adding electrical lights, but that was about all.

Despite being undeveloped though, the cave managed to attract hundreds of visitors every year who wanted to be shown through it. Bill always obliged although was always puzzled about how they found the place. There were no signs to point the way at that time but somehow people tracked down directions to the site and they always asked to hear the stories of the witch, and the stories that Eden spun from his own weird experiences at the place.

Many of the strange experiences actually happened to Bill Eden himself, while others involved visitors to the cave. For instance, a woman came to visit one day and asked to go down and see the cave. She had brought a group of friends along and in all, about fifteen people followed Eden down the rather treacherous path to the cave's entrance. All at once, the woman in charge of the group abruptly sat down in the middle of the path. One of the people who was with her asked why she was sitting there, and she answered that she wasn't! She claimed that a heavy weight, which felt like a ton of lead, was pressing her down to the ground and she couldn't get up. Several members of the group managed to get the lady to her feet and half carried her back up the hill to her car.

Bill Eden could also recount a number of encounters he had on his own in the cave. "You can hear footsteps in there all the time and I saw one thing," he once said in an interview. "Lots of people come out here expecting to see a ghost or a witch of whatever you want to call it. I just call it a spirit - and it looked like a person with its back turned to you. Looked like it was built out of real white-looking heavy fog or snow, or something real solid white. But you couldn't see through it. It had the complete figure of a person till it got down to about its ankles. It wasn't touching the floor at all. It was just drifting - bouncing along."

As Eden mentioned, a lot of people came to the cave hoping to see, or experience, a ghost. While many of them went away disappointed, some got a little more than they bargained for.

Eden had taken a group of young people into the cave one evening for a tour. They had been inside for about an hour and had stopped in the back room where they talked for awhile and Bill told of his experiences in the area. As they were starting to leave, one of the girls in the group started to make some remarks about the authenticity of the place, whether or not it was really haunted, and about how disappointed she was that nothing had appeared or had happened. She continued this monologue into the passage connecting the two rooms, which is quite narrow. Everyone else in the group seemed to be having a good time and Eden was used to the squeals, giggles and laughter that often accompanied young people on tours of the cave. The girl who was complaining was walking directly in front of Eden at this point.

She was walking along and then all of the sudden, stumbled backwards as if she had been pushed. She took a couple of step back and then sat down hard on the floor of the cave. "Somebody slapped me!" the girl yelled.

Eden shook his head. "You must have bumped your head," he told her and explained that the ceiling is pretty low in spots and sometimes people had to duck down to avoid being injured.

"No," the girl insisted. "I didn't bump my head, whatever it was hit me on the jaw."

Eden helped the girl to her feet, still skeptical, and they all moved to the front room of the cave. Once there, he shined his light on her face to see how badly she had been hurt. He looked at her cheek and was surprised to see a red welt - and the prints of fingers that were still visible where she had been struck! He certainly had no explanation for how bumping her head on a low ceiling could have accomplished that.

Another young woman came to the cave one day, also in hopes of catching a glimpse of the resident spirit. According to Eden, she had visited the cave several times before and returned again with a group of friends who wanted to try and conduct a séance to get in touch with Kate.

The group arranged themselves in the position that they wanted to be in and then asked Eden if he would mind shutting off all of the lights in the cave. Amused, Bill decided to go along with their experiment and so he shut them all out. The light switch was located just inside of the gate at the front entrance to the cave and when Eden turned the lights off, he stayed nearby, waiting to switch them back on again when needed. A few moments after the lights went out, he heard the group of young people begin calling for the spirit to appear.

It was only a few minutes later before one of the members of the group inside began calling for Bill to turn the lights back on -- and to do so in a hurry! Eden said that he could tell by the sound of the young man's voice, and by all of the hollering coming from the cave, that something had happened. Turning on all of the lights, he started down the passage to see what was wrong and ran into two boys who were carrying the girl who had so badly wanted to arrange the séance and to see Kate. They were holding her under her arms and were simply dragging her out of the cave. The girl had fainted and was now completely unconscious. They took her outside and Bill splashed some cave water on her face to bring her around.

When she came around and was able to talk, she told Eden about seeing a figure in the darkness. Apparently, their summoning had worked! Not surprisingly, the girl's description of the apparition matched closely with others who claimed to see a ghost in the cave. The figure was said to float just off the floor and to be made up of a misty white form -- strangely though, the girl also said that she appeared to be young and pretty, with dark hair hanging down her back.

Could the unusual sighting have been merely her imagination at work -- or did she really see a ghost on that afternoon in the cave? Although hallucinations can certainly have a strange effect on people, it seems possible that the fainting spell can be accepted as evidence that the girl saw something that day. What it may have been though, could still be anyone's guess!

In the early summer of 1977, several soldiers from Fort Campbell, Kentucky came over to visit the cave. Eden took the young men on a tour and ended up in the back room, where all of them sat around talking and Eden told his stories of the odd events on the farm.

One of the men politely expressed some doubts about the validity of the story. He had been to many places that were supposedly haunted and nothing out of the ordinary had ever occurred to him. Eden laughed and shrugged his shoulders. The man could believe whatever he wanted to, but as for Bill, well, he had seen enough things on the farm to know that something unexplainable was going on. "If something happened, you probably wouldn't ever come back here again," Bill added with a grin.

The group sat and talked for a short while longer and then they all got up to leave -- all except for the young man who had spoke up about his disbelief in ghosts. "Mr. Eden! Come here and help me," the soldier said. "I can't get up."

Eden and the man's friends all assumed that he was joking and they all began to laugh. It wasn't until Bill took a good look at the man that he realized that something really was wrong. The young man was now begging for help and his face was drenched so badly with sweat that it looked like someone had poured a bucket of water over him. When Eden took hold of his hand to help him up, he could feel the man's hand was cold and clammy as if he were going into shock.

The man continued to call for help and claimed that he could feel strong arms wrapped around his chest. They were squeezing him tightly, he said, and he was unable to breathe. Eden and the other men helped their friend to his feet and while the soldiers supported him, Bill wiped his face off with some run-off water from the cave. When the soldier got to feeling better, they took him outside of the cave. By the time they were ready to leave, the young man had completely recovered and was suffering no ill effects from his harrowing experience.

As he was heading to his car, he stopped and shook Bill Eden's hand. "Well, you were right about one thing, Mr. Eden," the young soldier said. "I won't ever be back here again."

The winter rains in Tennessee wreak havoc on the Bell Witch Cave, which is why Bill Eden (and the current owners) usually only opened the cave during the summer and early autumn months. Each spring, Bill always had a lot of work to do on the floor of the cave where the rushing water had carved out small holes and ditches.

One Sunday morning, Eden had taken his shovel and rake and was working back some distance in the cave, trying to level out the more damaged portions of the floor. He was chopping at and smoothing over the gravel when he heard a noise that he was not making himself. He spun around because he realized that it was coming from behind him, from the further recesses of the cave.

In the darkness, he could hear the distinct sound of someone walking down the passage, their feet crunching in the gravel on the floor. The sounds kept coming, moving toward him, until they stopped a few feet away. Eden strained his eyes to peer into the shadows, but he could see no one there.

"Something I can do for you?" he called out, but he got no answer. He called again, but still no answer came.

Although he most likely would have hated to admit it, I imagine this incident raised the hairs on the back of Bill's neck. He decided that he would probably get more work done near the entrance of the cave -- where it was much lighter -

so he picked up his tools and headed in that direction. He walked up front and as he passed through the first room, he noticed his dog sleeping on the little ledge over on the left side of the room.

For the next thirty minutes or so, Eden worked on the floor between the iron gate at the mouth of the cave and the first room. He had just stopped for a moment to rest when he heard the familiar footsteps, tracking through the gravel once more. They were once again coming from the back of the cave and quickly approached the first room, where Bill's dog was sleeping.

Suddenly, the animal's ears pricked up and he jumped to his feet. The hackles rose on the back of his neck and Bill saw his lips curl back to reveal the dog's rather intimidating set of teeth. The animal didn't move though. He just stood there, looking directly at the spot where the footsteps had last been heard. The gravel began crunching again and moved forward, in the direction of where Bill was standing. As the sounds moved past the dog, he stared ahead, as though watching someone that Eden was unable to see. The footsteps came directly toward Bill, passed by him, and then continued to the outside of the cave.

Immediately after, both Bill and the dog hurried outside into the sunlight. He admitted later that he did not have the nerve to go back inside right away, nor for several days afterward. From that time on, that particular dog never entered the main part of the cave again. He would follow people to the steel gate, which is about 30 feet inside, but then he would either wait there or return outside.

Whatever he had seen that day had frightened him away for good!

Just about anyone who visits the Bell Witch Cave, and who brings along a camera, wants to snap a photograph of the entrance to the cave.

This is a shadowy and forbidding spot, but on the other hand, quite beautiful. As you walk down the gravel path from the top of the bluff and cross the last wooden walkway, you find yourself standing just outside of the gaping mouth of the cave itself. The overhanging rock succeeds in cutting off a great portion of the overhead sky and a damp chill filters out from the cave, provoking goose pimples on your exposed skin. Behind you, over the edge of the bluff, you can hear the dull roar of the Red River and you can't help but ponder the distance to the water below.

If you have brought a camera along, this would be the perfect opportunity to use it. By standing back toward the spot where the bluff comes to a sudden end, you should be able to take a photo of the cave entrance and the rocks overhead.

The reader may have noticed that I have written that you should be able to take such a photograph - the problem is that few are ever able to do so! Believe me, hundreds have tried and failed. For some reason, there is a spot outside the cave where not only cameras fail, but sometimes flashlights and batteries refuse to work. In 1997, I was present at the cave when an entire computer system that had been set up to monitor activity in the area refused to work properly. Thanks to whatever anomaly exists here, there are very few photographs in existence of the entrance to the cave. According to the current owners, I have been lucky and have managed to take several good shots of the outside of the cave, but I am one of the few.

Even in Bill Eden's time, the cave entrance was hard to photograph. One day, after finishing a tour of the cave, a man was standing and talking to Bill and he asked one of his sons to pose for a picture in front of the cave. The boy took his dog and stood near a large rock in front of the cave. It would be a perfect shot. The man was using a brand new Polaroid camera and he had taken a number of very nice photos inside of the cave. He asked Bill to hold onto the developed shots while he took another one. The man then aimed the camera at the boy and snapped the photo.

After the photo developed, the gentleman noticed something strange about the picture - something that he had not noticed when the photo was being taken. The photo showed the dog and the lower part of the boy's body, but the boy's head and shoulders were missing. It looked as though someone had stretched a white, cloudy sheet from one side of the cave to the other, completely covering the boy's face.

A young woman named Leslie Seay had a similar experience at the entrance to the cave in 1989. A friend of hers was visiting from up north and wanted to see the sights of middle Tennessee. Since Leslie lived in Clarksville at the time, she decided to take her to the Bell Witch Cave. As this was between the time when Bill Eden owned the cave and before the current owners had taken over the property, no tours were being offer of the place. However, Leslie and her friend did convince the caretakers to allow them to go down and take a look at the cave, but promised not to go inside. They hiked down the trail and ended up in front of the cave entrance.

There is a large rock that rests directly in front of the entrance and Leslie's friend decided that she wanted her photo taken while sitting on it. Leslie obliged and snapped the picture and then the two of them walked back up the bluff and let the owners know that they had returned safely.

"About two weeks later, I sent the film to be developed," Leslie told me. "When I picked up the pictures, the girl told me that one of the photos did not process correctly and that I did not have to pay for it. I didn't look at the pictures until I got to my mother's house and as we were going through them, my mother said that the one in her hand looked rather odd."

She handed the photograph to her daughter and Leslie felt a chill go down her spine. The photo that her mother handed her was the one that she had taken of her friend on the rock outside of the Bell Witch Cave. The photograph was perfectly ordinary --- except for the fact that a large white mist was looming over her friend's head!

"It looked almost like a death shroud", Leslie remembered. "Growing up, I had always heard stories about Kate, but we always considered them to be ghost stories to be told while roasting marshmallows around the campfire. Not until that photo was taken did I ever believe them!"

The current owners have a scrap book of strange photos they have taken, along with photos that are sent to them in the mail by people who have visited the cave. They receive dozens of them every year, some showing strange balls of light, misty shapes and fogs and then there are the really weird photos -- photos that simply have no explanation at all! Many of these have been taken outside the entrance to the cave.

One such photo shows a girl seated outside of the cave on a large rock. The photo also shows the apparition of a boy who seems to be looming directly behind her. Despite the odd configuration of the images in the photo, it does not at all appear to be a double-exposure.

And this isn't the strangest one! Another photo was taken of two Girl Scouts during a trip to the cave. In the photo, one of the girls is visible, but the other is only partially present and she appears in the photo turned at an impossible angle! Worse yet, is the completely unexplainable image of a two-headed snake that is slithering up the leg of the first girl. Obviously, this was not there when the photo was taken and how it could have appeared in the photograph is totally without explanation.

The present-day owners of the Bell Witch Cave, and the piece of the old Bell farm made so famous by Bill Eden, are Chris and Walter Kirby. Walter is a tobacco farmer and Chris manages to stay busy managing the upkeep and offering tours of the cave. In the summer months, this task is more than a full-time job. Luckily, she also has her daughter, Candi, to help out.

The Kirby's purchased the land in April 1993. The place had been empty for several years, after the death of Bill Eden, but by that summer, the cave was open again for business. Over the course of the next year or so, they made a number of improvements to the cave, which included new lights, a new electrical system, an improved path to the cave, wooden walkways to cross the most treacherous areas of the trail, and a number of other things. These improvements continue today.

It wasn't long after the Kirby's moved to the farm, and began conducting tours in the cave, before they realized things were not quite right on the property. They began to notice first that there were strange noises that didn't have an easy explanation. "We've heard them in the cave and we've heard them in the house," Chris has said on occasion. "I feel like if there's anyplace that could be haunted, it's this place here. First of all, it's got the legend of being haunted. There's an Indian burial mound right above the mouth of the cave on the bluff. And the previous owner of the cave died in our bedroom."

Shortly after moving onto the farm, Chris was photographing parts of the property and one of the photos on the developed roll of film managed to capture something pretty amazing. She saw nothing when she took the photo and yet, on the developed print, was a misty shape that hovered above a sinkhole leading down into the cave. The photo continues to defy explanation and was even submitted to Kodak in 1997 for analysis. They stated that there appeared to be nothing wrong with the film or with the developing of the photograph. They also added that there appeared to have been no manipulation with the print and that it was not a double exposure. In short, none of the technicians who examined the film had any explanation for what they saw in the photograph. These were almost identical replies to queries that I would make a year later concerning photos that I had taken myself at the cave!

I first met Chris Kirby in the spring of 1997. I had long been interested in the Bell Witch case and knew that there was a cave located on the property that was purported to be haunted. My wife and I were on a trip down south at the time and decided to take a side trip over to Adams. After seeing the Bellwood Cemetery and the old Bell School, we headed for the cave.

Over to the right of the parking lot is a large, wooded area that contains the sinkhole near where Chris took the photograph of the strange mist. Behind the house is the trail that leads down to the cave. As we walked back along that way, we crossed an abandoned road that is really not much more than a depression in the earth now. Later, I would have the chance to walk some distance on this old road and I would learn more about the historical footsteps that I was following. It had been this road that Andrew Jackson had traveled on when he came to visit the Bell farm. It once linked up with an old trace, a last remaining piece of the old Nashville to Clarksville road that now serves as nothing more than a lane for farm equipment. It was along this stretch of road that Jackson's wagon became mysteriously stuck on his way to the Bell farm.

My own journey along this road would later take me back to the site of the Bell home and the cemetery where the bones of John Bell, several family members and some 30 slaves were laid to rest. It is an eerie roadway in some places and even on a bright and sunny afternoon, you can often understand why locals refer to some of the woods back here as being "haunted". I found one of the most unnerving places on the old Bell property to be the family cemetery. I can't really explain what bothered me about it so much, for it was not because it was a burial ground. There is just something about the forest on that part of the old farm that will leave you with little doubt that the stories of the Bell Witch are true! I was not surprised to learn that others who have come to this place have felt much the same that I did and still others claims to have encountered ghostly apparitions, and cold chills and have heard voices and sounds that cannot be explained.

After walking past the house and across the old road, we started down the gloomy pathway that would take us to the Bell Witch Cave. As mentioned earlier, the entrance to the cave is closed off by a locked, heavy steel gate. It is supposed to stop unauthorized visitors from entering the cave, which can be very dangerous, especially in the darkness. There are many sections of the cave that remain unexplored and this fact, along with the ghost stories, proves to be a real magnet for teenagers and curiosity seekers. Chris stated they always worry that someone will be hurt in there because the gate does not always stop the trespassers. They even had two break-ins within a few weeks of buying the property. In fact, the trespassing becomes so bad at certain times of year that the Kirby's have been forced to prosecute anyone caught inside of the cave at night.

And as it has been suggested that perhaps the gate is not always there to keep people out, but to keep something else inside? One afternoon in the late fall of 1977 (during Bill Eden's ownership of the cave), a group of people drove up from Nashville, hoping to take a tour of the place. When they arrived on the property, they found that Eden was not home. Disappointed after having driven so far to get there, they decided that they would at least go down the bluff to have a look at the cave entrance before going home. The visitors hiked down the trail and then entered the mouth of the cave, walking back just far enough to peer into the shadows beyond the gate. As they stood there, one of the group commented that he could almost feel someone watching them from the darkness. Perhaps he was right, for a few moments later, the clear sound of a woman singing could be heard from inside of the cave! They later described it as a high pitched keening noise that was certainly an attempt at singing, although they could not distinguish the words. The group quickly left and climbed to the top of the bluff in about half the time that it took for them to come down!

Although I have since traveled the path a number of times over the years, I still remember my first descent down the bluff -- and my first look at the cave entrance that I had heard so much about. I could imagine Betsy Bell and her friends having their picnics on the spot where I was now standing and I hoped that if I listened closely, I might hear a voice as the trespassers of 1977, so eerily did. While I heard no supernatural sounds emanating from the cave that day, I was introduced to the strange incidents that Chris Kirby and her family had experienced since purchasing the property a few years before. The oddities had been weird and frightening enough that Chris told us that she had never been into the cave by herself -- nor did she ever intend to come here alone!

One day, Chris and her dog were leading a tour of the cave for a group of visitors. She was just opening the steel gate that leads inside when she heard a strange sound - the same sort of sound described by Bill Eden and one of his tour groups years before. "It sounded like real raspy breathing sounds," she said, "like someone couldn't get their breath. It only lasted for a minute and then it was gone." Chris looked back to her tour group, but they were quietly talking amongst themselves and hadn't heard a thing.

The tour continued through the first room, down the narrow passage and into the second room. Here, as is the tradition in Bell Witch Cave Tours, Chris began telling stories of the witch, the haunting and strange incidents on the farm. As she was talking, the dog suddenly reacted to something that no one else could see. The hair on the animal's back stood up and she began showing her teeth and growling. The tour group asked what was wrong with the dog, but Chris had no idea. She was finally able to calm the dog down, but then the animal began whining and tucked her tail between her legs. She cowered back against Chris and at that same moment, the flashlight in Chris' hand suddenly went out!

"I guessed that it was just the battery at first," Chris remembered, "but then a lady's video camera stopped working too. We were all standing there in the dark and I'll tell you, I was ready to get out of there and everyone else was too!"

Chris also told us about the strange apparitions that she and visitors to the cave have reported. Some of these shapes are misty and fog-like, sometimes appearing in different parts of the cave, only to vanish when approached. She also recalled another type of image they had seen. "It looked like heat waves that come up over the highway in the summer time," she explained. "You can see them out of the corner of your eye and then they're gone."

One of the ongoing traditions (or legends, if you will) of the Bell Witch Cave involves the removal of any sort of artifact from the premises, be it rocks or anything else found inside of the cave. Some believe that perhaps the energy of the area is imbedded in some way within the actual makeup of the place and by removing a portion of the cave, you are inviting the phenomena that occurs here to travel with you. Others are not so scientific -- they believe that the spirit of the witch will follow anyone who removes something from the cave!

It's likely that this tradition got started a number of years ago when the remains of a young Native American woman were discovered by men doing construction work on one of the local roads. Because it is well known that the former Bell farm contains a burial mound, it was requested that the bones of the Indian woman be entombed within the Bell Witch Cave. The remains were laid out in the first room of the cave in a shallow indention that was then lined with limestone slabs. Unfortunately, they did not remain there for long.

A short time later, trespassers into the cave made off with the bones, but according to local lore -- not without a price! Gossip in the community has it that each of the persons who removed one of the relics suffered a series of misfortunes, accidents and injuries within days of the theft. For this reason, it has come to be believed that it is bad luck to remove anything at all from the cave. Over the last several years, I have received a number of accounts from people who claim to have taken away stones from the Bell Witch Cave, only to then experience not only bad luck, but strange happenings in their previous un-haunted homes! Chris Kirby has assured me that she has received a number of packages in the mail over the years that have contained rocks and stones that were removed from the cave. After getting them home, the folks who removed them began to suffer all sorts of problems and weird events. They believe that by mailing them back to the cave, they might alleviate their problems.

Even the Kirby's themselves have not been immune to the strange happenings! Candi Kirby can recall the time that she was exploring the cave one day and found a small and unusual looking rock, which she proceeded to slip into her pocket and take home. She knew that there was a story about bad luck occurring to anyone who removed something from the cave, but she didn't take it seriously. Just one week later though, the family's tobacco barn collapsed without warning, ruining a portion of their crop and doing expensive damage. Just a coincidence? Candi didn't think so and has taken no further chances by removing anything else from the cave.

Since the late 1970's, the Bell Witch Cave has a destination point for ghost hunters, curiosity seekers and paranormal enthusiasts. In recent years, there have been a number of investigators who have attempted to document the supernatural events at the Bell Witch Cave but I don't think that any of them have done so with the same enthusiasm, or with the same chilling results, as Bob Schott. In 1997, Schott, a film and television producer with a company called Global Media Productions, became interested in the story of the Bell Witch and the hauntings at the old Bell farm. He contacted me about the stories and in perhaps working with him on a (now sadly defunct) series called *Adventures Beyond*, which specialized in intense paranormal phenomena. As it turned out, the Bell Witch Cave was featured on one of the only installments of the series, an episode called *America's Most Haunted*.

The format of Schott's series was different than most seen on television in that it was not a documentary with historical re-enactments but rather about paranormal investigations using the most advanced types of equipment and techniques available. For this particular installment, Schott and the investigative team (which I was lucky enough to be a member of) were equipped with high-tech temperature monitoring equipment, electro-magnetic field fluctuation detectors, military quality night vision equipment, infrared cameras, and a computer system that was capable of detecting any type of change in several different energy fields. As mentioned earlier, the computer system failed completely while it was set up at the mouth of the cave -- something that had never happened before and has not happened since!

"I was looking for a place that was really haunted, really active," Schott reported. "I was familiar, of course, with the story of the Bell Witch and when Troy told me about the phenomena still encountered on the property today -- I knew this was the place."

During the investigation, we spent several days on the Kirby farm, exploring the cave, the sinkhole where Chris had photographed the strange energy, and even the cemetery where John Bell is buried. Our best results came during our late-night forays into the cave itself.

At one point, using two different infrared temperature probes, we picked up a sudden drop in the temperature of the cave. It was as if something very cold moved past us and then continued on through the cave passage. A photograph taken at that same moment was developed and revealed a glowing ball of light. The energy inside of the globe is so intense that it appears to be giving off light. Examinations by independent photography labs, including Kodak, revealed that the image in the photo was not a reflection, nor was it any artificial or natural part of the cave. They could offer no explanation for what it might have been.

In addition, we also had some interesting (and rather chilling) results using a video camera that had been fitted with a Generation III Night Vision lens, which was reportedly 5 times more sensitive than the equipment used by the U.S. Military during the 1991Gulf War. The lens was so advanced that it had not been available on the civilian market until a short time before the investigation. It had been loaned to Schott by the manufacturer, a company that deals specifically with sensitive government and military contracts.

During the investigation, the camera and lens picked up what can only be described as a "doorway effect" that appears in the long passage between the first room and the second room in the cave. This "doorway" appears to be an array of light that crosses from one side of the passage to the other, lasting only a few seconds, and then vanishes. What is especially eerie about the effect is when it is watched frame by frame. As the light moves across and then back, two very distinct faces emerge from the "doorway", remain for a second or two, and then retreat back into the light array again!

I have never been able to explain what this "doorway" could be, nor what the images are in the light, other than faces of unknown origin. Not only have I been stumped, but so were the manufacturers of the night vision equipment, as well as independent labs and analysts.

One of Bob Schott's aggressive investigative techniques was to present whatever evidence he obtained to a skeptical, but fair, laboratory for analysis. "We knew that we had good evidence," Bob said, "but it really proves nothing unless we can stump the experts with it."

This is what he did with the film footage from the passageway. The company that made the equipment took a look at a copy of the film and were puzzled by what they saw. They, along with other film experts, ran the clip over and over and put it through all sorts of tests to determine if it had been hoaxed, or merely an accident of light that had created the "doorway effect" and the faces. In their final report on the footage, they stated that they had no explanation for the strange anomalies and that these images could only be paranormal in origin.

"This is some of the best evidence ever obtained for the existence of the supernatural," stated Schott. "We came to the Bell Witch Cave because we heard that it was haunted - I think that after this investigation, I can say with a lot of certainty that it is!"

The Bell Witch Cave is located just outside of Adams, Tennessee. To reach Adams, take Highway 76 from Interstate 24 (Near Clarksville) until reaching Highway 41. The cave can be reached by turning off Highway 41, right next to the Bell School. You can't miss the sign for the cave alongside the roadway and a right turn takes you onto a curving gravel road and up to a small brick house, which was built by Bill Eden. There is a sign here that reads "Bell Cave Parking".

THE TIPTON-HAYES FARM CAVE
Near Johnson City, Tennessee

One night, a number of years ago, a man named Robert McCormick decided to camp in a small cave near Johnson City, Tennessee with his young son. After passing a pleasant evening talking and eating an outdoor meal around the campfire, the man and his son bedded down for the night. It was a beautiful summer night and so McCormick and his boy spread their bedrolls out near the mouth of the cave.

In the early morning hours, both of them were awakened from a deep sleep by the sound of voices. McCormick opened his eyes and was surprised to find that he was surrounded by a small group of Native Americans. Thinking that perhaps his friends had decided to play a practical joke on him, he laughed and told the "Indians" to leave them alone and let them sleep. When there was no reply, and in fact the men seemed not to notice him at all, he called out to them again. This time, the Indians abruptly vanished -- disappearing into the darkness away from the fire. They did not walk away though, they just disappeared.

Now, terrified, McCormick's son began screaming hysterically. He jumped out of his bedroll and began to run up the hill away from the cave with his father close behind. As they made it to the top of the hill, McCormick turned and looked back but the entrance to the cave was dark and silent. He saw nothing but the dim glow of the embers from their campfire. The Indians, if they had ever been there at all, were gone. In the distance though, McCormick would later swear that he heard the faint sound of laughter and he realized that the vanishing Indians had not simply been his imagination at work after all.

And McCormick was not the first (nor will be likely be the last) to have strange experiences around this small cave. The small underground chamber is located on the Tipton-Hayes Farm near Johnson City and for many years it has been considered a haunted place, especially in the summer months. There have been many who have reported strange sights and sounds around the mouth of the cave after dark. The stories say that ghostly campfires can sometimes be seen, flickering against the walls of the cave, and shadowy men are sometimes gathered around it, laughing and talking amongst themselves. One witness claimed to see a man dressed in buckskin stoking a fire. The specter could have been that of Daniel Boone, who often camped in this cave, or that of many other frontiersmen who also used the cave. As this latter witness tried to approach the cave for a closer look, he made a noise and the eerie scene before him suddenly disappeared. When he reached the entrance though, he claimed that he could still smell the aroma of burned wood in the air.

What causes this tiny cave to be so haunted? And who are the spirits that linger here? With the kind of history that this location has seen, and the number of colorful characters who have passed through it over the years, those questions may be difficult to answer.

For centuries, the cave was used as a shelter and overnight campsite for Indians and for the white explorers who came here as well. Some believe the history of the cave may even date back to the prehistoric era. Beyond that, the cave has hosted more than its share of distinguished visitors, including the first white men to ever explore this region, James Needham and an indentured servant named Gabriel Arthur. The ghosts of these two Englishmen are among those who are alleged to haunt this cave.

The two men were agents for Colonel Abraham Wood, the owner of a prosperous trading post in Virginia. In 1763, they were sent by Wood to explore the wilderness regions south and west of the Appalachian Mountains and to establish a trade with the Tomahitan Indians. They were accompanied by eight Tomahitan guides and another guide of questionable reputation, an Occaneechee man called "Indian John". In his previous trading with the Indians, Wood had been forced to use the often hostile Occaneechee as middlemen. He hoped to eliminate this problem by having Needham and Arthur set up contacts of their own. The Occaneechee were not eager for this to happen however for they had made a good profit reselling Indian goods to Colonel Wood.

The explorers traveled west and entered the lands that were now Tennessee. According to tradition, they spent at least one night in the shelter of the cave near present-day Johnson City. After this, they headed south and came upon a village of Tomahitan Indians. The tribe already had an active trade with the Spanish in Florida and were happy to speak with the Englishmen about a similar agreement. Gabriel Arthur, who was less than 20 years-old at the time, remained at the Tomahitan village to learn their language while Needham returned to Virginia to report to Colonel Wood and to arrange for the first shipment of goods into the region.

The return trip to Virginia did not go smoothly. At some point on the route, Needham and Indian John got into a violent argument and before the Tomahitan guides could intervene, Needham was stabbed to death. The Tomahitan's were terrified that the English would retaliate against them but Indian John somehow convinced them that if they returned to the village and killed Arthur too, no one would ever know what happened to the men. It would be assumed, he told them, that they had simply vanished into the wilderness.

The guides, led by Indian John, returned to the Tomahitan village and learned that the village leader and some of the warriors were away. Taking advantage of this, Arthur was captured and taken to the public square. He was lashed to a post and wood was stacked around his feet as the men planned to burn him alive. Moments later, the chief returned to the village with his men and saw what was taking place. One of the original Tomahitan guides quickly told him what had happened to Needham and what Indian John planned to do to Arthur and the chief was infuriated. He shouted for the execution to stop but the Indian who was about to set the wood at Arthur's feet on fire refused to listen. With the Spanish musket that the chief had over his shoulder, he fired and shot the man dead. Then, he cut Arthur free from the post and sent him to his lodge under the protection of his men. With words of warning to the rest of his village, the chief dealt severely with Indian John and banished him from the region.

Once the furor died down though, Arthur decided not to leave the village. He stayed on with the Tomahitan and lived as one of the tribe, even accompanying them on their raids against other tribes. On one such raid against the Shawnee, in what is now West Virginia, he was wounded twice and was captured by the enemy. About one year after Needham's death, Arthur finally ended up back at Colonel Wood's post in Virginia.

Into the 1800's, the cave near Johnson City continued to host travelers and explorers and to provide a resting place for them. During that time, few Indians lived permanently in the upper portion of East Tennessee. The Cherokee, the dominant tribe in the area, had long since driven out the weaker tribes but did not live in this area. Upper Eastern Tennessee was mostly a hunting ground in those days.

Although not close to any established Indian settlement, the frontiersmen and the Native Americans still seemed to find the cave. This was largely because it was along a well-used Indian trail called the Great Path. There were many trails in this area, although most were crudely cleared paths that made little impression in the forest. When Daniel Boone was laying out the Wilderness Road in 1769, he stumbled upon the long and well-used Great Path. The trail extended from the vicinity of Staunton, Virginia and ended near Echota, the capital of the Cherokee nation, which was then located around the present-day area of Chattanooga, Tennessee. Daniel Boone is said to have stayed many nights at the little cave near Johnson City after he discovered the Great Path.

This area was located at about the midway point of the trail and when white settlers began coming to this region, they gravitated toward this central area. One settler wrote in his journals about a night that his family sheltered for the night in the cave with a hunting party of about a dozen Cherokee Indians. They spent several hours that night around the fire good-naturedly trying to communicate with signs and what common words they could conjure up.

Such meetings continued for decades until the Native Americans were eventually driven out of the area. After that, the cave continued to be used for some time, still providing a shelter for travelers until the area became largely settled. The passage of all of these people, over such a long period of time, has undoubtedly left an impression here -- and one that has been experienced by the unaware for years.

The cave is now part of the Tipton-Haynes Farm, a historical recreation area that is administered by the Johnson City Recreation Department. There is a restored clapboard house on the property and it sits on a hill just off the old Erwin Highway. Below the home is a springhouse and about thirty yards away, and in plain sight of the house, is the cave. As mentioned, it is small and only extends back about 30 feet before it branches off into two main corridors, neither of which leads very far. There is little to see as far as caves go but remember that the cave was not used for its scenic beauty but rather for the shelter that it provided to the early travelers. It is open to the public today and may be visited by anyone with an interest in the rich history -- and the hauntings -- that can be found here.

ROBBER'S CAVE
Lincoln, Nebraska

When the settlers and the explorers first came to what is now Nebraska, it was the home of the Pawnee Indians. High on the summit of a place called Pahuk Bluff was where the nation met in high council. The bluff was considered to be a sacred place and it was here in 1854 that the Pawnee met in peace talks with General John M. Thayer, who later became governor of Nebraska. Despite an agreement that was met with the Indians, Pahuk Bluff was chosen by the settlers as the perfect place to build "Neapolis", the planned state capital. The Pawnee were then moved to reservations in the south. The Indian's villages were burned and they were driven out --- but some say that they left a little bit of their magic behind.

Beneath Pahuk Bluff was a place that the Pawnee held in awe, a cave system where young men were initiated into the spirit world and taught their animal powers and the healing virtues of plants and roots. Beneath this bluff is the underground Nebraska, caves of porous sandstone where for centuries, water has carved out an elaborate system that runs for miles. These caves were used for many years by the Pawnee and it was said that the sounds of drums and chanting could often be heard here. Stories told by the Indians spoke of tribe's ancestors, who lived here in spirit form, and whose voices and drums could still be experienced.

One of these portions of the spirit caves would later be dubbed "Robber's Cave" by later residents and for many years it was a popular site to visit in Lincoln, especially for teenagers and curiosity seekers. The cave was said to be haunted by sounds from the past. Visitors had long been reporting the sounds of unexplained voices, cries, screams, and unintelligible laughing and talking. Were these the spirits of the forgotten Pawnee or the ghosts of the cave's later inhabitants? In this cave, there were many former inhabitants to choose from.

Robber's Cave is only about 500 feet long, although later passages that were sealed off may have gone much further. It plunges down to a depth of about 60 feet, not including the old well that was created by a seepage of ground water.

This massive hole disappeared down into total darkness and while I have corresponded with a number of different people about this cave over the years, no one seemed to know just where this well ended up.

The various people that I have talked to have also offered much in the way of conflicting stories and information too. According to legend, the cave saw many uses over the years, including as a way station for slaves who escaped from the south via the Underground Railroad. In 1863, the original entrance was destroyed in a quarrying operation, only to be purchased a few years later in 1869 by brewers from Wisconsin. They hired local laborers to dig out the tunnels and renovate them for use in storing beer. At that time, before the widespread use of electric refrigeration, breweries would often lager German-style beer in underground caverns so that it would age in a cool location.

The brewery failed in 1873 and from that time, the cave became a meeting place for gamblers, outlaws and horse thieves. The most famous outlaw alleged to have visited Robber's Cave was Jesse James, who supposedly hid out here after a robbery in 1876. This has confused the cave with another Robber's Cave, which is also located in Nebraska, which Jesse James was also alleged to use as a hideout. This is an entirely different cave though and has nothing to do with the legends associated with the cave in Lincoln.

Of course, growing up in the Midwest, and having an interest in the violent careers of the western outlaws, I often heard of locations connected to Jesse James. He turns up quiet a bit in our regional lore, as you may remember from my introduction to this book, and even in my own family history. According to my father's great aunt, she was Jesse's second cousin -- which makes my connections to the outlaw about as tenuous as those of the Robber's Cave in Lincoln. But whether Jesse James ever used the cave as a hideout of not, it has been documented that the cave was used as a layover for outlaws and gamblers.

One room in the cave was most closely associated with the outlaws and a visitor could find it by climbing up about five feet along the cave wall. A narrow passage here then led into a vast hidden chamber. On one side was a fire pit with a natural stone chimney above it and beyond that was a stone wall that had been filled in with bricks and sealed off. It was said that if you listened carefully, you could hear the sounds of the ghosts of Robber's Cave behind this wall. Visitors who came here in years past said that the voices of men talking and laughing could be heard, muffled as though coming from a distance.

What many of the visitors did not realize is that the cave originally continued on for quite some distance beyond this brick and stone wall. According to the stories (and again, I have received many conflicting reports about this location) the passageway met up with tunnels that once connected the state penitentiary and the State Hospital for the Insane. One story claims that this tunnel was used as an escape route for some prisoners and this is why it was finally sealed off.

In 1906, a story spread about a treasure box that was found in the cave. This tale brought so many visitors that its more recent life as a tourist attraction was born. Brave tourists and sightseers visited the cave for years, braving slick pathways, ghost stories and scores of bats -- so many bats that reports sometimes claimed the ceiling looked like a "seething mass of fur and fluttering wings".

In the early 1970's, the cave was closed to the public because of the dangerous conditions. It was re-opened for a time in 1985 and but then closed down again a few years later. Today, the cave is no longer in existence in any form. The site has been filled and a business was constructed on top of what was the cave entrance. According to sources, the location is only known to those who once visited the cave because of a familiar landmark (a grain elevator co-op) that is located nearby.

And while the cave is now gone and only exists as a memory, one has to wonder if perhaps those lost passages -- located far beyond that brick wall -- still exist. If they are still down there, forgotten by the passage of years, do the sounds from the past still echo in the corridors and tunnels? Does the laughter and groans of the gamblers or the eerie chants of the Indians still drift down the through the cavern? It's likely that we will never know....

SPECTERS OF THE CAVE-IN-ROCK AREA
Cave-in-Rock & Anna Bixby's Cavern
Southeastern Illinois

The rivers and waterways of southern Illinois have always played a dominant role in its history and folklore. The early settlers, like the French, established themselves along the rivers and later, farmers would come to realize how much more simple it was to use the river to transport grain to market. The era of the steamboat created towns like Chester, Elizabethtown, Cairo, Metropolis, Golconda and Shawneetown. These towns became shipping ports with flour and lumber mills and even an iron foundry in Grand Tower. Travelers came to the towns by boat and hotels and establishments on the riverfront flourished.

Many stories have emerged from the rivers and the towns surrounding them, of wrecks, lawlessness, pirates and even ghosts. Perhaps the most famous pirate location on the river was an outlaw hideout called Cave-in-Rock, which is located along the Ohio River at the southeastern edge of the state. The cave became the stronghold of pirates who plundered flatboats on the river and who murdered and robbed travelers. It was also here, around 1800, that a robber named Samuel Mason began operating a tavern and gambling parlor in the cave. He used whiskery, cards and prostitutes to lure travelers in off the river and many of these customers found themselves beaten, robbed and sometimes dead, after tying up at the crude wharf.

Cave-in-Rock, located close to the town of the same name, was a perfect place for criminal enterprises along the river. At that time, it boasted a partially concealed entrance and a wide view up and down the river. The cave is about

100 feet deep, with a level floor and a vertical chimney that ascends to the bluff above.

Samuel Mason operated here for several years. He was said to be a man of gigantic size and possessing no conscience, he killed for both pleasure and profit. He also operated along the Mississippi River and on the fabled Natchez Trace, a series of trails in the south that became known as a haven for thieves and pirates. Eventually a reward was offered for Mason, $1000 dead or alive, and a hatchet was put into his back by one of his own men. This traitorous wretch never collected the reward though as he was in turn killed by other members of the gang. Mason's cronies eventually scattered to the wind and other outlaws took their place at Cave-In-Rock.

The pirates were also said to have preyed upon ferryboat passengers at Ford's Ferry, a few miles upriver. The ferryman himself, James Ford, was said to have been in league with the pirates. He was also said to be one of the "slave catchers" in the employ of John Hart Crenshaw, a plantation owner who operated Hickory Hill. This house is popularly known in southern Illinois as the Old Slave House and is one of the few locations where slavery actually existed in Illinois. Ford eventually came under attack by a vigilante group called the "Regulators" and this would lead to his demise. One night, in 1834, he was having dinner at the home of a Mrs. Vincent Simpson, the widow of one of Ford's men. He was eating his food at the table and someone brought him a candle and asked that he read a letter aloud for him. Using the candle as a signal, the "Regulators" outside opened fire, aiming between the logs of the cabin. Ford died with 17 bullets in his body!

For years after his death, the slaves told stories about how Jim Ford had died and "landed in Hell head first". At his funeral, attended only by his widow, a few family members, neighbors and some slaves, a terrible thunderstorm came up. Just as Ford's coffin was being lowered into the ground, lightning flashed and a deafening clap of thunder filled the air, causing one of the slaves to loose his grip on the rope holding the coffin. The box dropped into the grave head first and wedged there at a strange angle. The heavy rain that began to fall made it impossible to move the casket, so it was covered over the way that it had fallen. This left Ford to spend eternity standing on his head.

Ford's death would not bring an end to the thievery at Cave-in-Rock. Many of the remaining pirates continued to prey on travelers from the sanctuary of the cave, while others joined with villains like John Murrell and his "Mystic Band". Murrell was a "slave catcher", thief and murderer, who killed his first man when he was only sixteen. He later died after serving time in prison.

By the late 1830's, most of the outlaws, pirates and counterfeiters were driven away from Cave-in-Rock and the bloody past of the place began to fade with time. As years passed, the cave became more of a recreation area than a den of thieves and remains a natural attraction in southern Illinois today. The legends have never died completely though and many still remember the area's blood-soaked past -- and the stories of ghosts. In years gone by, travelers passing on the river often claimed to hear the keening moans of the dead echoing out from the mouth of the cave. These same cries are still sometimes reported today. Do these eerie voices belong to the crime victims of long ago, who were lured to their death at Cave-in-Rock? That answer remains as mysterious as the history of the cave itself.

One of the greatest mysteries of the Cave-in-Rock region, and perhaps of southern Illinois in general, involves a woman named Anna Bixby (or Bigsby, according to some accounts). There are so many stories and legends, and various versions of the legends, about this woman that it is impossible to know what to believe. According to the census records of southern Illinois, she was a real person though and it has been generally accepted that she discovered a cure for what was then called "milk sickness". Amazingly, she did so almost 70 years before the medical establishment acknowledged that the source of the sickness was the plant that Anna had discovered long before.

Among the myriad of legends that still exist about Dr. Anna in southern Illinois is that of a cave in Hardin County, a lost treasure -- and of course, a ghost.

Anna Bixby was a doctor who lived years ago in southeastern Illinois. She was a talented midwife and healer who visited the sick, tended the wounded and traveled around the area to help those who were sick. She likely had no real medical education and even more likely was unable to read or write, as would have been common at this time. Because of the work that she did and the discovery of the root that was causing milk sickness, some historians refused to believe that she would have done all of this with no formal education. Perhaps for this reason, an alternate version of the story of Anna Bixby came to be. According to this version, Anna was the daughter of a wealthy pioneer named Norman Pierce, who came west to Illinois from Philadelphia in the early 1800's. Thanks to her family's wealth, she was able to train as a doctor in Pennsylvania (which would have been fairly unheard of at the time) and also as a school teacher.

This is unlikely though. Most recent historians believe that Anna was a midwife from Tennessee who came to Illinois with her husband, Isaac Hobbs. According to the census records, they were already married when they came to Illinois, which disputes the version of the story that says they were married after she went to medical school. Anna's medical training came from her study of herbs and healing techniques and she traveled widely to assist those in what would have been a wilderness at that time. When a strange disease began to break out in the region, which was killing both people and cattle, Anna was baffled. She watched, treated as best she could, observed the illness and studied the habits of those who were stricken. As hard as she worked though, she was unable to stop the scourge.

The number of deaths increased alarmingly and whole herds of cattle were wiped out. The superstitious came to believe that the illness was caused by a poison that was being scattered by a witch. There was even talk of retaliation against various persons who were suspected. Anna did not believe the witch theory though and felt that the cause of the illness was likely a plant that the cattle were eating and then passing on through their milk. The milk cows themselves did not fall ill but the other cattle, and the people, who drank their milk fell victim to the malady. Anna spread the word to the surrounding communities that they should refrain from drinking milk until after the frost in the autumn. Her warning saved many lives but did not save the young cattle, which the settlers depended on. Greater tragedy had been avoided for the time being, but the sickness was sure to return in the spring. Anna was determined to solve the mystery of the disease and became even more so after her husband fell ill and died from the milk sickness.

Anna puzzled over the illness through the winter and when spring came, she set off into the woods and fields to look for the plant that had caused so much misery. The solution to the problem came almost by accident when she chanced to meet in the woods an elderly Native American woman that the local people called "Aunt Shawnee". She was also a herbalist and healer and showed Anna a plant that we now call "milkweed", which had caused the same symptoms as the milk sickness did in her own tribe. The plant had killed many of the Shawnee cattle and she told Anna that it was probably what she was looking for.

Anna again spread the word and according to tradition, troops of men and boys prowled the woods, destroying the plant, for many years afterward. The plague was finally wiped out and in 1928, more than 60 years later, medical scholars acknowledged Anna's find as the cause of the ailment. For this reason, she has long been considered something of a legend in southern Illinois as a healer and medical worker --- but this was not the end of her story.

While the story of Anna Hobbs Bixby's solution for the milk sickness mystery has been accepted as truth, there are elements to the story (such as how much medical education she actually had) that remain open to question. The same can be said for the next great incident in Anna's life, which took place during her second marriage to Eson Bixby, who it is believed was involved in a number of criminal enterprises. The legend does have some elements of truth but unfortunately, much of it turned out to more fancy than fact. The legend originated in the book *The Ballads of the Bluff* by Judge W.M. Hall, who allegedly had a diary that belonged to Anna Bixby. Historians have since disputed much of the story, although it was believed that Hall was simply passing along stories that he had heard. Here is the basic version of the story:

Legend holds that John Murrell and his gang, along with James Ford and other disreputable characters, distilled whiskey and made counterfeit money in a headquarters in Hardin County that has since become known as Bixby's Cave. Enos Bixby, Anna's husband, took over after these men were driven out or killed and continued their operations, along with committing robberies and stealing timber. Bixby married Anna when she was an old woman because he hoped to steal her money from her. Finally, he attempted to kill her by tying her up with ropes and heavy chain and pushing her off a bluff. As it happened though, she fell into a tree and managed to escape. Not long after, Anna died suddenly and she was buried with the rope and chain that her husband tried to kill her with. Her ghost has haunted her burial site ever since, often appearing as a shimmering light.

But, despite the popularity of the tale, it only contains elements of the truth. The time period when all of this allegedly occurred seems to be the biggest problem with the story. Bixby's Cave did (and does still) exist, however after 1811 it is unlikely that it would have been big enough to house a moonshine distillery and certainly not a counterfeiting operation. The cave was heavily damaged in the earthquake that rocked the New Madrid Fault at that time and afterward was much less accessible than it had been before. Several of the men who were involved in the criminal aspects of the story were dead long before Anna married Eson Bixby and others who allegedly worked together were children during the time of the opposite criminal's heyday. If the story had involved these men, then it would have had to have taken place in the 1820's. This seems odd since Anna's first husband died in 1845 and Anna survived into the 1870's.

On the other hand, recent historians believe that the story may have occurred in some fashion but it was told and re-told using well-known outlaws as the key players in the tale, when the real culprits may have been much lesser known. There were counterfeiters operating in Hardin County at the time and it has been learned that Anna's second husband was involved with criminals.

In 1935, the *Hardin County Independent* newspaper published what was likely a more accurate account of Anna's escape from her murderous husband. The writer of the account, Charles L. Foster, had left Hardin County in the 1880's but had grown up in the Rock Creek area, a few homes away from Anna Bixby. He had been born in 1863 and vaguely remembered Eson Bixby when he was alive, which seems to date the escape to the late 1860's, in the years following the Civil War.

According to the account, a rider came to the Bixby household late one night during a terrible thunderstorm. He called out to the house that someone needed Anna's medical skills and of course, she immediately came out. She mounted the rider's second horse and they rode into the woods. The trail was shrouded in darkness, thanks to the heavy storm clouds overhead, and Anna soon became disoriented and unsure of their route. However, at one point during the ride, she looked over and when a flash of lighting illuminated the night, Anna saw the identity of the mysterious rider -- it was her husband Eson.

When he realized that she had discovered his identity, Bixby brought the horses to a halt and he quickly bound her hands and gagged her. It was obvious that he intended to do away with her and Anna began to panic. When she heard the jingle of chains being removed from his saddlebags, Anna became so frightened that she began to run, dashing into the dark woods. As she plunged into the forest, her fear became even stronger as she realized that she had no idea where she was. The storm continued to rage, sending rain lashing down on her and causing the wind to whip through the trees in a wild fury. Anna ran for some distance and then suddenly, the ground beneath her vanished and she tumbled over a large bluff and crashed to the ground far below. The fall broke the ropes that bound her hands but also broke some of her bones, seriously injuring her. Nevertheless, she managed to crawl a short distance to a fallen tree and slithered in behind it.

A few moments later, a light appeared in the darkness at the top of the bluff and Eson Bixby came into view carrying a burning torch. He climbed down from the top of the rocks and searched around for Anna, but he did not find her. After a few minutes, he returned to his horse and rode away.

Once he was gone, Anna began crawling and stumbling out of the forest. It took her until sunrise to find a nearby farmhouse but when she reached it, she found herself at the doorstep of friends -- only a few houses away from her own. They quickly took her in and she told them the story of what had happened.

Bixby was soon arrested and taken to the jail in Elizabethtown. He escaped though and vanished for a time. He was later captured again in Missouri, but once again, he escaped. This time, he disappeared for good and was never seen again.

Anna lived on in the Rock Creek community of Hardin County until the 1870's and when she died, she was buried next to her first husband and only a simple "A" was inscribed on her tombstone. But there are those who believe that Anna, or at least her spirit, lives on.

The legend of Anna Bixby states that her husband wanted to do away with her because of a fortune that she had managed to collect over the years. What may have amounted to a "fortune" in that day and time may have been much smaller than what we would consider to be one today but most believe that it was a large amount of money. The legend further states that when Anna learned of Eson's greed, she hid the money away somewhere, just before he attempted to do away with her. It is believed that the hiding place for the treasure was the cave beside Rock Creek in Hooven Hollow, which was also said to have been the hiding place of the outlaw gang.

The cave is still known as Anna Bixby Cave today and it is along the bluff, in the vicinity of the cave, where people have reported seeing a strange light appear over the years. The large, glowing light moves in and out of the trees and among the rocks, vanishing and then re-appearing without explanation. It is believed that the light may be that of Anna Bixby, still watching over the treasure that she hid away her years ago.

One of the most detailed accounts of the Bixby ghost light was collected by folklorist Charles Neely in his 1938 book *Tales & Songs of Southern Illinois*. The story of the spooklight was told by Reverend E.N. Hall, a minister who once served the Rock Creek Church and who had a number of the brushes with the uncanny in this part of Hardin County. One evening in his younger days, Hall and a friend of his named Hobbs, walked over to a nearby farm to escort two of the girls who lived there to church. When they got to the house, they found there were no lights on. It appeared that the girls left without them and the two young men stood around for a few moments, wondering what to do.

They stood at the edge of the yard as they talked and looked toward the darkened house. The house itself stood on a short knoll with a hollow that ran away from the gate to the left for about 100 yards and then joined with another hollow that came back to the right side of the gate. Hobbs was looking eastward along the bluff when he saw what appeared to be a "ball of fire about the size of a washtub" going very fast along the east hollow.

At first, the young men thought that it might be someone on a horse carrying a lantern, then realized that it was moving much too fast for that. The light followed the hollow to the left of the gate and along a small curve where one hollow met the other. It followed the opposite hollow and came right up the bank where the two men were standing. It paused, motionless, about 30 feet away from them and began to burn down smaller and smaller and then turned red as it went out. Finally, it simply vanished.

The two young men decided not to go to church. They went directly to the farm where they had been working and went to bed. The next morning, at the breakfast table, they told Mr. Patten, the farmer they had been working for, what they had both seen the night before. He laughed at them and said that it had just been a "mineral light" carried by the wind. He had no explanation though for how fast the light had moved or for the fact that there had been no wind the previous evening. He could also not explain why the light seemed to follow the two hollows and then stop in place and burn out.

Later, Hall had the chance to speak with the woman who owned the farm, a Mrs. Walton, and to ask her what the light might have been. She then told him the story of Anna Bixby, who had owned the property before she had, and explained that to protect her money from her criminal husband, she had hidden her fortune in a cave that was located on the property. Mrs. Walton always believed that the spooklight was the ghost of Anna Bixby checking to see that her money was still hidden away. She had seen the light herself on many occasions, always disappearing into the cave.

Hall asked her, if she knew so well where Anna's money was hidden, why she had never bothered to go and get it. "I would," Mrs. Walton answered, "if I thought that Granny Bixby wanted me to have it."

Cave-in-Rock is located just outside of the small town of the same name in extreme southeastern Illinois. There is a wonderful state park and lodge also located nearby. The cave is easy to find and although small, manages to give many visitors the goosebumps when they consider the bloody history of the place.

Anna Bixby's Cave is located near the former Rock Creek Community, a short distance from Cave-in-Rock. It is located on private property, so permission must be obtained before visiting. It is also not recommended to go to the cave during the summer months because the hollow is infested with rattlesnakes.

HAUNTED CAVES OF ST. LOUIS
Cherokee Caverns, English Cave & Others -- Beneath St. Louis, Missouri

The caves of St. Louis, Missouri represent one of the most strange and mysterious elements of this fascinating city. The entire city of St. Louis is built upon a huge and complex system of natural caves. In fact, no other city on earth has as many caves beneath its streets, sidewalks and buildings. While most of them have been abandoned and closed off, they have not been forgotten and many tales, stories, legends and accounts of their unusual history are still told today.

Caves were used as man's earliest storage cellars. Thanks to the natural coolness of them, food and other items could be stored in them and kept from spoiling. This was perfect for the lagering that was done to beer by St. Louis brewers. Adam Lemp, who first brought lager beer to thirsty St. Louisans, was the first of the German brewers to put the caves to work for him, but he was far from the only one. These brewers altered the caves beneath the city to suit their purposes. They constructed stone arches and brick ceilings to prevent water from seeping in and paved the uneven cave floors. They also constructed staircases and walkways and installed massive wooden kegs where the beer could be aged. While the brewers did save money by having the cave as a starting point, the caverns were expensive to open and renovate. For this reason, many of them did double duty as not only a place for beer storage, but for sales as well. A number of beer gardens and taverns were once located in St. Louis caves and became popular drinking establishments and night spots.

Many of the caves would also boast a rich history. In some cases, breweries might not have been built at all but for the existence of the cave beneath the earth. The Anheuser-Busch brewery cave was first discovered in 1852 by a German brewer named George Schneider. He built a small brewery on the land above it and operated for three years before going out of business. The company was taken over by a competitor, Urban & Hammer, who renamed the property the Bavarian Brewery. The company was funded by Eberhard Anheuser and when they defaulted on their loans at a later date, brewing history came to pass. Later, when Anheuser-Busch began using artificial refrigeration in its plant, the cave beneath the brewery were abandoned and forgotten. It was rediscovered in the 1930's though when excavations were being done for underground storehouses. Although no longer used today, the cave is a piece of Anheuser-Busch and St. Louis history.

There were a number of other breweries that also used the natural cave systems of the city during the heyday of beer brewing in St. Louis. Ironically, many of them used different portions of the same caves, never realizing that they were actually connected. This was mostly because there were so many breweries operating in the city in those days.

It was the huge tide of German immigration to St. Louis that created the beer brewing industry that we know today. Soon, breweries and beer-gardens began to appear all over town and none of them suffered for lack of patronage. A number of smaller breweries began to appear as the residents of the city began to join the Germans in their appreciation for beer.

The first brewery of any size was that of Adam Lemp, who came to St. Louis in 1838. Here, he established a small mercantile store and marketed items that he manufactured himself, including vinegar and beer. In 1840, he officially began producing the first lager beer in St. Louis. Lager beer was different than the thick ales that were common at the time and the term "lager" came from the German word "lagern", meaning to store. Early German brewers stored their product in cooling caves during the summer and this aging process would allow the yeast to settle, improve the flavor of the beer and allow it to be stored for a longer period of time. The end result is a crisp, clean, sparkling beer and not only did it taste better, but it created a product that did not have to be consumed as quickly before it went bad. Lemp helped to start a revolution in the industry and he is rightly considered the "father of modern brewing in St. Louis".

Other breweries also came along like the Julius Winkelmeyer Brewery, Phoenix Brewery, Lafayette, Home, Excelsior and many others. Another well-known company was the Griesedieck Bros. Brewing Company, which was started by Joseph Griesedieck in 1912. Five years later, Griesedieck left the company that he had started with his brother and opened a company that made beer and soft drinks. In 1921, the changed the name to the Falstaff Brewing Company, having purchased the "Falstaff" trademark from William Lemp. In 1860, there were 40 breweries operating in St. Louis, producing about 23,000 barrels of beer each year.

And while a good many of the forgotten caves of St. Louis were used by the brewing industry for lagering beer, there were many others that were not. As mentioned already, the city is literally honeycombed with caves and there were probably a large number of them that were never found. It's possible that some of these caves still exist today, still untouched by human hands. In addition, there are also a large number of caves that were known to our ancestors but have been forgotten over time. These caves are seldom seen or mentioned today and are kept secret by small bands of spelunkers who still roam the world under the city streets. The strange history of the caves of St. Louis have left an indelible mark on the city and on those who discover their legacy today as well.

HAUNTED ENGLISH CAVE

One of the most famous St. Louis caves is one that few living people have ever seen. Now filled with water and inaccessible, English Cave has long been a place of legend in the city. It is the one such cave that has been regarded as "haunted" since it was first discovered and the stories have it that it brought bad luck and misfortune to every person who owned it!

The original entrance to English Cave, as it came to be known, was located just east of Benton Park, between Arsenal and Wyoming Streets in south St. Louis. The only entrance was by way of a natural shaft that extended about 60 feet below ground. At the bottom of the shaft, a visitor would then enter a chamber that was close to 400 feet long.

In the early days of the city, the cave was known only to the Native Americans of the region. There came to be a legend associated with the cave that not only may account for the alleged curse attached to the place, but also for the reports of hauntings that followed in the years to come. According to the story, there was a young Indian woman who fell in love with one of the men from her village. The young man reciprocated her feelings but was unable to marry the girl as she had already been promised to the tribe's war chief, a violent and disagreeable man. Rather than see her in the arms of another, the man convinced his lover to run away with him. They managed to find refuge in the cave and hid there, waiting for the danger to pass. The chief somehow tracked them to the cave though and he and his warriors stationed themselves outside, determined to take back his intended bride. Rather than surrender to the chief, the couple stayed in the cave until they starved to death.

Many years later, this tale was repeated to the white explorers who entered the cave and seemed to have a ring of truth after the bones of two people were discovered inside. If there is any truth to the story, it might explain the accounts that were passed on about the cave, including the ghostly sounds of crying and weeping reported here and the eerie voices that speak in an unknown dialect. Could the spirits of the two Indians have lingered behind in the cave and if so, could they account for the curse that was believed to plague the owners?

Ezra O. English was the first of the luckless proprietors of the place. In 1826, English built a small ale brewery next to the cave and east of the commons. He later set up the brewery inside of the cave and became the first person in St. Louis to use a cave as a commercial property. Unlike those who followed his example, English did little to improve the cave's interior, although he did wall up the mouth, removed some of the stone and earth from the floors and carve out 50 stone steps into the first chamber. Beyond this was the second chamber, which was ten feet lower than the first. Here, a small spring emerged from the ceiling and created a small waterfall. The first chamber was the principal part of the early business though. He used it as a place to store ale and he also provided accommodations for customers who wanted to sample cool drinks.

In 1839, English took on a partner named Isaac McHose, a local businessman, and they began calling the place the St. Louis Brewery. The business grew and by 1842, they had developed the first subterranean beer garden and resort in the city. While the men were expanding the business, they gained a new neighbor. The city was also converting the commons next door to the brewery into a public burial ground. Cholera epidemics had been striking the city and the graveyard began to grow.

By 1849, the renovations to the cave had been completed and English and McHose re-named their project Mammoth Cave and Park, perhaps borrowing the name from the cave of the same name in Kentucky, which was just then starting to attract visitors from all over the country. English and McHose also did their bit to attract visitors to their cave. They built gardens and arbors around the property and hired a family of vocalists to entertain in the cave on Sundays. Later, they constructed a sail swing, arranged hot air balloon rides and hired a military band to play full-time.

Unfortunately, they saw little success. The year 1849 is remembered by most in the city as the "year of misfortune", thanks to the terrible cholera epidemic that swept through the city and the great fire that devastated the riverfront. No one seemed to have much interest in the attractions that the cave offered and by 1851, English was the sole proprietor of the cave again. Within a few years, he faded from public records.

Several years later, the city passed an ordnance for the removal of all bodies from the cemetery that adjoined the site. They were to be taken to the "Quarantine Burying Grounds" that were located some distance south of Jefferson Barracks. When all of the bodies were removed from the St. Louis Cemetery, another ordnance established it as a public park in 1866. It was named after Thomas Hart Benton and the cave was largely forgotten.

However in 1887, two businessmen named F.K. Binz and George Schaper attempted to resurrect English Cave as a commercial mushroom farm. They hoped to fare better than their predecessors had and were constantly reminded of the cave's failures. Even a newspaper article that was released at the time wished the men well "in spite of the history of failure that has hung around the place." The operation was soon in full swing and the men tended their crop by light of kerosene lanterns. For a time, the business was moderately successful and regular customers reportedly came and paid 75 cents for a pound of mushrooms. It didn't last though and in less than two years, the cave was abandoned once again.

The next unlucky occupant was Paul-Wack Wine Co., which became widely acclaimed for the fine wines they offered. Great wines or not though, they didn't stay around much longer than the mushroom farm. In 1897, the company used the cave for storage for their nearby winery but soon closed down. The winery was the last company to use the cave for business purposes, but its history had not yet ended.

Shortly after the turn of the century, a St. Louis park commissioner suggested opening a portion of the cave as a part of Benton Park. He recommended that an ornamental entrance be constructed from the park for he believed the cave would draw visitors from all over, as there was no other park with such a unique attraction connected with it. The plans were never realized though and eventually the cave really was forgotten.

During the 1960's though, interest in the cave was revived thanks to Hubert and Charlotte Rother, the authors of the excellent and indispensable book, *Lost Caves of St. Louis.* They proposed a plan for re-opening the cave with the help of the Hondo Grotto, a local chapter of the Missouri Speological Society, a group of cave explorers. The society surveyed Benton Park and used sounding equipment to try and detect an approximate depth of the cave. They discovered that the ground under Benton Park was catacombed with large rooms and ten passageways that left the park and travel in all directions. They tried to interest two different St. Louis mayors and the City Park Department in their plans, but no one was interested.

Instead of giving up though, their interest in the cave grew. They began digging through old records and searching for information. They discovered that although the cave had been closed in 1897, it created a myriad of problems for the park years later. It seemed that periodically, the lake in Benton Park would suddenly lose all of its water. Apparently, the water was flooding down into the cave below. The Park Department constructed a concrete bottom for the lake and sealed off the leak but it would later be discovered that this would not be enough to keep water out of the cave.

The problem faced by the Rother's back in the 1960's though was how to get into the cave again. The original entrance had been closed off, but thanks to newspaper accounts that were written about their plans for the cave, many older people in the area came forward with their memories of the cave. One woman told them that she recalled entering the cave in 1889 and had gone in through the backyard of a confectionary, just east of Benton Park. The owner of the confectionary charged his customers 25 cents to see the cave. Another man claimed to have visited the cave in 1911 by way of a staircase in the back of an old shed. Another remembered a spiral staircase and yet another told of an entrance through an abandoned frame building off an alley. He and some friends had pried two wooden cellar doors away from the entrance and had gone down a flight of steps.

They continued to pick up promising clues and bits of information and tried to follow as many leads as possible. They learned of an entrance that had once been located in a boarded-up shed that stood near the intersection of the alley behind Provenger Place. There was also an alleged entrance from a basement of a house near Benton Park. The Rother's check out the address, but there was no building there so they asked about the basement entrance at houses up and down the block. "All we received," Charlotte Rother later wrote," were suspicious looks and blank faces." They followed every story and every possible lead, but ran into a blank wall. There was seemingly no way into the cave.

Unfortunately, it turns out that all of their searching may have been for nothing. At the time of this writing, I have learned that the cave is completely underwater and inaccessible today. I have been told that there are some grates in Benton Park that would look down into the cave, if they were not filled with water. A few years ago, in the middle 1990's, a group of amateur cave explorers were able to get into the cavern during a time when the water levels were very low. Even then, the water was more than waist-deep in spots. The group managed to come out with some priceless video footage of the cave, showing brick walls and arched ceilings that had been installed during the expansion done by English and McHose. Since that time, as far as I am aware, no one has been back into the cave.

Is the curse of English Cave finally ended then? Will curious visitors and unlucky brewery owners no longer disturb the rest of the Indian girl and her lover? Perhaps now the two can live out their eternity within the damp and murky darkness of English Cave and be no longer bothered by trespassers from the world above.

CHEROKEE CAVE

There is no question that the most famous of St. Louis' caves was a place that would become known in later years as Cherokee Cave. Originally, this was part of the same cave that was discovered by Adam Lemp and used for his brewery. Thanks to the unusual additions made by the Lemp family to the cave in later years, it remains as perhaps the most enigmatic in the city.

The saga of the Lemp family is one that is well known to not only those in St. Louis but also to readers and researchers of the supernatural. I devoted a very large section to the Lemp family in my book *Haunted St. Louis*, but for those who are unaware of their strange and dark history, I will try and briefly recount some of it here.

The Lemp Family came to prominence in the middle 1800's as one of the premier brewing families of St. Louis. For years, they were seen as the fiercest rival of Anheuser-Busch and the first makers of lager beer in middle America but today, they are largely forgotten and remembered more for the house they once built than for the beer they once brewed.

The story of the Lemp brewing empire began when Johann Adam Lemp, a German immigrant came to St. Louis in 1838. He opened a small mercantile store at what is now Delmar and Sixth Streets and in addition to common household items, he also sold vinegar and beer that he made himself. Apparently, Lemp began to see that he did better business with these items than with anything else and he soon established a small factory to make them at 112 South Second Street, between Walnut and Elm. This would be approximately where the Gateway Arch now stands along the St. Louis riverfront.

The new plant produced both vinegar and beer and for the first few years, Lemp sold his beer in a pub that was attached to the brewery. It is believed that during this period, Lemp introduced St. Louis to the first lager beer. This new beer was a great change from the English-type ales that had previously been popular and the lighter beer soon became a regional favorite. Business prospered and by 1845, the popularity of the beer was enough to allow him to discontinue vinegar production and concentrate on beer alone.

The company expanded rapidly, thanks to a demand for the beer, but Lemp soon found that the brewery was too small to handle the production of the beer and the storage needed for the lagering process as well. He found a solution to his problem in a limestone cave that had been discovered just south of the city limits of the time. The cave, which was located at the present-day corner of Cherokee and De Menil Place, could be kept cool by chopping ice from the nearby Mississippi River and depositing it inside. This would keep the cavern cool enough for the lagering process to run its course.

Lemp purchased a lot over the entrance to the cave and then began excavating and enlarging it to make room for the wooden casks needed to store the beer. The remodeling was completed in 1845 and caused a stir in the city. Other brewers were looking for ways to model their brews after the Lemp lager beer and soon these companies also began using the natural caves under the city to store beer and to open drinking establishments.

The Lemp's Western Brewing Co. continued to grow during the 1840's and by the 1850's was one of the largest in the city. Demand for the beer continued to increase too, as it was highly regarded by almost everyone. In 1858, the beer even captured first place at the annual St. Louis fair.

Adam Lemp died on August 25, 1862, a very wealthy and distinguished man. He had created the leading brewery in St. Louis, the country's most competitive beer market, and had lived the American dream, discovering riches and happiness in the new world.

Adam Lemp left a thriving business in the hands of his son, William, and under this new leadership, it began to grow in ways that its founder could have never conceived of. He began construction of a new brewery above the cave where the beer was stored. By the 1870's, the Lemp factory was regarded as the largest in the entire city.

By the middle 1890's, the Lemp brewery was becoming known all over America. They had already introduced the popular "Falstaff" beer and it became a favorite across the country, something that had never really been done by a regional brewer before. Lemp was also the first brewery to establish coast-to-coast distribution of its beer. It was transported in about 500 refrigerated railroad cars, averaging about 10,000 shipments per year. They operated their own railroad, the Western Cable Railway Company, which connected all of the brewery's main buildings with the shipping yards along the Mississippi. From here, they connected to major railroads and then spread out around the country.

The brewery had also grown to the point that it employed over 700 men and as many as 100 horses were needed to pull the delivery wagons in St. Louis alone. The brewery was now producing up to 500,000 barrels of beer each year and was ranked as the eight largest in the country. Construction of new buildings, and renovations of the current ones, continued on a daily basis at the Lemp brewery. The entire complex was designed in an Italian Renaissance style with arched windows, brick cornices and added Lemp shields and eventually grew to cover a five city blocks.

In addition to William Lemp's financial success, he was also well-liked and popular among the citizens of St. Louis. He was on the board of several organizations, including a planning committee for the 1904 World's Fair and many others. His family life was happy and his sons were very involved in the business. In November 1892, when the Western Brewery was incorporated as the William J. Lemp Brewing Co., William Jr. was named as vice-president. William Jr., or Will as he was commonly known, was born in St. Louis on August 13, 1867. He attended Washington University and the United States Brewer's Academy in New York. He was well-known in St. Louis for his flamboyant lifestyle and in 1899, married Lillian Handlan.

William's other sons were Frederick, Charles and Edwin and he had three daughters, Anna, Elsa and Hilda. In 1897, Hilda married the son of one of William's best friends, Milwaukee brewer Frederick Pabst. William and Julia also had one other child, an infant that died that was not carried to term.

During the time of the Lemp Brewery's greatest success, William Lemp also purchased a home for his family a short distance away from the brewery complex. The house was built by Jacob Feickert, Julia Lemp's father, in 1868 and was likely financed by William. In 1876, Lemp purchased it outright for use as a residence and as an auxiliary brewery office. Although already an impressive house before, Lemp immediately began renovating and expanding it and turning it into a showplace of the period. The mansion boasted 33 rooms, elegant artwork, handcrafted wood decor, ornately painted ceilings, large beautiful bathrooms and even an elevator that replaced the main staircase in 1904. The house was also installed with three room-sized, walk-in vaults where paintings, jewelry and other valuables were stored. It was a unique and wondrous place and one fitting of the first family of St. Louis brewing.

Ironically, in the midst of all of this happiness and success, the Lemp family's troubles truly began.

The first death in the family was that of Frederick Lemp, William Sr.'s favorite son and the heir apparent to the Lemp empire. He had been groomed for years to take over the family business and was known as the most ambitious and hard working of the Lemp children. Frederick had been born on November 20, 1873 and attended both Washington University, where he received a degree in mechanical engineering, and the United States Brewers Academy. In 1898, Frederick married Irene Verdin and the couple was reportedly very happy. Frederick was well-known in social circles and was regarded as a friendly and popular fellow. In spite of this, he also spent countless hours at the brewery, working hard to improve the company's future. It is possible that he may have literally worked himself to death.

In 1901, Frederick's health began to fail and so he decided to take some time off in October of that year and temporarily move to Pasadena, California. He hoped that a change of climate might be beneficial to him. By December, he was greatly improved and after his parents visited with him after Thanksgiving, William returned to St. Louis with hopes that his son would be returned to him soon. Unfortunately, that never happened. On December 12, Frederick suffered a sudden relapse and he died at the age of only 28. His death was brought about by heart failure, due to a complication of other diseases.

Frederick's death was devastating to his parents, especially to his father. Brewery secretary Henry Vahlkamp later wrote that when news came of the young man's death, William Lemp "broke down utterly and cried like a child... He took it so seriously that we feared it would completely shatter his health and looked for the worst to happen."

Lemp's friends and co-workers said that he was never the same again after Frederick's death. It was obvious to all of them that he was not coping well and he began to slowly withdraw from the world. He was rarely seen in public and only seldom seen outside of his office in the brewery.

On January 1, 1904, William Lemp suffered another crushing blow with the death of his closest friend, Frederick Pabst. This tragedy changed Lemp even more and soon he became indifferent to the details of running the brewery. Although he still came to the office each day, he paid little attention to the work and those who knew him said that he now seemed nervous and unsettled and his physical and mental health were both beginning to decline. On February 13, 1904, his suffering became unbearable.

When Lemp awoke that morning, he ate breakfast and mentioned to one of the servants that he was not feeling well. He finished eating, excused himself and went back upstairs to his bedroom. Around 9:30, he took a .38 caliber Smith & Wesson revolver and shot himself in the head with it. There was no one else in the house at the time of the shooting except for the servants. A servant girl, upon hearing the sound of the gunshot, ran to the door but she found it locked. She immediately ran to the brewery office, about a half block away, and summoned William Jr. and Edwin. They hurried back to the house and broke down the bedroom door. Inside, they found their father lying on the bed in a pool of blood. The revolver was still gripped in his right hand and there was a gaping and bloody wound at his right temple. At that point, Lemp was still breathing but unconscious.

One of the boys called the family physician, Dr. Henry J. Harnisch, by telephone and he came at once. He and three other doctors examined William but there was nothing they could do. William died just as his wife returned home from a shopping trip downtown. No suicide note was ever found.

William Lemp's tragic death came at a terrible time as far as the company was concerned. In the wake of his burial, all of St. Louis was preparing for the opening of the 1904 World's Fair, perhaps the greatest event to ever come to St. Louis. Not only had William been elected to the fair's Board of Directors, but the brewery was also involved in beer sales and displays for the event. William Jr. took his father's place and became active with the Agriculture Committee and with supervising the William J. Lemp Brewing Company's display in Agriculture Hall, where brewers and distillers from around the world assembled to show off their products. The St. Louis brewers also combined for the restaurant and pavilion at the Alps section of the Pike, one of the fair's most popular attractions.

Finally, in November 1904, William Lemp Jr. took over as the new president of the William J. Lemp Brewing Company. He inherited the family business and with it, a great fortune. He filled the house with servants, built country houses and spent huge sums on carriages, clothing and art.

In 1899, Will had married Lillian Handlan, the daughter of a wealthy manufacturer. Together, the two of them had one child, William J. Lemp III. Lillian was nicknamed the "Lavender Lady" because of her fondness for dressing in that color. She was soon spending the Lemp fortune as quickly as her husband was. While Will enjoyed showing off his trophy wife, he eventually grew tired of her and decided to divorce her. Their divorce, and the court proceedings around it, created a scandal that all of St. Louis talked about. When it was all over, the "Lavender Lady" went into seclusion and retired from the public eye.

But Will's troubles were just beginning that year. The Lemp brewery was also facing a much-altered St. Louis beer market in 1906 when nine of the large area breweries combined to form the Independent Breweries Company. Of even more concern was the expanding temperance movement in America. The growing clamor of those speaking out against alcohol was beginning to be heard in all corners of the country. It looked as though the heyday of brewing was coming to an end.

The year 1906 also marked the death of Will's mother. It was discovered that she had cancer in 1905 and by March 1906, her condition had deteriorated to the point that she was in constant pain and suffering. She died in her home a short time later. Her funeral was held in the mansion and she was laid to rest in the mausoleum at Bellefontaine Cemetery. Her death seemed to affect Will the most. Combined with his scandalous divorce and the problems at the brewery, his mother's death surely made 1906 one of the worst years of his life.

In 1911, the last major improvements were made to the Lemp brewery when giant grain elevators were erected on the south side of the complex. It was also in 1911 that the Lemp mansion was converted and remodeled into the new offices of the brewing company. A number of changes were made to the structure, including the addition of the immense bay window directly atop the atrium on the south side of the house. Inside, the front part of the house was converted into private offices, lobbies and rooms for clerks. Even with these changes though, the park-like settings of the grounds and the carriage houses were retained.

Like most of its other German competitors, the Lemp brewery limped along through the years of World War I. According to numerous accounts though, Lemp was in far worse shape that many of the other companies. Will had allowed the company's equipment to deteriorate and by not keeping abreast of industry innovations, much of the brewing facilities had become outmoded.

And to make matters worse, Prohibition was coming.

Unlike when it had been in his father's hands, the Lemp Brewery did not prosper in Will's hands. The combination of poor management and the passing of the 18th Amendment, which made Prohibition the law of the land, had a devastating effect on the Lemp Brewery.

The coming of Prohibition seemed to signal the real death of the company. As the individual family members were quite wealthy aside from the profits from the company, there was little incentive to keep the brewery afloat. Will gave up on the idea that Congress would suddenly repeal Prohibition and he closed the Lemp plant down without notice. The workers learned of the closing when they came to work one day and found the doors shut and the gates locked.

Will decided to simply liquidate the assets of the plant and auction off the buildings. He sold the famous Lemp "Falstaff" logo to brewer Joseph Griesedieck for the sum of $25,000. He purchased the recognizable Falstaff name and shield with the idea that eventually the government would see Prohibition for the folly that it was and that beer would be back. Lemp no longer shared the other man's enthusiasm though and in 1922, he saw the brewery sold off to the International Shoe Co. for just $588,000, a small fraction of its estimated worth of $7 million in the years before Prohibition. Sadly, virtually all of the Lemp company records were pitched when the shoe company moved into the complex. International Shoe Co. would use the larger buildings, and portions of the cave, as warehouse space.

With Prohibition finally destroying the brewery, the 1920's looked to be a dismal decade for the Lemp family. As bad as it first seemed though, things almost immediately became worse with the suicide of Elsa Lemp Wright in 1920. She became the second member of the family to take her own life. She committed suicide in her husband's home under what have been described as mysterious circumstances. The police were not called for hours, there were conflicting accounts of whether or not Elsa was depressed and her husband became very "agitated" while be questioned about the authorities.

And while the circumstances around Elsa's death have had some suggesting there was more to the story than was told, her brothers seemed to find little out of the ordinary about her demise. Will and Edwin rushed to the house as soon as they heard about the shooting. When Will arrived and was told what had happened, he only had one comment to make.

"That's the Lemp family for you", he said.

Will was soon to face depression and death himself. He had already slipped into a dark state of mind following the end of the Lemp's brewing dynasty, but he took an even sharper turn for the worse after the sale of the plant to the International Shoe Co. He was downcast and bitter and had always believed that the brewery could have been turned into something great, even after Prohibition, and now it was nothing more than a warehouse. His family's hopes, dreams and legacies had turned to dust.

The months that followed the auction were difficult ones for him as not only had the family business died, but Will himself had been responsible for selling off the last pieces of Adam and William Lemp's life's work. It was likely this indignity that bothered Lemp the most. He never really recovered from his role in the company's dissolution and his state of mind began to deteriorate. Perhaps it was a "curse" that ran in the Lemp bloodline, or perhaps they were all simply sad products of their time, but mental instability and depression seemed to be a common factor among members of the family. Will soon began to follow in the footsteps of his father and he became increasingly nervous and erratic. He shunned public life and kept to himself, complaining often of ill health and headaches.

By December 29, 1922, he had reached the limit of his madness and committed suicide himself in his office at the Lemp Mansion. Lemp had shot himself in the heart with a .38 caliber revolver. He had unbuttoned his vest and then fired the gun through his shirt. When discovered, Lemp was still breathing, but he had expired by the time a doctor could arrive.

Oddly, Lemp seemed to have no intention of suicide, even a short time before. Apparently, the final turn in his downward spiral had come on quite suddenly. After the sale of the brewery, he had discussed selling off the rest of the assets, like land parcels and saloon locations, and planned to then just "take it easy". Not long after that announcement, he had even put his estate in Webster Groves up for sale, stating that he planned to travel to Europe for awhile. Even a week before his death, he had dined with his friend August A. Busch, who said that Lemp seemed "cheerful" at the time and that he gave no indication that he was worrying about business or anything else. "He was a fine fellow," Busch added, "and it is hard to believe that he has taken his own life."

With William Jr. gone and his brothers involved with their own endeavors, it seemed that the days of the Lemp empire had come to an end at last. The two brothers still in St. Louis had left the family enterprise long before it had closed down. Charles worked in banking and finance and Edwin had entered a life in seclusion at his estate in Kirkwood in 1911. The great fortune they had amassed was more than enough to keep the surviving members of the family comfortable through the Great Depression and beyond.

But the days of Lemp tragedy were not yet over.

By the late 1920's, only Charles and Edwin Lemp remained from the immediate family. Throughout his life, Charles was never much involved with the Lemp Brewery, although he was named as treasurer around 1900 and was second vice-president in 1911. His interests had been elsewhere, but when the family home was renovated into offices, he made his residence at the Racquet Club in St. Louis.

He ended his connections with the family business that same year and took the first of what would be many positions in the banking and financial industries. In 1917, he became vice-president of the German Savings Institution and then on to Liberty Central Trust in 1921. He stayed on here for several years and eventually got into the automobile casualty business as president of the Indemnity Company of America. In 1929, Charles also moved back to the Lemp mansion and the house became a private residence once more.

Despite his very visible business and political life though, Charles remained a mysterious figure who became even odder and more reclusive with age. He remained a bachelor his entire life and lived alone in his old rambling house with only his two servants, Albert and Lena Bittner for company. By the age of 77, he was arthritic and quite ill. Legend has it that he was deathly afraid of germs and wore gloves to avoid any contact with bacteria. He had grown quite bitter and eccentric and had developed a morbid attachment to the Lemp family home. Thanks to the history of the place, his brother Edwin often encouraged him to move out, but Charles refused. Finally, when he could stand no more of life, he became the fourth member of the Lemp family to commit suicide.

On May 10, 1949, Alfred Bittner, one of Charles' staff, went to the kitchen and prepared breakfast for Lemp as he normally did. He then placed the breakfast tray on the desk in the office next to Lemp's bedroom, as he had been doing for years. Bittner later recalled that the door to the bedroom was closed and he did not look inside. At about 8:00, Bittner returned to the office to remove the tray and found it to be untouched. Concerned, he opened the bedroom door to see if Charles was awake and discovered that he was dead from a bullet wound to the head. Bittner hurried to inform his wife of what had happened and she contacted Richard Hawes, Lemp's nephew, who then summoned the police to the mansion.

When the police arrived, they found Lemp still in bed and lightly holding a .38 caliber Army Colt revolver in his right hand. He was the only one of the family who had left a suicide note behind. He had dated the letter May 9 and had written "In case I am found dead blame it on no one but me" and had signed it at the bottom.

Oddly, Charles had made detailed funeral arrangements for himself long before his death. He would be the only member of the family not interred at the mausoleum at Bellefontaine Cemetery and while this might be unusual, it was nearly as strange as the rest of the instructions that he left behind. In a letter that was received at a south St. Louis funeral home in 1941, Lemp ordered that upon his death his body should be immediately taken to the Missouri Crematory. His ashes were then to be placed in a wicker box and buried on his farm.

He also ordered that his body not be bathed, changed or clothed and that no services were to be held for him and no death notice published, no matter what any surviving members of his family might want.

On May 11, 1949, Edwin Lemp picked up his brother's remains at the funeral home and took them to the farm to be buried. And while these instructions were certainly odd, they were not the most enduring mystery to the situation. You see, even after all of these years, there is no indication as to where Charles Lemp's farm was located!

The Lemp family, which had once been so large and prosperous, had now been almost utterly destroyed in a span of less than a century. Only Edwin Lemp remained and he had long avoided the life that had turned so tragic for the rest of his family. He was known as a quiet, reclusive man who had walked away from the Lemp Brewery in 1913 to live a peaceful life on his secluded estate in Kirkwood. Here, he communed with nature and became an excellent cook, gourmet and animal lover. He collected fine art and entertained his intimate friends.

Edwin managed to escape from the family "curse" but as he grew older, he did become more eccentric and developed a terrible fear of being alone. He never spoke about his family or their tragic lives, but it must have preyed on him all the same. His fears caused him to simply entertain more and to keep a companion with him at his estate almost all the time.

His most loyal friend and companion was John Bopp, the caretaker of the estate for the last 30 years of Edwin's life. His loyalty to his employer was absolute and it is believed that Bopp was never away from the estate for more than five days at a time during his entire time there. He never discussed any of Lemp's personal thoughts or habits but would sometimes speak of the famous parties held at the estate and the well-known guests who attended them. He remained faithful to Edwin even after his friend's death.

Edwin passed away quietly of natural causes at age 90 in 1970. The last order that John Bopp carried out for him must have been the worst. According to Edwin's wishes, he burned all of the paintings that Lemp had collected throughout his life, as well as priceless Lemp family papers and artifacts. These irreplaceable pieces of history vanished in the smoke of a blazing bonfire.

And like the Lemp empire ---lost forever.

After the death of Charles Lemp, the mansion was sold and turned into a boarding house. Shortly after that, it fell on hard times and began to deteriorate, along with the nearby neighborhood. In later years, stories began to emerge that residents of the boarding house often complained of ghostly knocks and phantom footsteps in the house. As these tales spread, it became increasingly hard to find tenants to occupy the rooms and because of this, the old Lemp Mansion was rarely filled. These stories seem to contradict the skeptics who claim that the ghosts are a more recent addition to the house!

The decline of the house continued until 1975, when Dick Pointer and his family purchased it. The Pointer's began remodeling and renovating the place, working for many years to turn it into a restaurant and an inn. But the Pointer's were soon to find out that they were not alone in the house...

The bulk of the remodeling was done in the 1970's and during this time, workers reported strange things happening in the house, leading many to believe the place was haunted. Reports often varied between feelings of being watched, vanishing tools and strange sounds. Many of the workers actually left the job site and never came back.

Since the restaurant has opened, staff members also have had their own odd experiences. Glasses have been seen to lift off the bar and fly through the air, sounds are often heard that do not have explanation and some have even glimpsed actual apparitions who appear and vanish at will. In addition, many customers and visitors to the house report some pretty weird incidents. It is said that doors lock and unlock on their own, the piano in the bar plays by itself, voices and sounds come from nowhere and even ghostly apparitions have appeared on occasion.

In addition to customers, the house has also attracted ghost hunters from around the country, who have come partly due to the November 1980 LIFE magazine article, which named the Lemp Mansion as "one of the most haunted houses in America". It remains a popular place for dinner and spirits today.

For our purposes here though, the subject of the mysterious tales is not the Lemp Mansion but rather the caves that were discovered and first used by Adam Lemp beneath the mansion and the brewery.

A reporter for the *Missouri Republican* newspaper wrote that Lemp's cave had three separate chambers and that each one of them contained large casks that were capable of holding 20-30 barrels of beer. The lagering cellars were opened for use in 1845, but Lemp soon expanded them to store more than 3,000 barrels of beer at a time. The beer cellars had been created by simply clearing out the natural underground river channels that had been carved from the limestone. They were divided off by the construction of masonry and brick walls into artificial rooms. During the early period of the brewery's history, Lemp was still brewing the beer on Second Street and taking it by wagon to the cave for the lagering period. After the death of Adam Lemp, his son, William, would construct a new brewery above the cave.

Around 1850, and around the time that the Lemp Brewery was just beginning to grow, fur trader Henri Chatillon built a home on a piece of property that adjoined Lemp's property at the crest of Arsenal Hill on Thirteenth Street. In 1856, Dr. Nicholas DeMenil purchased the house and land and he began enlarging and expanding the farm house a few years later.

DeMenil added several rooms to the house and a magnificent portico that faced eastward and looked out over his large garden and the Mississippi River. The Greek Revival mansion became a favorite landmark for river pilots rounding a landmark known as Chatillon's Bend.

In 1865, DeMenil leased the southwest corner of the property to the Minnehaha Brewery and they built a small, two-story frame brewery on the site. For several years, DeMenil had been using a cave that was located beneath his house as a place to store perishable goods and he also leased a portion of this to cave to Charles Fritschle and Louis Zepp, the owners of the brewery. Like Adam Lemp, they planned to use the caverns as a place to lager beer and over the course of the next year, they made a number of improvements to the cave. Unfortunately though, the brewery went out of business in 1867 and DeMenil acquired the buildings.

During the years of both operations though, both the Lemp's and the Minnehaha Brewery were using different parts of the same cave. A wall had been constructed between the two businesses but the Lemp's had little to fear from this short-lived competition. It is also believed that they must have been on good terms with Dr. DeMenil. When the Lemp family renovated their home just down the street from the DeMenil mansion, an arrangement was made to run three pipelines through DeMenil's cave, furnishing the Lemp mansion with hot water, cold water and beer from the brewery complex down the street.

The Lemp's continued to use the cave until the time when artificial refrigeration was installed at the factory. After that, the cave no longer played in role in beer production, so it was turned into a private playground for the Lemp family. A tunnel exited the basement of the house and entered into a portion of the cave that Adam Lemp had discovered for his beer lagering years before. Traveling along a quarried shaft, the Lemp's could journey beneath the street, all the way to the brewery. One large chamber was converted into a natural auditorium and a theater with constructed scenery of plaster and wire. Crude floodlights were used to illuminate the scene and the Lemp's were believed to have hired actors on the theater and vaudeville circuits of the day to come into the cave for private performances. This section of the cave was accessible by way of a spiral staircase that once ascended to Cherokee Street. This entrance is sealed today and the spiral stairs were cut away to prevent anyone from entering the cave.

East of the theater was another innovation of the Lemp family. Just below the intersection of Cherokee and De Menil was a large, concrete-lined pool that had been a reservoir back in the days of underground lagering. In the years that followed, the Lemp's converted it into a wading pool by using hot water that was piped in from the brewery's boiler house, which was located only a short distance away.

After Prohibition, the caves were abandoned and the entrances sealed shut.

However, this was not the end for the Minnehaha portion of the cave. In November 1946, a pharmaceutical manufacturer named Lee Hess bought not only the Minnehaha portion of the cave but the old DeMenil Mansion and grounds as well. He set to work developing the cave as a tourist attraction after first tearing down the deserted brewery buildings and a row of ten buildings that Dr. DeMenil had constructed as stores and homes between Cave and Cherokee Streets. In their place, he erected a museum building and parking lot to serve what he dubbed "Cherokee Cave". The cave became a popular tourist attraction but staff members at the DeMenil House talk about Hess and his strange obsession with the cave. He nearly lost his entire fortune trying to develop it and only two rooms of the sprawling DeMenil house were used during his time there. He and his wife shared one room and Albert Hoffman, who managed the cave for Hess, lived in the other. Staff members say that he moved all of the house's antiques and furniture into the attic while he was living here.

Before the cave was opened, Hess hired workmen to tear open an entrance into the Lemp part of the cave and in the process found that the passageway between the two cellars had been filled to the ceiling with clay. In the course of digging it out, workers found a number of bones that were linked to extinct animals and rare creatures that had no scientists had thought had lived in this area. Scientific research was conducted and Hess later got back to re-opening the cave. In April 1950, Cherokee Cave was opened to the public and it was a popular attraction for more than ten years. Visitors to the cave were able to stroll along on a tour that took them to Cherokee Lake and the Petrified Falls and of course to the famed Spaghetti Room, where slender cave formations hung down from the ceiling like strands of pasta.

The cave remained open until 1960 and in 1961, it was purchased by the Missouri Highway department to clear the way for Interstate 55. Hess battled to the end of his life to keep the state from destroying the DeMenil mansion and he eventually succeeded, although the cave museum and entrance could not be saved. The building and the entrance that Hess had created were demolished in 1964. Today, the only reminder of this unique place is a short street near Broadway and Cherokee in St. Louis called "Cave Street". The De Menil Mansion became a historic site and museum.

For years after the Interstate tore though this historic portion of the city, it was believed that Cherokee Cave had been filled in and completely destroyed. However, those with an interest in that sort of thing can tell you that portions of the cave do still exist today. While not in any way accessible to the public, the mystery of the place still remains alive.

Cave researchers and spelunkers have toured these passages in recent years but the last real documented visits took place in the middle 1960's. During the visit, accounts told of the labyrinth of rooms that were constructed by the Lemp's and revealed the remains of broken and rotted wooden casks where beer was once aged in the cellars. Visitors also passed through oversized doorways and into rooms lined with brick and stone. The wading pool remained as well, now filthy and covered with mud. The theater still existed, although it was hard to imagine audiences who might have assembled here to watch a performance. When the theater was built, the Lemp's tore out the natural formations of the cave and replaced with them with formations made from plaster and wood. Tinted in odd colors, this formed the backdrop for the stage.

And while many can attest to the haunting that occurs in the Lemp mansion, once accessible from the cave, there are others who insist that the cave is haunted too. Stories have been told about strange sounds and shapes that have been seen and heard down here and cannot be explained away as the weird, but natural, happenings of a cave. In recent times, the brewery above the cave has occasionally been the site of a "haunted house" attraction that has been put on by the current owners of the Lemp Mansion Restaurant. While a standard attraction of that type, in some cases, the customers sometimes got a little more than they bargained for. On at least one occasion, the attraction was reportedly closed down after a staff member spotted someone in an off-limits area that led down to the cave entrances. The customers were stopped at the door while employees tracked down this wandering visitor and escorted them out. However, after a thorough search, there was no one found. The trespasser had completely vanished!

On other occasions, apparitions had been seen and one staff member, who entered the cave itself, claimed to hear the sound of someone with hard-soled shoes walking behind him in some of the abandoned passageways. Unnerved, he began walking faster, only to have the mysterious footsteps keep pace with him. Suddenly, perhaps thinking that it was only his imagination or an echo of the cave playing tricks on him, he stopped abruptly, fully expecting the tapping of the shoes to stop as well -- but they continued on for several more steps before stopping too. Now, feeling quite frightened, he turned and illuminated the passage behind him with his flashlight but there was no one there! Needless to say, he immediately left the cave.

And the stories have continued to be told of the past few years. Lemp Mansion owner Paul Pointer told me recently that he hopes to possibly re-open the caves some day, and especially the Lemp brewery buildings, perhaps featuring a cave museum or some other attraction to highlight the natural history that still exists under the city. He had no idea if such a dream would ever come to fruition and if it did, it might be a long time in the future.

Forays into the caves for research purposes have added to the haunted lore of the place but unfortunately, it was unlikely that I would ever get to experience this for myself. The Lemp Caverns, and legendary Cherokee Cave, were now closed and forgotten, perhaps for all time. I had finally resigned myself to the fact that it was a place that I would never get to see.

Or that's what I thought at the time.

A NIGHT IN THE LEMP CAVERNS

In March 2003, I received an invitation from the G.H.O.S.T.S. research group in St. Louis, including Joe Immethun, Cathy Immethun-Voege, Terry Gambill and Luke Naliborski, to come with them on an excursion into the one place in St. Louis that I never imagined that I would get to see -- the Lemp Caverns and Cherokee Cave. They had been able to arrange a private tour of the caverns with Paul Pointer and when they asked me along, I immediately said that I would come.

On a chilly night in early March, we assembled at the nearby Lemp Mansion and then followed Paul as he took us to one of the rear entrances to the brewery buildings, now the only access into the caves. We entered one of the buildings with the gigantic grain silos and first had the rare treat of touring the brewery building itself, even riding one of the original elevators to the top floor and going out on the roof for an incredible view of south St. Louis. The warehouse buildings of the brewery are utterly massive with huge open floors that once held the workings and storage casks for the beer. In later times, after artificial refrigeration, the beer had been stored in various locations in the building. As we would descend to the lower areas of the brewery though, we would literally go back in time to the earliest days of the company, when beer had to be stored in low, cool areas to lager.

Staircases and elevators began to take us lower into the brewery until we finally entered areas that were underground. Here, we found more of the massive rooms with curved archways, detailed stone and brick work and unique ceilings that had been built with individual, arched sections to add extra support for the gigantic stone buildings overhead. When the brewery had been opened, the foundations would have had to support incredible weight in machinery, men and the huge casks of beer.

In each section that we explored, as we went deeper underground, remnants of the brewery and the heyday of the Lemp empire remained. In the upper sections, we found only occasional, worn away emblems in the shape of the famous Lemp shield (which later became the Falstaff logo), original light fixtures, hidden designs in doors and glass fixtures but little else. As we descended deeper underground however, the remains of the brewery became more noticeable and some locations appeared almost untouched, as though the last people to walk there before we did had been men who received a paycheck from the Lemp brewery each week.

Leaving the gigantic, arched rooms behind, we descended once again, this time through a smaller doorway, traveled along more passages and then went down a long, curved staircase to what would be considered the sub-basement of the brewery -- at the same level as the first portion of the cave. It was through this level that the Lemp's would ascend to the brewery as they walked to work on many mornings, using the cave to travel from the mansion to their offices. It was here that William Lemp had walked as he began his descent into the depression and madness that would later claim his life. He became so withdrawn that he refused to appear in public and chose these subterranean passages to travel to the brewery each day.

Our flashlights illuminated this area of the complex, which seemed well on its way to being reclaimed by the cave that it had been carved out of. The floors were covered with mud, moss and algae in some places and water dripped constantly from the walls and the ceilings. The brick was slowly crumbling beneath the decades of dampness and moisture that was covering it. It was this area of the brewery, the actual cave, where Adam Lemp had stored the first lager beer in St. Louis. There are several chambers that had been created here with high, curved ceilings and it was inside of these chambers where the original casks were placed. Ice was cut from the river during the winter months and then placed in the chambers to keep the beer cool. As it melted, the water would drain off into the sides of the chambers and into the water that flowed through the cave itself. On the sides of these long rooms, the cave water was visible and while extremely clear, left behind mineral deposits on the stone floor, making it plain that it was not fit to drink.

We then left the finished areas of the cave, with its stone floor and brick-lined walls, and entered a passageway that would take us into the wild areas of the cave that remained. To reach this section, we passed through a long, rugged corridor that was so damp and filled with moisture that many of the photographs that we took that night were so fogged that it was impossible to make out details. Several of my own photographs were lost but by continuing to clean my lens throughout the evening, I was able to take some of the first photos of the caverns that had been captured in years.

This long passageway, which led deeper into the cave, was littered with fallen stone, mud and refuse from the old days of the brewery. Above our heads were metal brackets and chains that had once been part of a conveyor belt system for transporting ice into the lager vaults. A motor from the conveyor belt is still resting on the side of the path through the passage. At the end of it, a metal ladder dangled from the ceiling and led upwards into a narrow, shadowy hole. During the early days of the brewery, this had been a shaft that was used to dump ice down into the cave. It was loaded onto cars on the conveyor belt and then mechanically moved to the lagering areas. This hole was sealed off many years ago and the metal ladder has fallen into disrepair.

Our first area of exploration took us to the left of the passage and we traveled down a wide tunnel toward what was once the Lemp's theater. In a number of areas, cave formations, mostly stalactites, were visible. Unfortunately though (as we would see in other parts of the cave), many of the formations had been broken off and damaged. This was presumably done in less enlightened times, when people didn't realize that such formations not only take hundreds of years to be created but are very harmful to the life of the cave. There are formations in the caverns that still exist but they are now somewhat rare.

The old Lemp theater is literally in ruins today. An archway at the back, which led to another chamber, was really one of the only remaining architectural pieces, as the false scenery that had been created for the theater now lay in heaping piles on the floor. It has long since been destroyed but some of the garish colors that had been painted on the plaster and stone can still be seen. Overhead, an old electric light bar that once illuminated the small stage does still remain. Its bulbs have long since been darkened and have been shattered though. I couldn't help but wonder as I stood here, looking around a room that was shrouded in a heavy mist, just how much privacy the Lemp's must have craved? I couldn't imagine huddling down here, far underground in this damp and dark chamber, just so I could attend private performances of popular programs. And how much did the Lemp's offer to be able to get the actors to put on these command performances? The theater remains an eerie and downright spooky place. I would not be surprised to learn that the ghosts of these actors still linger here -- still walking a stage that vanished long ago.

The theater marks the end of this passage and so we turned back in the direction we had come from and once more ended up beneath the ice chute to the surface. Just beyond this is the famed "swimming pool" of the Lemp family. The pool was actually just a wading pool and it was only used for this purpose after electric refrigeration was installed in the brewery. Before this, it was a reservoir for run-off from the melting ice. To visit the site today, you can still see the smooth walls of the reservoir but over the years, it has been heavily clogged with falls of rock from the cave's ceiling and by copious amounts of mud and clay. It bears little resemblance to any sort of wading pool now and was certainly not inviting enough for me to want to consider rolling up my pant legs and walking in. The pool is still filled with water though, which is approximately two feet deep or so, and is a habitat for the blind, white fish that dwell in caves. The animals are fairly rare but they can be found in the old Lemp Caverns.

Once we traveled past the reservoir, we entered what I considered to be the actual passages of Cherokee Cave. Here, the natural contours of the cave had been opened up and the floor had been artificially smoothed and fitted with curbs on each side of the path to keep the majority of the water away. These improvements, along with the remains of electrical wiring and light boxes, had been left behind when Lee Hess had been forced to abandon the cave back in 1961. They were just a few of the signs of the commercial cave that we would find in the passages ahead.

As the trip progressed, the commercial aspects of the cave became more and more obvious. At one point, we reached a ravine that cut across the path and had to use a metal ladder to climb down and cross to stone steps on the other side. An alternate route opened to the right and we descended another flight of steps, along which metal hand rails had been installed nearly 50 years ago. Here, we discovered more signs of the commercial Cherokee Cave in stripped out electrical lines and carefully constructed walkways. It was this passage that had originally connected the cave and brewery to the Lemp

Mansion. The entrance from the house has long since been sealed off and is no longer accessible but I looked forward to seeing it anyway. However, as we began to get nearer to the house, the water that now covered the floor grew deeper and deeper. To make matters worse, Paul began to get very concerned about the quality of air in this passageway. This has been a problem with some of the cave exploration that has been done in recent years. On one occasion, one member of a group of spelunkers had to be bodily carried out of the cave after passing out. We tried checking the air with a flame from a lighter and we watched as the flame grew weaker and weaker as we progressed along the passage. Eventually, it flickered and went out and we had to turn and go back. I was the last to return, feeling a great sense of loss for the now forgotten cave. I wondered if the others had the same sense of the history that we were privileged enough to be experiencing, walking where very few had walked in nearly half a century. This was, I realized, a haunted place -- whether by ghosts or by time though, I was unable to say.

One final passage awaited us and led us deeper into the cave or, if we had visited Cherokee Cave when it was in business, would have led us out of the cave. This was the original shaft that had been opened by Lee Hess and would have ended at the cave's visitor center and parking lot if they had not been demolished in the early 1960's.

The passage made a sharp right turn, although ahead of us was a man-made basin that had been built to catch run-off from a small spring that flowed from the cave wall. A trickle of water was still running into the basin even now. We turned into this last passageway but only traveled for a short distance before coming to what had been dubbed "Cherokee Lake" by Lee Hess. A stone bridge had been built across the lake decades ago but the path on the opposite side of it ended abruptly at a stone wall. This wall had been placed here by the Missouri Department of Transportation during the construction of Interstate 55. When they had razed the visitor's center, to replace it with the highway, the cave had also been sealed off, bringing to an end an element of St. Louis' most mysterious and colorful history.

Our return journey back through the labyrinth of cave passages, doorways, staircases, lagering chambers and brewery corridors took us much less time to complete than it had when we were descending. I was surprised to discover that we had actually been underground for several hours.

I remember walking back down the corridor where the conveyor belt system had been, which led from the cave to the lagering caverns, and looking back into the darkness and mist behind us. I am not sure what I expected to see or hear -- the sound of other, more ethereal explorers following behind or perhaps the specters of the Lemp's themselves still trudging to the brewery after all of these years? I don't know for sure, but I know that I expected something.

I wish that I could tell you that I had had some ghostly experience while exploring these haunted caverns but unfortunately, I cannot. The ghosts were certainly there though, at least in a figurative sense, because no one can come here and not feel the very tangible spirit of the past. It was a night that I may never be able to experience again --- and one that I will certainly never forget.

The Lemp Mansion is located on DeMenil Place in South St. Louis, just off of Cherokee Street. The historic DeMenil Mansion, where Lee Hess lived when renovating Cherokee Cave, is located on the same street. Interstate 55 runs just behind both houses and in the area beyond the property was once located the visitors center and parking lot for the cave. Officially, Cherokee Cave no longer exists but it portions of it still run beneath the earth here, stretching from the Lemp Mansion to the brewery buildings at the end of the block. Access to the caves is only available through the former brewery buildings but no trespassing is allowed here. This is private property and is kept locked at all times. Trespassers will be prosecuted to the fullest extent of the law.

WYANDOTTE CAVE
Near Leavenworth, Indiana

Many of us do not think of Indiana as a place to find caves, but the southern portion of the state is not only a beautiful region on the surface, but below the surface as well. Two of the most amazing caves in America can be found here, Marengo Cave and Wyandotte Cave. There is much to draw the visitor to either of these caverns, including fantastic formations, incredible and massive chambers, a rich history --- and tales of ghosts and hauntings.

The history of Wyandotte Cave began in prehistory, with the Native Americans who hunted the region and used the cave for both shelter and for mining the natural resources of the caverns. Their main interest was in the chert, an important raw material that could used to manufacture arrowheads, spear points and scraping tools. Another mineral, aragonite, was also taken from the cave to fashion jewelry, amulets and pipes. Remains that were discovered in the cave in more modern times also suggest that the Indians used the cave for food storage as well.

According to legend, Wyandotte Cave was discovered in 1798 by an unknown trapper who used the cave for shelter when an Indian that he befriended fell into the Wyandot Creek (now the Blue River) during the winter months and nearly died from hypothermia. Three years later, a man named F.I. Bentley apparently found the cave and he left a mark here that has been dated as the oldest inscription in the caverns. Bentley was an Englishman and apparently searching for minerals and potting clay when he came here. This date has been disputed somewhat but it is known that the cave was again visited, and written about for the first time, in 1806. The esteemed visitor to the site was William Henry Harrison, the Territorial Governor of Indiana and the future president of the United States. He was accompanied by Major Floyd and Major Warren of the state militia and was likely in search of saltpeter, which could be used in the manufacturing of gunpowder.

In 1810, the cave was purchased by Lev Brashear of Nelson County, Kentucky with plans to mine the cave for the saltpeter that had been discovered here, as well as for the Epsom salts and the gypsum. Brashear was related to not only Charles Wilkins, one of the owners of famous Mammoth Cave, but William Henry Harrison as well. Brashear was one of the leading salt producers in Kentucky and despite the fact that operations were hampered at the cave by the lack of available water, which was needed to remove minerals from the soil; he managed to remove salt from the cave and also to produce saltpeter. There has been speculation that slave labor was used in the cave, but this remains unknown. It is also thought that production here ceased for about six months following the great earthquake along the New Madrid Fault in 1811. When operating, saltpeter from this cave was taken to Dupont, Kentucky and used to make gunpowder for American guns during the War of 1812. When demand for gunpowder dropped off, the land reverted back to the federal government when Brashear ceased making payments on it.

After the war ended, the cave and surrounding property was purchased by Dr. Benjamin Adams from Louisville, Kentucky. In 1814, a hunter who had visited the cave gave Dr. Adams some samples of Epsom salts that he had removed from the location. Adams wanted the salts for his apothecary and so he offered $600 for two cartloads of them. Soon after, he contacted the land office in Jeffersonville, Indiana and found that no one owned the property. He and a partner, Dr. William Burrell, purchased the site and made plans to mine it for the salts and for the saltpeter. However, the market never really rallied and the operation proved to be unprofitable. His partnership with Dr. Burrell dissolved and Adams gave up his rights to the cave in 1818.

Around 1819, a man named Henry Rothrock acquired the land around the cave and set up a cabin and sawmill on the Blue River, about a half mile from the cave entrance. He cut the timber here, mostly cedar and chestnut, and built rafts that traveled as far as New Orleans during periods of high water. Rothrock made no mention of the cave in his record though until 1847.

In spite of this, Dr. Henty McMurtrie from Louisville published one of the first real accounts of the cave, about ten years after Rothrock bought the property. In his book *Environs of Louisville*, he called it the "Mammoth Cave of Indiana". In June 1832, William B. Oaks toured the cave in the company of Henry Rothrock and wrote a popular description that called it "The Great Cave".

No efforts were made to develop the cave until 1847 though, shortly after Rothrock purchased more of the surrounding land to continue his lumber operations. The cave was starting to attract a few local visitors by this time but it likely would have remained nothing more than a local curiosity if not for the explorations of two renowned spelunkers, Norman Colman and Harvey Link.

They heard about the cave in 1850 and obtained permission from Rothrock to explore it. In November, they descended into the cave with the assistance of Andrew Rothrock, Henry's 11 year-old son, who was already adept at cave exploration, having roamed the passages for some time already. "The Great Indiana Cave", as they called it, kept them busy for several months and they discovered and named several of what have become the most famous chambers and formations in the cave, including Odd Fellows Hall, Wallace's Dome, Pluto's Chasm, the Pillar of Constitution and many others.

A slight movement of air, which was detected by a candle flame, led an exploration party into another section of the cave and here they found even more wonders, like Monument Mountain, a vast chamber that was filled at one end with a massive rock fall that rose to heights of over 120 feet. The cave was filled with formations, which they noted in their journals, as well as streams and pools that contained colorless fish.

The men wrote several accounts of the cave and it was mapped for the first time in 1851. Not long after, an article that appeared in the *New York Weekly Tribune* and the *Cincinnati Commercial* newspapers quoted former Indiana Governor David Wallace in which he refers to the cave for the first time as "Wyandotte Cave". Many of the names of the cave's formations and attractions appeared in this print here for the first time as well.

The public soon took notice of the cave and tourists began traveling to this remote area. The cave was opened for a fee and became the fourth commercial cave to operate in the United States. In the years that followed, guides and explorers employed by Rothrock continued to discover new sections of the cave, as well as new passages and formations. A third level that was discovered in 1858 served to double the number of tourists who were already flocking to the region.

In 1860, Rothrock constructed a new house on his property, a two-story building that served as a cave hotel and a residence for his family. Wyandotte Cave had become big business and with this came the hiring of additional cave guides and regularly scheduled tours. Even during the Civil War, the cave continued to be a popular attraction and the first guidebook was written about the caverns by James Parish Steele in 1864.

Seven years later, in 1871, Henry Rothrock died and the cave passed into the hands of his family. They continued to operate it, just as Rothrock had, and also continued the extensive explorations. They also rented out portions of the cave for various enterprises. For instance, in 1883, men from the G.H.S. & Company in Evansville hauled onion sets to the cave for storage in an attempt to corner the market. The cave was particularly wet that season and the plan failed miserably.

The Rothrock family continued to own and operate the cave until 1966, when the state of Indiana purchased it, along with 1,100 acres of the surrounding property. The state made a number of further improvements to the caverns, adding electric lights, concrete stairways, and a walled gate and enlarged the passageways to make them more accessible. In the 1980's, more renovations were completed as a nature center and a campground were added to the property. Today, Wyandotte Cave is operated by Cave Country Adventures, a company that also operates nearby Marengo Cave, and visitors who come here can take a comfortable journey beneath the rocks, forests and hills of southern Indiana.

As modern and safe as explorations in the commercial portions of the cave are these days, most visitors become acutely aware of the utter blackness that exists just beyond their reach -- and just beyond the illumination of the fallible electrical lights -- in the darkest passages of the cave. Even seasoned cave visitors become unnerved on occasion when they gaze into the shadows and down the passageways where the tours never go. It is human nature to wonder what might be down there -- lingering in the dark.

GHOSTS OF THE WYANDOTTE CAVERNS

There are at least two ghosts that are said to haunt the cave passages here and both of them date back to the middle 1800's. Their history is firmly entrenched in the period when Henry Rothrock was the owner and operator of the cave.

The first story has been called the "Counterfeiter's Ghost" by some of the tour guides and folklorists of the region. For those who question the authenticity of the story, it does have it roots in a real event that occurred at the cave around 1829 when a visitor actually discovered a wooden crate just like the one described in the legend. This find was mentioned in Dr. Henry McMurtrie's book *Environs of Louisville*, then further embellished in 1853 and 1864 and soon was used to explain the haunting that occurs here as well. The story of this ghost was started many years ago and is kept alive today by tour guides and staff members.

The legend has it that soon after the cave started to attract the attention of cave explorers and the public, Henry Rothrock began hiring men to excavate the openings of the cave and some of the nearby passages to make it more accessible for future visitors. A few of the men that he hired worked the diggings at night, long after the other men had gone home of the day. Since the excavation progressed according to schedule, Rothrock didn't make a fuss about it and allowed them to continue working on their own time.

One afternoon though, one of the dayshift workers came to Rothrock and told him about a wooden crate that he had found in one of the small passages in the lower section of the cave. Usually, no one had any reason to be down there but the worker had been exploring on his own and stumbled across the box. Rothrock decided to go down to the cave and take a look at the crate for himself. After looking it over, he opened the lid and was surprised to find a small printing press, engraved plates and stacks and stacks of what was apparently counterfeit money. He soon realized why some of the workers insisted on digging after dark.

Rothrock left the crate where he had found it and after saddling his horse, rode to nearby Leavenworth, where he shared the news of the discovery with the local sheriff. During that time period, counterfeiting was a frequent, but serious, offense by criminals. The United States faced a real crisis at this time as counterfeiting bedeviled the government and posed a serious threat to the nation's banking system. In the 1860's, it was estimated that as much as one-third to one-half of all U.S. currency was counterfeit. Some 1,600 state banks designed and printed their own money and with all of these varieties of genuine notes flooding the nation, counterfeiters had a field day. The sheriff realized the seriousness of the situation as Indiana, like so many other states, was infested with counterfeiters and he devised a plan to capture the culprits. As Rothrock only usually saw the night shift workers on Friday mornings, when they came to collect their pay, the sheriff planned to apprehend them at that time. He and some of his deputies hastily worked out the plan and then rode out to Rothrock's property just before dawn the following day.

As the sun began to come up over the horizon, Rothrock waited at the entrance to the cave while the sheriff and his men crouched nearby, waiting for the workers to emerge. At the usual time, the three men walked out of the cave, unaware that anyone but their employer was waiting for them. Suddenly, the lawmen appeared from hiding and the counterfeiters bolted in surprise. Two of the men were immediately captured but the third managed to slip away from his captors and he ran back into the darkness of the cave. With torches lit, several deputies pursued him but he quickly vanished into the maze of passageways and chambers. They heard his footsteps echoing ahead of them and they pushed ahead to the Mountain Room. The vast chamber was utterly silent and no trace of the counterfeiter could be seen or heard. He had simply disappeared.

The deputies searched for a time but finding nothing, they returned to the mouth of the cave. They thought that perhaps he had doubled back on them and had emerged from the cave where the sheriff was waiting. When they went back outside though, they learned that the counterfeiter had not come back out. He was still in the cave and the decision was made to simply wait him out. The cave was almost completely uncharted, which ruled out a thorough search of the place, but without food or water, the man would have to come out at some point. The sheriff decided to post guards outside and wait until the man emerged again.

Days passed and the lawmen kept a constant vigil but the counterfeiter did not appear. After three weeks, some surmised that the man had escaped through some other unknown entrance, that he had an accident in the cave and had died or that he had simply starved to death. In any case, he was not coming back out and so the sheriff removed the guard and closed the case. To this day, no physical trace of the counterfeiter has ever been found.

However, many feel that some trace of him does remain.

After the cave opened officially to tourists, and visitors began to arrive in great numbers, many spoke of seeing a shadowy figure walking among the rocks in the Mountain Room. In recent times, guides use this section of the cave to demonstrate what the cave was like without electric lights and to show the tourists how early cave exploration was accomplished. They usually turn off the electric bulbs and then light lanterns for a historic effect. There have been many times, in the eerie, flickering light, when tourists and guides alike have reported seeing the figure of a man wandering about the edges of the room. He always vanishes when the lights are turned back on.

Others claim to have heard strange voices in the cave and one afternoon, a guide reported that he heard someone calling for help in the darkness. As he moved through the cave in his search, the voice seemed to change directions and to come from different areas, moving ever deeper into the lowest portions of the cave. Finally, when no one was found, and he had not heard the voice in some time, he returned to the office to report a lost tourist -- only to be told that no one had been in the cave all afternoon. Some believe this unexplained voice may have been the sound of the trapped counterfeiter, calling out for assistance from the other side.

But if this lost criminal still lingers here, he likely does not walk these dim passageways alone. There is another legend that persists here as well and while this ghost has only manifested in the cave on one occasion, if a similar situation would arise again -- who can say that he would not put in another appearance?

During the early days of exploration at Wyandotte Cave, Henry Rothrock remained actively involved in the discovery of the new passages, levels and chambers. And while his thriving lumber business often kept him away, nothing deterred his young son Andrew from exploring in his place and on most occasions, by his side. Andrew was only 11 years-old when the exploration began but he was both a courageous and skilled spelunker. He knew the cave better than any adult who lived in the area and many of the explorers, if not carefully guided into the lower depths, could have been lost or even killed in the treacherous passageways. Andrew was always available to guide these men into the depths and seemed to thrive on the excitement of the descents into the cavern.

Unfortunately though, when Andrew was in his teens, he began to develop a strange, hacking cough. Thinking that perhaps he had developed a cold from all of the time that he spent in the cave, his parents forbid him to go back until he was well but Andrew would sneak away and go exploring anyway. When Andrew's illness refused to get better, the Rothrock's took him to all of the local doctors and then finally to the hospital in Indianapolis. The doctors here were finally able to diagnose his illness as an affliction of the lungs that is spread through exposure to bat guano in caves. There was no cure but the progress of the disease could be slowed by staying quiet and by staying out of the cave. By this time though, it was too late -- Andrew took to his bed and was unable to gather the strength to leave it. His cough grew worse and worse but even as he lay dying, he constantly pleaded with his father to go to the cave one last time.

Andrew turned pale and his eyes sunk deep in their sockets. His choking cough caused his whole body to shake. Henry Rothrock knew that his boy had little time left and so he wrapped Andrew up in blankets and carried him down into the cave one last time. They went down to the Mountain Room and Henry propped him up against the wall so that he could see into the cavern. It was such a beautiful place, Andrew told his father, and wished that he would never have to leave it. Then, with one last shuddering breath, the young man died.

Andrew was sorely missed and fondly remembered by the explorers who came to the cave and most of them had learned so well from him that they could now guide themselves through the more dangerous sections of the cave. In this way, the boy's legacy lived on and as a little more time passed, Andrew was largely forgotten by everyone except for his family. This is what made what happened on the anniversary of his death a few years later even stranger.

One day, two amateur spelunkers came to Wyandotte Cave and decided to do some exploring on their own. They entered the cave and began traveling through the passageways, descending deeper and deeper below the earth. They wandered without a map or guide and at one point, one of the men stumbled and the lantern he carried was shattered on the floor. Undaunted though, they continued on with just one light and as ill luck would have it, their other lantern was soaked by falling water and they suddenly found themselves without any light at all. The two men found themselves immersed in total and complete darkness.

The gravity of their situation was now realized. Without a light, there was no way that they would be able to find their way back to the entrance. To make matters worse, no one even knew they were in the cave, making a rescue party impossible. The men knew that they could hold out for a little while, as water was readily available in the cave, but they had only a little food with them. They were left with nothing but hope --- hope that a miracle might somehow occur.

For three days, the men waited in absolute darkness. They had no idea of the time of day or how much time had passed. One of the men was sleeping but his companion remained awake, praying for deliverance. He was sure that he was hallucinating when in the distance, a faint light appeared. Scarcely able to believe what he was seeing, he shook his friend awake to ask him if he saw the light too. His befuddled companion also saw the flickering in the darkness and the two men realized that someone had entered the cave. They called out hoarsely and the light abruptly brightened and began moving in their direction.

The light came around a corner in the passage and suddenly, the figure of a young man appeared. Later, the men would realize that they had never seen the lantern the boy carried -- all that they would recall is that he seemed to be bathed in light. He walked toward them and stopped, asking if he could help them. The explorers gratefully embraced him and explained that they had become lost in the cave and after losing their lights, had been trapped there for several days. The boy told them that if they followed him, he would be happy to lead them out.

Thrilled, the men grabbed their packs and followed as the young man led them through the twisting passages of the cave. He always stayed a little ahead of them, but close enough so that they could follow his light. When they finally saw daylight coming from the entrance of the cave, the two men ran past the boy and out into the bright sun. Blinking and laughing, they turned to the young man to thank him but he had already turned and disappeared back into the cave. Thinking that they would simply return to the cave and thank the boy properly, the pair went home for a reunion with their families, who had no idea where the explorers had been for the past several days.

True to their promise though, the men returned to the cave the following day with presents for the young man as a way to express their thanks. They went to the home of the Rothrock family and knocked on the door. Henry Rothrock answered and led the two men inside. They asked after the boy they assumed lived there and quickly told Rothrock of their perilous experience in the cave and how the young man had rescued them. Rothrock shook his head though -- no young man lived in the house and the incident they described could not have happened. The two men insisted though and even described what the boy had looked like to the older man.

Suddenly, Henry Rothrock turned pale and excused himself from the room for a moment. When he came back, he brought with him a small tintype photograph. He held it out to the two spelunkers and asked if they recognized him. Both men immediately identified the boy in the photograph as the boy who had rescued him from the cave. They asked once again to see the boy so that they could thank him in person.

Sadly though, Henry Rothrock shook his head and explained to them that they would be unable to thank the boy in person. In a quavering voice, he told the two young men that the boy had been his son, Andrew -- but that he had died several years before.

He had loved the cave, Rothrock said, and apparently he had never left it after all.

Wyandotte Cave is located in southeastern Indiana, just a few miles south of Interstate 64 and near the small town of Leavenworth. The cave is open to the public between March 1 and October 31.

MARENGO CAVE
Near Marengo, Indiana

Located just a few miles away from Wyandotte Cave is another commercial cavern that is known as Marengo Cave. As a traveler, amateur spelunker and cave enthusiast, I can say that I have found very few caves during my excursions that can compare to the beauty of Marengo Cave. The formations and passageways here are not only amazing, but breath-taking as well.

I discovered this cave for myself in 2002 while I was traveling to Louisville, Kentucky. I happened to see a roadside sign for it and made it a point to stop. Not only did this side trip turn out to be one of the best cave trips that I have ever taken but I also discovered a ghost story in the process!

Marengo Cave is located within the limestone hills and forests of southern Indiana and aside from being designated as a U.S. National Landmark; it is also one of the most stunning show caves in the eastern United States. The cave is also extremely rich in history and the events of the past, and at least one of the characters involved with it, have left a lingering legacy as a haunting.

Marengo Cave was discovered on September 6, 1883 and unlike Wyandotte Cave, there is no evidence to suggest that anyone ever entered this cavern before its discovery. The cavern was located near a small community that had sprung up on land that was originally deeded to Henry Hollowell in 1814. The area remained largely undeveloped until 1817, when the land was sold to David Stewart. Marengo Cave would later be discovered on Stewart property and the family would retain control of the land and the cave (which had not yet been discovered at the time) until 1955.

In 1839, David Stewart plotted out a town site around where the small settlement stood and after discarding several names like Proctorville, Springtown and Big Springs, he settled on Marengo as a permanent name in 1852. Marengo had been the name of the famous battle fought by Napoleon at Marengo, Italy in June 1800.

Until about 1881, Marengo was little more than a cluster of log cabins, a couple of stores, a saloon, a church or two and a graveyard. The completion of the Louisville & St. Louis Airline Railroad changed all of that though and the business district and main part of town shifted about a half mile south to the site of the new railroad depot. After the railroad crossed Crawford County, commerce began to move away from the Ohio River towns of Leavenworth and Alton and to the growing railroad towns like English and Marengo.

The only notable addition to the Marengo community prior to the coming of the railroads was the construction of a boarding school in town in 1869. This essentially made Marengo the education center of south central Indiana. The Marengo Academy was founded by Professor J.M. Johnson and was a well known school for more than 40 years. Thanks to the rough roads in the region, which were nearly impassable in the winter, students who lived outside of the immediate region had to board during the school term. Its excellent reputation attracted students from all over the surrounding area.

A young woman who was employed at the academy would play an vital role in the discovery of Marengo Cave. Blanche Hiestand was a 15 year-old girl who was employed as a cook at the school in September 1883. She overheard some of the students discussing a hole that they had found in a deep depression, about a half mile from the academy building. There were rumors that there might be a cave, which had Blanche very intrigued. After school ended that day, she went home and fetched some candles and then tracked down her brother, Orris, who was four years younger.

The two of them crossed Whiskey Run Creek and then hiked up the hill to where the local church and cemetery was located. Just beyond the graveyard was a stand of trees and it was here that Blanche had overheard that a cave might be located. She and Orris peered into the sinkhole and as they climbed down to the bottom of it, they saw a small opening in the rocks that was partially hidden by dangling tree roots. Blanche slid down closer to the opening and she could feel cool air streaming out against her face. She leaned inside but could see little in the hole but some loose rock that descended into utter darkness. She was unable to see what awaited them but she lit a candle anyway and climbed into the hole. Orris followed closely behind.

Together, the two of them slid down the loose rock into what turned out to be a cave. As they continued downward, they could feel the wet rock underneath them and could hear the dripping of water in the blackness beyond the light from their candles. The floor soon leveled out and they found themselves in a massive chamber that was more than 100 feet below the surface of the earth. The candles only created a dim circle of light but even from what little the children could see, they sharply drew in their breath. The chamber was filled with brilliantly colored formations, shimmering pools of crystal clear water, glistening mounds of stone, dangling pendants and sights so overwhelming that the Hiestand's lost their courage and decided to turn back without going any further into the cavern. They hurried back up the slope to the sinkhole and covered with mud, ran all of the way home.

Blanche and Orris told no one of their discovery until they went to church on the following Sunday. When Samuel Stewart, who now owned the land, heard about the cave, he gathered a small group of men and boys and led them on an expedition of his own. They soon found long and twisting passageways and chambers with such splendor that few caves could compare with the number, and beauty, of the cavern's magnificent formations.

The news of the discovery spread quickly and soon hundreds of citizens from Marengo and the surrounding communities arrived to tour the cave. Samuel Stewart soon recognized the commercial possibilities of the location and almost immediately opened the cave for public exhibition. The Stewart's initially charged a 25 cent admission to view the cave and they also began making improvements to facilitate the larger crowds that were beginning to come. The entrance was enlarged and a wooden staircase was constructed down through the steep sinkhole entrance. Since the majority of the cave was level, little had to be done to the interior passages to make them accessible to the tourists and only a handful of now famous spots in the cave were not available during the early months of operation. Incidentally, the improvements were paid for by doubling the admission price soon after the wooden staircase was completed.

Stewart and his son, Mitch, soon began working to improve the access to the cave itself, constructing wooden stairs and a walkway that climbed the hill, surrounded and then covered the sinkhole. A trap door was put into place that would open to allow entrance to the cave itself. This entrance was used until about 1910, when the present entrance was completed. The entrance at the sinkhole was always damp and often dangerous and most visitors didn't care to climb the 156 steps required to take them in and out of the cavern. To make matters worse, during wet seasons, a small stream of water would flow into the sinkhole and turn the staircase into a slippery waterfall.

In 1908, the cave company decided to employ some surveyors to try and fine a new entrance. The ceiling of the cave in one area was found to be only 11 feet from the surface and so the current Crystal Palace entrance was blasted into the cave.

Samuel Stewart owned the cave from the time of its discovery until his death in 1895. Apparently, soon after the development of the cave began, a dispute erupted between Samuel and his brother, Lewis, over the cave. The natural entrance was located close to the property line between their separate lands and Lewis claimed that since part of the cave ran beneath his property, he had as much right to it as his brother did. He sank his own entrance into the cave, which entered what is now dubbed the Pillared Palace. For a brief period after this, the cave was divided up. Lewis ran tours of the portions of the cave under his property and Samuel was only allowed to show the part of the cavern that was under his land. A wire fence ran through the cave, separating the two sections. Eventually, the two men realized that their behavior was ridiculous and so they reached the agreement and the entire cave was opened again. Lewis sheepishly sealed off the entrance on his property.

After Samuel died in 1895, his wife, Mary, inherited the cave and it was managed for her by James M. Weathers, Jr. She attempted to sell it off for several years but still owned the cave at the time of her death in 1899. After Mary passed away, the control of the cave was divided among ten heirs and in order to manage it, the Marengo Cave Co. was incorporated in 1900. The ten family members owned various amounts of stock in the company and each year, the individuals would bid a percentage of the gross income for the right to operate the cave.

Mitch Stewart was chosen as the first manager of the cave and he operated it until 1911, when J.M. Weathers, Jr. was hired back to run it. A year later, the cave was put up for sale and while Weathers was interested in buying it, something occurred (that remains unknown) that kept him from doing so. He was still the manager though when Charles Fitzgerald, a lawyer from Louisville who had married Minnie Weathers, began buying up stock in the cave company. He eventually gained a controlling interest in the cave.

Weathers remained the manager of the cave, hiring new guides and exploring new parts of the cave, until his death in 1918. Mitch Stewart, or "Uncle Mitch" as he was fondly called, once again took over as manager. He remained in this position until the middle 1920's, when Charles Fitzgerald moved to Marengo and took over the running of the cave.

Around this same period, a number of changes and additional improvements were made to the cave. Trails were dug out to raise the ceiling height, concrete steps were added in several locations and handrails were put in to ease visitors through the most treacherous spots. Cinders and boards were also placed in damp areas to improve footing and after the new entrance was completed, a stone wall was installed to seal off the natural entrance at the sinkhole. A new cave house was erected near the new entrance and the old building near the sinkhole was torn down. Later, a large shelter was built northwest of the cave entrance, along with a fish pond, a dance pavilion and a landscaped flower garden.

More changes came in 1923. At this time, a cistern with an elaborate pipe system was built to bring water from a small spring uphill to the cave house. Prior to this, the only water source at the cave was an old crock that had been placed under a small waterfall in the cave. Visitors could drink from the crock using a metal cup. In the past, when there were periods of heavy rainfall in the area and the creeks turned too muddy, the owners of the cave would allow the locals to take drinking and cooking water from the crock as well. The crock and cup, now covered with mineral deposits, can still be seen in the cave today.

The first electric lights were also installed in the cave in 1923, although only in the section known as the Crystal Palace. Lanterns were used throughout the rest of the cave but this major improvement again doubled the admission price, raising it to $1.

Business began to increase at the cave in the early 1900's. Since travel to the cave was still difficult by road, most visitors came by railroad. The Louisville, Evansville & St. Louis Airline Railroad ran frequent excursion trains from all three cities (although less often from St. Louis) for the express purpose of visiting Marengo Cave. Local farmers and town residents would bring their wagons to the train depot and would transport visitors the mile or so to the cave. These same visitors often stayed at the Murphy House Hotel, or simply dined there on their famous chicken dinners, and then caught the train back home in the evening or the following morning. Railroad excursions began to decline in the later 1920's, thanks to the popularity of automobiles, but excursions continued to Marengo until the time of World War II.

In 1929, another property dispute developed over the cave. This time it was between the cave company and John E. Ross, a nearby landowner to whom Mitch Stewart had once mentioned that several rooms in the cave were under his land. Charles Fitzgerald, who was managing the cave, wanted to buy the rights to the portions of the cave under Ross' land and Ross agreed to sell, but wanted a survey completed. Fitzgerald then decided not to allow the survey and Ross filed suit in court. In 1932, a court-ordered survey was completed and showed that about 700 feet of cave passages were under Ross' property. The case made its way through appeals processes and eventually ended up in the Indiana Supreme Court in 1937. It was decided in the favor of John Ross.

The Marengo Cave Co. claimed the right to use the cave through what is called "Adverse Possession", since they had controlled it for 46 years. The courts ruled otherwise and it has since become known as a leading, historical "Adverse Possession" case and it still studied in law schools today. Modern property scholars believed the court ruled in error in this case though. Regardless, Ross remained stubborn and a fence was built between the two sections of the cavern underground. No deal was ever made with the cave company and the section remained closed until Ross' death in 1972.

Charles Fitzgerald continued to operate the cave through the Great Depression and through World War II. Business declined sharply during this time but word of mouth advertising and the beauty of the cave brought in enough customers to keep things running, even during the worst times.

Shortly after the war, Fitzgerald's health began to decline and his son-in-law, Wilbur Lindley, took over management of the cave until June 1955, when Floyd Denton, a well-known local businessman purchased the cave. He had recently sold his drug and appliance store in Marengo and had used the proceeds to buy up stock in the cave company from various heirs. He had big plans for the cave and immediately set to work on them. He built a new ticket office and gift shop to replace the old clapboard cave house, which had fallen into disrepair. He hired a local electrician to finally install electric lights in the cave for the first time and began to actively promote the cave, which had not been done to any extent in years. He also hoped to install overnight cabins and a restaurant on the property. Sadly, Denton did not live to see his dreams for the cave fulfilled. He died in June 1960, soon after suffering a heart attack while working on the lighting system in the cave.

After Floyd died, his wife, Lucille, managed he cave for a time but since she was never in favor of her husband buying it in the first place, she never actively continued his plans. However, she did repair the original electrical lighting system, which had never worked correctly. In 1965, she washed her hands of the place though and turned over the management to her son-in-law, Jack Hollis.

Hollis wanted to expand the cave and considered making another offer for the Ross section of the cave. Eventually though, thanks to the damp and muddy conditions of this area, along with the expenses that would be incurred by installing more electric lighting, he opted to fund a swimming pool for the cave park instead. The pool was constructed in 1966 and a new entrance to the park was opened along the hillside above Whiskey Run Creek. This new entrance provided direct access to the newly completed State Highway 64 and the owners thought that people driving into the park by way of the new road would be so impressed by the new swimming pool that they would visit the cave also. As it turned out, the pool was never profitable and after a season, it was leased to tenants and was never a part of the cave again.

After Floyd's death, the cave operated mostly by word of mouth but attendance remained fairly strong. It was open daily in warm weather months and closed when it was cold. Jack Hollis continued to run the cave but Lucille, who had remarried by this time, periodically put the place up for sale.

In 1973, Gordon Smith, a spelunker from Louisville, was visiting the cave and mentioned that he heard that it was for sale. Lucille told him that if he bought it quickly, she would sell it to him for half what they were asking for it. Smith jumped at the opportunity and began calling friends and other cave explorers to try and raise money. In a couple of weeks, Smith formed a corporation with three other enthusiasts to buy the cave. The other three men included Terry Crayden, the manager of Squire Boone Caverns; Gary Roberson, who had helped Crayden develop the caverns; and Pat Stephens, a well-known Louisville spelunker. Terry Crayden soon left Squire Boone Caverns and moved to Marengo to take over the management of the cave.

Faced with a large loan payment and little personal equity, the cavers soon began an aggressive promotional campaign. They decided to keep the cave open all year around, even though the only heat in the gift shop and ticket office came from a drafty fireplace. Whenever they wanted to have a meeting that first winter, the four men had to huddle in the bathroom of the ticket office, where a small electric heater had been placed to keep the pipes from freezing. They knew that they needed customers to keep the cave open all the time, so they began erecting highway signs throughout southern Indiana and began cranking out brochures that could be handed out all over the place. They sank what money they had into producing splashy color brochures but it paid off, increasing their attendance from 7,500 people to over 13,000 after their first year.

In spite of this, the other stockholders were not happy with Crayden's management of the cave and he was replaced by Gary Roberson. One of the first guides that Roberson hired was Bob Wyman, a high school student with an interest in archaeology. Wyman was incredibly shy at first but his hard work and dedication to the cave would later elevate him to the positions of the cave's Operations Manager and later as the Vice-President of the corporation.

In 1974, Roberson began developing a campground along the Whiskey Run Creek bottom and also started a program for Scouts and youth groups that would allow them to spend the night in the cave. After touring and exploring portions of the cave, the groups would learn about cave safety and then bed down for the night after being chilled by a ghost story. The program was an immediate success and continued for five winter seasons. The income from this kept the cave running during the slow months and is fondly remembered by many who still live in the area today.

Other programs were implemented in the cave as well, including some that were a bit odd. Throughout the history of the cave, it had been used for a variety of purposes, including church services, weddings and even square dances. In 1971, Arthur Eve, the music director at the Marengo School, decided to produce the musical "Oliver!" in the cave, complete with pit band, a stage and seating for about 300 people. This production led to the formation of the Crawford County Cavern Coral Theater group, which produced two seasons of plays in the cave. The cool temperatures and dampness of the cave doomed it to failure though and the novelty eventually wore off.

In 1974, the low budget company, American International Pictures, filmed a segment of their film *Abby* in Marengo Cave. The segment filmed here involved an evil spirit that was accidentally released from a cave by archaeologists and in the resulting chaos, one of the archaeologists was impaled on a stalagmite. After taking up residence in the body of a woman, the movie then continued outside of the cave. Since that time, other films have also been filmed in the cave.

Also in 1974, the owners were approached by Boyd Campbell, a local lumber man, who wanted to sell them the Ross section of the cave. He had purchased the land from Ross' heirs and after logging the useful timber from it, he wanted to sell it off. A deal was worked out and after 44 years, the entire cave was again under one ownership. Unfortunately though, because of the amount of money needed to develop this area, it was only used for exploration programs during the overnight stays and for occasional lantern tours in the summer.

By the later 1970's, business had improved to the point that modern indirect lighting was installed in the cave and a decision was made to finally open the Ross section of the cavern. A new entrance point was chosen, which would make Marengo Cave one of the few multi-tour caves in the United States. The new tour would enter the new entrance, would go through the Ross section, down the to end of the cavern and out through the existing entrance. The owners dubbed it the "The Dripstone Trail" tour. The other tour would use the present entrance, go to the left at a crossroads in the Crystal Palace section and then return to the exit at the same entrance. It was called the "Crystal Palace" tour and both excursions retain these same names today, visiting some very different portions of the cave over a several hour period.

As it turned out though, the development of the Dripstone Trail was plagued with problem after problem. The tunnel was supposed to be completed by Christmas 1978 but was not finished until the following March, thanks to mud, freezing water, ice deposits and extremely cold temperatures that made progress impossible at times. Gary Roberson became so disgusted with the whole thing that he eventually gave up. If not for the determination of Bob Wyman (now the assistant manager) and Roberson's brother-in-law, Darwin

Groves, the project would have never been completed. These two forged ahead, assisted by other dedicated staff members and guides.

In the midst of all of these problems, Pat Stephens decided to get out of the cave business and wanted to sell of his stock. After putting so much blood, sweat and tears into the business, Smith and Roberson decided to go deeper into debt and purchase his stock. They were teetering on bankruptcy at this point and the problems with the Dripstone Trail were still not over.

After the tunnel was finally completed, only nine weeks were left to install the walkways and the electric lighting. If the trail was not completed on time, due to the large cost overruns and the numerous problems, the business would likely be finished. The staff members began working almost around the clock and while not completely finished, the trail was ready in time for the Memorial Day weekend. The owners breathed a sigh of relief -- not realizing that more problems were coming just a few weeks later.

The area surrounding the cave was hit with two major floods that summer, one in June and then a massive one in July. Nearly 11 inches of rain fell in less than 24 hours and flooded highway bridges leading into Marengo. At the cave, the water crested nearly 16 feet deep in the campground. The water pouring into the cave became huge ponds in the main levels and it was possible at one point to actually canoe through the cavern to the Dripstone Trail section of the cave. Even though the water soon receded and the cave opened for tours the next day, the summer was ruined thanks to the media. Not long after the flood, President Jimmy Carter landed at the nearby town of English to inspect the damage. The media coverage destroyed business for the cave and six weeks after the flood had been forgotten, people were still calling to see if the cave was closed. There was no way to track how many did not call and assumed that it was not open. Only government assistance through the Small Business Administration helped the cave and other local businesses to survive.

Attendance rebounded through the 1980's but the early years of the decade marked one of the strangest events to ever occur at the site -- a cave robbery! On July 28, 1982, a tour group of 27 people was passing under the famed Penny Ceiling area on the Dripstone Trail Tour when a masked gunman with a sawed-off shotgun appeared on a ledge and announced "this is a hold-up!" The visitors, thinking this was a joke and somehow part of the tour, started to laugh. This angered the would-be robber and he fired off the shotgun into the ceiling. The crowd quickly sobered, realizing that the man was not kidding. The gunman took the flashlight from tour guide Pete Crecelius and had Pete put all of the visitor's wallets and valuables into a plastic bag. He turned off the lights and ran away, leaving the group standing there in complete darkness. Pete managed to find his way to a light switch using a guest's lighter and then took his group out of the cave, shaken but unharmed.

As it turned out, the robber wasn't nearly as clever as he thought he was. He was obviously someone who was familiar with the cave and Pete was sure that he recognized the voice of the masked thief as belonging to a former employee. He was right and the man was arrested two weeks later and served a 10-year prison sentence for the robbery.

The following year, the cave celebrated its centennial and then in 1984, one of the most important events in the site's history occurred when Marengo Cave was designated as a National Natural Landmark. The cave was awarded this status mainly on the basis of it being a textbook example of a cave in the middle, or mature, stage of development. It is also the most decorated cave located in the Interior Lowlands Province of the United States, with high quality formations. From this point on, the cave was monitored and protected by the National Park Service, although it remained privately owned.

This new designation greatly enhanced the public image of the cave and attendance soared, soon setting and breaking new records. Today, the cave is owned and operated by Cave Country Adventures, which also operates Wyandotte Cave and Cave Country Canoes in the area. The grand tradition of cave entertainment and education continues today and the company offers many activities for groups and individuals, including various tours, group overnights, underground adventure tours, camping and much more.

In all honesty, I never imagined that by following a roadside sign would I discover such a place of history, mystery and natural beauty. If you have never discovered Marengo Cave for yourself, you are missing a rare treat and ghost story or not, it is well worth the trip!

THE GHOST IN MARENGO CAVE

As I may have already mentioned, I learned about a haunting at Marengo Cave by accident. Thanks to a passing comment by one of the excellent tour guides here, I heard about a former guide who may have never left the cave at all. He loved the place so much that he retired under protest and after his death, has allegedly returned to wander the passageways and (oddly) to continue making music on cave formations -- as he first did more than 75 years ago.

Bill (Willie) Clifton often boasted that he had walked more miles underground that any person in history -- and perhaps he did. Willie was a guide (although he preferred the name "caretaker") for over 50 years at Marengo Cave. As a young man, Willie had traveled the country, working at various jobs, until he was hired by J.M. Weathers, Jr. as a guide in 1913. He was 27 when he came to work at the cave and retired under protest at the age of 80 in 1965.

Bill claimed that he had walked as many as 80,000 miles underground during the time he worked at the cave. He was almost always in duty, whether he was being paid or not. Before Floyd Denton bought the cave in 1955, a bell was kept outside of the cave house. When visitors came to the cave during the off season, or often after hours, they would ring this bell for a guide. Bill would walk over from his house, which was a short distance away, and would take them on a tour, no matter what time it was. He loved the cave and took pride in the fact that he knew just about everything about it that there was to know. His wife Mary often stated that "the cave was his life."

He also loved music and would sing for his visitors during the tours. He would stop during the tours and play music on the cave formations using a wooden mallet. In those days, before anyone knew the damage that could be done by handling or touching the various stalactites and formations in the cave, Willie would hammer out all sorts of tunes and melodies on the stone. He would play the pillars of the Pipe Organ formation in the Crystal Palace, would strike the folding draperies near the Elephant's Head and even left a wooden ladder in place to that he could climb up and strike the Chimes on the Palisades. He had found that the stalactites would elicit different notes and once, early in his career, provided the music for a wedding that was held in the cave. Before the blessed event, he spent hours practicing in the cave each night.

Interestingly, Bill never made much more than $10 a week for most of his career. Even after more than 50 years in service, his salary topped out at twenty-some dollars for a week's salary. He never asked for more though and once had the opportunity to go to work for Wyandotte Cave for more money but he wouldn't leave because Marengo Cave needed him.

Bill continued to work until 1965 and he was finally forced to retire just short of his 80th birthday. Everyone thought that he was getting too old to be a guide but he fooled everyone by living another 16 years! This was even in spite of the fact that he fell off his roof while doing some repair work when he was in his 80's and broke his neck.

At the age of 88, Willie made his final trip through the cave, although he lived seven more years and finally passed away in 1980. Since that time, he has become known as a genuine legend of Marengo Cave and some believe that his last walk through the cave in 1973 may not have been his final journey after all. There are those who suspect that he still lingers in the cave today. Bill Clifton may be the cave's greatest legend in more ways than one...

According to tour guides and some local folks, Willie Clifton never left his beloved cave. A number of strange incidents have taken place here in recent years and not surprisingly, Bill's ghost has been blamed as the culprit. One guide that I spoke with was in the cave late one evening, long after the attraction had closed for the night. As he was walking along one of the passageways, he heard the distinctive sound of the metal door that leads in from the main entrance suddenly slam shut. Thinking that someone had come into the cave, he quickly went to see who it was. He searched for some time, but couldn't find anyone. Finally, he went to the office to ask who was in the cave and was informed that no one was in the cavern with him.

Other odd incidents have occurred as well and the accounts that are passed on by the guides are perhaps the most believable of all of the stories that come from caves. These are people who are well aware of the natural happenings of the cavern and events that might seem strange to a tourist can be easily explained by someone who is more intimately aware of the strangeness that normally occurs underground. When the guides, staff members and cave explorers are unnerved or shaken by events that take place -- these oddities cannot be so easily explained away.

Reports say that visitors and guides have often heard the sound of someone singing in the cave and have been unable to track down whoever might be responsible. Needless to say, this has been blamed on Willie, as have the times when the sounds of musical melodies have been heard as well. One guide said that he was in the cave and during a tour, he and several visitors heard what sounded like a hammer tapping on stone. Instead of just a random clanging though, the tapping actually played out a tune. It went on for several minutes and then faded away. The group picked up the pace and when they reached the area where they were sure the sound had been coming from -- they realized that it was deserted. There was simply no one there.

Could it have been Willie Clifton, still wandering about the passageways of the cave that he loved so well? Perhaps it is, or at least I would like think that it is. What better afterlife could we hope for than to spend eternity in a place that was so important to us in life? Keep that in mind if you ever get a chance to see the wonders of Marengo Cave. Watch out for Willie Clifton and if you see him -- be sure to say hello for me!

Marengo Cave is located in South Central Indiana, a short distance from Interstate 64, and just outside of the small town of Marengo. The town and cave can be reached from the Interstate by taking Highway 66 to Marengo and then right to the cave. The cave is open daily, except for major holidays.

MAMMOTH CAVE
The World's Largest Haunted Place!

Hidden among the forests and hills of southwest Kentucky is Mammoth Cave National Park. It is the largest cave in the world and impossible for any casual visitor to see in one day, or probably even in one week. There are many passages, paths and tunnels that are not open to the general public, thus adding to the mystery of this place. But in addition to the secrets of nature, there is much in the way of legend and lore about the cave. The place has a strange and unusual past and there are thousands of secrets in the dark corridors of the cave and according to some --- a myriad of ghosts as well!

THE HAUNTED HISTORY OF THE CAVE
The first people came to Mammoth Cave more than 12,000 years ago, when bison and mastodons still roamed the wilderness of what would someday be called North America. During this period, small groups of nomads wandered the

territory and many of them came to Mammoth Cave seeking shelter. No one knows what these primitive people may have called the cave, but modern researchers are sure that it had great value to them. They traveled deep into the cave, seeking mineral deposits of gypsum, mirabilite and selenite. It remains a mystery as to why these people were willing to risk their lives in the depths of the cave for the minerals, but perhaps they believed them to have medicinal or even magical qualities.

Regardless, they did leave signs of their passage and some modern explorers have navigated narrow and nearly impassable crevices only to find that they were not the first to arrive in the deepest chambers of the cave. The naked footprints of aboriginal man have remained unaltered in some of these chambers for centuries.

These early cave explorers also used Mammoth Cave as a burial place for their dead, perhaps believing that it provided some sort of passage to the next world. There have been a number of "mummies" found in the cave over the years. Some of them have been left behind in former burial postures, while others have been the bodies of early explorers who lost their lives in the cave. All of the remains have been remarkably preserved thanks to the minerals found here.

The first mummy was found here in 1813 and others were found in connecting caves in the years that followed. One of the mummies, which gained the most notoriety, was heard about by a man named Nahum Ward of Shrewsbury, Massachusetts and he journeyed to Mammoth Cave to learn more about it. When he arrived, he convinced one of the owners to allow him to take a tour of the cave and then to take the mummy with him when he left. Ward then wrote a long and descriptive account of the cave and of *his* discovery of the mummy. Readers were curious to see the mummy (for a fee) and Ward traveled widely with it on display. Not only was his display based on a scientific hoax, claiming that had had found the mummy, but the fraud also served to bring scores of visitors to Mammoth Cave. It would be primarily Ward's published description of the cave, which was reprinted dozens of times all over the country, that made Mammoth Cave famous as a household word.

The most famous of Mammoth Cave's mummies was discovered by two guides in 1935 and dubbed "Lost John". The mummy was found more than two miles into the cave and trapped beneath a rock. It was believed that he had been a Native American mineral hunter who had perished in an accident. For many years, the "cave mummies" were a major tourist attraction for the cave but all have since been buried or removed from display.

In the early 1700's, there were few permanent residents of Kentucky (which was then part of Virginia) although the Shawnee and the Cherokee Indians used the region as a hunting ground. During the French and Indian War of the late 1750's, a British soldier became the first reported European to reach the Mammoth Cave region. By that time, many of the colonists along the eastern seaboard were starting to feel the crush of civilization. The more adventurous among them began crossing the Appalachians for the western territories. They recognized the lure of the wilderness and the frontiersmen often heard from their Native American friends of the natural wealth of "Kain-Tockee".

Despite the skills of these men when it came to living off the land for food and shelter though, they were still at the mercy of other suppliers when it came to gunpowder and a method of preserving food. It was in the discovery of the saltpeter deposits that Mammoth Cave's greatest riches were realized. The saltpeter led to the first legal ownership of the cave.

Legend has it that the first white man to venture into the cave was a frontiersman named Houchins, who chased a bear into an entrance to the cave in 1797. Valentine Simmons, however, was the first owner of the cave. He claimed 200 acres of land, which included the cave, in 1798. He then sold the cave to the McLean brothers, who began processing the saltpeter deposits. In 1810, the operation was taken over by Charles Wilkins and Fleming Gatewood, who began mass production in the cave.

Prior to buying the rights to Mammoth Cave, Wilkins had already established himself as a saltpeter merchant, supplying the Dupont gunpowder works in Delaware with product from Kentucky. The men were excited at the promise of the cave, already realizing that a fortune was to be made from the increasingly hostile relations between the United States and Britain. The War of 1812 would drive up the cost of saltpeter and production in Mammoth Cave would follow suit.

The war progressed and Wilkins used more than 70 slaves to work the leaching operation that would remove the saltpeter from the cave. To prepare for the work, square wooden vats were built and wooden pipes were made from long, straight poplar logs. The logs were then bored out with augers and then tapered so that they would fit together end to end. The slaves dug into the soil, placed the dirt into the vats and then saturated it with water that was piped in using the wooden tubes. The water trickled through the soil and the calcium nitrate leached out. The solution was then filtered through ash and boiled to concentrate the saltpeter. It was bagged and transported to mills in Philadelphia, where it was combined with powdered charcoal and sulfur to make gunpowder.

The business proved to be quite profitable, netting the owners about 21 cents per pound. After the war ended though, the price of saltpeter plummeted and the mills were able to get the product more cheaply from other locations. The operations in Mammoth Cave were closed down for good.

Fortunately though, all was not lost. The fame of Mammoth Cave had started to spread. Numerous newspaper articles had been written about the cave's contribution to the war and had also discussed its natural wonders and the strange "mummies" that had been found in the cave. Soon, people began traveling from the east to the Kentucky wilderness and Mammoth Cave began to receive its first tourists.

In 1815, Hyman Gratz became a partner with Charles Wilkins in the ownership of the cave. Gratz was a showman and an entrepreneur and he quickly realized there was money to be made in exhibiting the cave. After Wilkins died in 1828, Gratz continued showing the cave to anyone who was interested and actually stepped up operations to make the place more profitable. He used veterans of the mining operation as guides to accompany curious travelers.

The cave was originally called "Flatt's Cave" but the name had been gradually changed to Mammoth Cave during the War of 1812. The "Rotunda", the first large room that was entered, prompted the name and gave visitors a taste of the massive chambers ahead. At first, the guides rarely ventured any further than the old mining operation and tunnels they were familiar with. As they grew more comfortable with the passages though, they started to venture a little deeper with each excursion. Travelers were then led into what were called the "Haunted Chambers" and they risked the dangerous, wet and rocky canyons known as the "Bottomless Pit" and the "Crevice Pit".

As the century grew older, the fame of Mammoth Cave grew larger and more widespread. Guidebooks began to boast of the cave's hundreds of miles of passages and word of mouth, combined with newspaper and magazine articles, travelogues and first-person accounts, brought people from all over the world. People came from everywhere to see the marvels of the cave and some said that "more visitors had come from England to see Mammoth Cave than those visitors hailing from Kentucky". Some of celebrity guests of Mammoth Cave included historic personages like Jenny Lind, Edwin Booth, Charles Dickens, Ralph Waldo Emerson, Prince Alexis of Russia and many more. People from all walks of life came to the cave however, not just the wealthy and famous. None of them walked away from it unimpressed!

While the list of early visitors is indeed impressive, it is hard for us to appreciate just how dangerous the cave could be at that time. These intrepid visitors were forced to brave slick floors, narrow passages and dangerous pathways. The greatest challenge though was lighting. Throughout the 1800's, a variety of lights were used in the cave. Visitors carried open-flame lanterns, fueled by refined lard oil on occasion, but the most popular method of light was the full flame torch. The guides would wrap wooden poles with oiled rags and set them ablaze. Then, to show off the wonders of the cave and their own skills, they would fling the torches onto ledges and into narrow gaps in a way that few could duplicate today.

The visitors of the 1800's were also fond of smoking their names onto the smooth, white ceilings of the cave. Today, you can still see names and dates, carefully scripted with fire, that were left behind by visitors more than a century and a half ago.

THE EARLY CAVE GUIDES
Mammoth Cave had many early guides, as the first flood of visitors began

arriving here in 1818. The cave was famous by that time, thanks to a number of writers and authors who were already beginning to spread the word about the place, but the lack of decent and accessible roads discouraged many of the tourists. Stagecoaches stopped miles from the entrance, at Bell's Tavern, and the remaining distance had to be covered by way of a narrow, rugged trail. The tavern was located in Three Forks, which is now known as Park City, and the place earned an excellent reputation as a dining and lodging place and the primary stepping off place for the eight-mile trip to Mammoth Cave.

There was an inn of sorts at the cave, but it was as bad as the roads were. It was simply a log building with two rooms on the ground floor and so most overnight visitors preferred to eat and sleep at Bell's Tavern, which was revered for its peach and honey brandy.

In 1838, the cave was purchased by Franklin Gorin, an attorney from Glasgow, Kentucky who envisioned great things for Mammoth Cave. He paid $5,000 to the Gratz family for rights to the cave and immediately began to improve the roads and accommodations and to bring in skilled guides. He became the most important man in the cave's early history. He improved the inn, renaming it the Mammoth Cave Inn and enlarging it to sleep up to 40 people, smoothed the roadways, added fences and stables and introduced a young slave to the cave named Stephen Bishop. This young man, who was just 16 years old at the time, would become a legend in his own lifetime. Bishop would go on to live the rest of his life in and among the passageways of Mammoth Cave, becoming the first man to explore and map the cave system. He was a self-educated man, with a remarkable wit and humor, and he acquired a considerable knowledge of geology.

During that first summer of 1838, Bishop familiarized himself with every room, corridor and passageway known to the previous guides. In addition, he began to explore parts of the cave that had been untouched before. He found confusing mazes, dead ends and hidden wonders. One of the passages led to a deep hole that had always been known as the "Bottomless Pit". On October 20, Bishop placed a rickety wooden ladder over the pit and carefully made his way across, becoming the first man to do so. It was soon spanned with a bridge and Bishop began leading visitors to share in the wonders on the other side. Bishop also became the first to discover the cave's underground water system and the strange, eyeless fish that lived in the caverns.

Reports of these discoveries brought even more visitors to the cave, so in 1839, Gorin hired two slaves from Thomas Branford of Nashville, Tennessee. He paid Branford the annual sum of $100. The new guides were brothers, Mat and Nick, and they have taken on the last names of their master in writings of the cave. They became known as the "Branford's" and along with Stephen Bishop, they became the leading explorers and guides of Mammoth Cave. The three of them would continue leading cave tours until the 1870's and their offspring would continue a tradition here for more than 107 years.

Time marched on and the Civil War brought unrest and trouble to southern Kentucky. However, the manager of the cave, a staunch supporter of the Union, continued to conduct tours throughout the years of the war. Stories that have been passed down tell of encounters within the cave between northern and southern soldiers, each taking a moment from the war to marvel at the natural wonders of the cave.

After the war ended, some of the former slaves in the Mammoth Cave community left the area to find new homes. Others, like the Branford's, chose to stay on. They, like Stephen Bishop, had been offered their freedom years before in return for their services in the cave. They had refused to leave though and they stayed on at Mammoth Cave. Stephen Bishop had died shortly before 1860, but his wife, Charlotte, and son, Thomas, remained at the cave.

Even though the cave had remained open through the war, tourism had been damaged and Reconstruction and continued problems between the north and the south kept things slow for years after. A revival in tourism did not occur until the middle 1880's, with the expansion of steamboat traffic, better connecting stage lines and the completion of the Louisville & Nashville Railroad, a spur of which was built directly to the mouth of the cave.

Another Bishop, Ed, became one of the cave's greatest explorers. Accompanied by a German cartographer named Max Kaemper, Bishop climbed and slid through a collapse of rock and dirt that had previously been thought of as "the end" of Mammoth Cave. The exploration, and the map that came from it in 1908, is still thought of as the most important accomplishment in the cave's history.

Bishop's discovery led to the realization that Mammoth Cave is actually several different caves that all connect in some way underground. No one knew this for many years and different people owned separate caves. It was so confusing that some people owned different parts of the same cave, with different entrances, on different parcels of land. In the early part of the 1900's, as automobile vacations became popular in America, the ownership of the caves would have strong consequences in southern Kentucky. And sometimes this would have dire results!

THE CROGHAN'S OF MAMMOTH CAVE

William Croghan and his wife, Lucy, built their brick home called "Locust Grove" in 1790 in what was then wilderness near Louisville, Kentucky. Their first child, John, was born that same year. He grew up at Locust Grove, spending many hours enthralled with the stories told to him by his famous adventurer uncle, George Rogers Clark.

After graduating from Priestley Seminary in Danville, Kentucky and from the College of William and Mary in Virginia, John studied medicine and received a doctorate from the University of Pennsylvania in 1813. He then returned to Kentucky and opened a medical practice in Louisville, taking an active part in the establishment of the Louisville Marine Hospital.

After the death of his father in 1822, John inherited Locust Grove and a large plantation, which he farmed and used to produce salt. In time though, John gained his own taste for adventure, perhaps remembering the stories told to him by his famous uncle, and he went abroad to tour the world. In 1839, he returned home and visited Mammoth Cave. He walked the passages with his guide and was amazed by the size of the rooms and the chambers they found.

While in London, John had heard much of Mammoth Cave and he agreed with the current owner's plans for publicizing the cave in the east and in Europe. He also understood the difficulties of getting tourists to the cave and then finding them suitable lodging once they arrived. He believed that not only should a grand hotel be built at the entrance to the cave, but underground in the cave as well! He envisioned a carriage road leading into the cave, a dining room, a library and a grand ballroom. Croghan quickly purchased the cave from Franklin Gorin in 1839 (the deal included the cave, the inn, Stephen Bishop and the Branford brothers) and set about turning his dreams into reality.

Mammoth Cave prospered under Croghan's ownership, although the underground hotel was never realized. He did however construct the spacious Mammoth Cave Hotel, a large inn constructed from two log buildings. It was equipped with rooms to sleep several dozen visitors, a dining hall and a ballroom. It would continue to serve travelers until it burned down in 1916. Croghan also spent huge amounts of money on advertising and continued to attract visitors from all over the world. He established a reputation for the cave as an international showplace.

At Croghan's own expense, he began building public roads to the cave. The first road was opened from Cave City to the Mammoth Cave Hotel and then continued on across Green River to connect to a road at Grayson Springs. Another road began at the Louisville and Nashville Turnpike near Rowletts Station and led to the hotel before continuing on to the southwest, where it connected with another turnpike. This was said to be an excellent road in those rugged times and also became the shortest route between Louisville and Nashville. It also just happened to travel right past the Mammoth Cave Hotel and bypassed Bell's Tavern completely.

Croghan not only saw the cave as a tourist attraction, he also saw medical benefits to it. As a doctor, he had read of underground hospitals in Europe in which those suffering from consumption (tuberculosis) had been cured. He believed that Mammoth Cave just might have the same curative powers. He and many other doctors believed that the moist air and the constant temperature of the cave might slow, or even reverse, the ravages of the disease.

In 1842, Croghan directed Bishop and the Branford's to construct wood and stone huts within the cave and then he invited 15 tuberculosis patients to participate in his experiment. Unfortunately, several of the patients died in the cave and the trial was considered a failure. The surviving patients were sent home and the huts were abandoned. They still exist though and can be seen in the cave today. Several of the patients who died were buried in the Old Guide's Cemetery near the cave entrance.

Ironically, Croghan also contracted tuberculosis and he died in 1849. Being a bachelor, he left the cave in trust for his nieces and nephews. In this way, his death began more than 70 years of tenants and resident managers at Mammoth Cave. The years that followed were strange ones for the cave, with no clear-cut route to follow. Mammoth Cave enjoyed success for most of these years, only slowing down after the Civil War.

David Graves of Lebanon, Kentucky leased the cave in the 1870's. His time at Mammoth Cave is best remembered for the fine food that he served and the billiard hall that he operated inside of the cave. He finally left Mammoth Cave after a number of legal disputes with the owners of the cave and with a competitive stage line that was used to ferry passengers to the cave.

At that time, stage lines were the best methods of bringing tourists to Mammoth Cave. But stagecoach travel was not without danger. One evening in 1880, a group of visitors were returning from the cave when they were stopped by bandits at the Little Hope Cemetery. The robbers took more than $1000 and many personal items from the travelers, including a fine gold watch that was engraved with the name of Judge R.H. Rountree of Lebanon. Later, a newspaper article reported that the same watch was found in the possession of Jesse James after his death. Was this famous outlaw responsible for the Mammoth Cave stage robbery?

In 1886, Francis Klett brought a mushroom farm to the cave but more importantly, W.C. Comstock established the Mammoth Cave Railroad and greatly improved travel for cave visitors. The railroad connected to the L & N line at Glasgow Junction. The rail cars were pulled by an engine called "Hercules" and the little train served Mammoth Cave and the surrounding communities until 1929, when automobiles made it obsolete. All that remains of the train today is an overgrown spur line, the engine, a single coach car and mostly forgotten memories of a bygone era.

THE CAVE WARS

The Twentieth Century did not come quietly to the cave country of southern Kentucky. The rivalry that flared up between David Graves and a rival stage line in the 1870's was only the beginning. As it turned out, there would be two realizations that brought about what has been called the "Cave Wars" of the early 1900's.

The first was that cave tourism could actually be profitable and that it was also very popular. The attention given to various caves in the area had been substantial already, but as the new century dawned, it became obvious that it was no passing fad. With this realization in southern Kentucky, it became necessary for the locals to simply get in on the idea.

The second event was the beginning of the automobile vacation era. More and more people in America were buying cars and they were using them to travel to places where they had never been before. To folks in the surrounding states, Mammoth Cave became a natural destination point. Soon, this type of travel would gain the attention of the entire country and historic monuments like "Route 66" would be born. Unfortunately though, the interstates would bypass the small highways and regional attractions in later years and many of them would die and fade away.

The area around Mammoth Cave today is like a time capsule of the past. The "boom years" of the 1920's through the early 1970's had a lasting effect on the region in the attractions and motor hotels, most of which barely eke out an existence in these modern times. There are faded signs here that depict the wonders of caves and petting zoos that have been closed down for years.

But it wasn't always this way.

From the early days, the residents of central and southern Kentucky used the caves for a wide variety of purposes. They provided shelter from storms, preserved their milk, canned food, turnips and potatoes, provided a playground for their children and even served as hiding places for moonshiners and their stills. But as the turn of the last century approached, it was becoming obvious that Mammoth Cave was a huge commercial success and so residents became less interested in the caves for their mundane uses and more interested in using them as a draw for tourists. Many of the local farmers and land owners began to pursue a sideline of cave hunting and developing.

Since the Croghan estate controlled most of the land on the ridge where Mammoth Cave was located, the exploration began to focus on neighboring Flint Ridge, which was separated from the Mammoth Cave ridge by narrow Houchins Valley. The locals desperately wanted to get into the cave business and to start promoting their own caves as competition for well-known Mammoth Cave, or at least to take away a bit of their business.

Flint Ridge became the site of a number of commercial cave operations and the source of a number of lurid and advertising campaigns as well. The owners were promoting and conducting tours of their own caves, located on their own property. As the years passed, and Mammoth Cave became a national park, many of these caves were absorbed into the park system. Most of these smaller caves merely made up portions of the much larger one. At that time however, people either didn't suspect this, or just didn't care. If a person had an entrance to a cave on his property, then he had his own cave. The caves were advertised and marketed wildly and each owner would extol the virtues of his cave above all of the others in the area. Each would post as many signs as possible between major roads and the entrance to Mammoth Cave, hoping to lure travelers away from the most popular attraction.

Prior to the 1890's, major interest in the caves along Flint Ridge had been confined mostly to Salts Cave, thanks to the artifacts that had been found here.

This remote offshoot of Mammoth Cave was the object of freelance exploration and exploitation and open to anyone, it had been plundered of old torches, Indian pottery, decaying moccasins and even a male mummy that had been discovered in 1875 by William Cutliff. Legend has it that he also found three other mummies and hid them away in the cave somewhere. To this day, they have never been found.

The development of the Flint Ridge caves really began in 1895, when Lute and Henry Lee opened up a sinkhole on the south side and dubbed their discovery Colossal Cavern. Officials of the Louisville & Nashville Railroad immediately began trying to purchase it and eventually succeeded. Afterwards, they blasted an opening about a mile and a half from the Mammoth Cave entrance but their intent was not so much to exploit the cave as to find out if it connected to Mammoth. Many had come to suspect that Mammoth Cave, as it had been explored by Stephen Bishop and other guides, was located under land that extended out from property owned by the Croghan estate. This was confirmed by Ed Bishop and Max Kaemper in 1908 but the Croghan heirs were so desperate to keep this a secret that they refused to publish the maps or findings of their expedition.

People suspected it anyway, including a man named Edmund Turner, a young civil engineer with a passion for underground exploration. He came to the Mammoth Cave region in 1912 and when looking for someone to act as a guide, he met another young man named Floyd Collins, a native who had given up farming for caving. With Collins, Turner explored Salts Cave and while finding some new unexplored passages, did not find any connections to Mammoth. Turner traveled all over the area and dug and blasted holes into any spot that he thought looked promising. At one point, he came close to discovering the Frozen Niagara entrance to Mammoth but ran out of dynamite and moved on to another spot. He boarded with many families in the region, including L.P. Edwards, whose farm he believed was located over a sizable cavern. The two entered into a verbal agreement to split anything they found and Turner believed that he could trust the man since Edwards was a preacher.

The result of this agreement was the discovery of Great Onyx Cave in 1915. Turner named the place, helped to build the entrance and developed the trails. Because the cave possessed the finest onyx columns in the region, Reverend Edwards was quick to capitalize on this and also took advantage of the verbal agreement that he had with Turner by cheating him out of his half and claiming the whole thing for himself. Turner died a pauper from pneumonia less than a year later and only a small fund, raised mostly by local cave guides, provided him with a decent burial. Edwards refused to donate a dime to the fund. Turner was buried in the Mammoth Cave Baptist Church Cemetery with small, uncarved sandstone rocks at his head and feet. The grave can still be found here today.

In the years that followed, Great Onyx Cave became one of the most successful of the caves on Flint Ridge, in spite of the fact that a number of adjoining neighbors filed lawsuits against Edwards, claiming that the cave was under their property. Although Edwards lost all of these suits, he still controlled the largest portion of the caves and later passed it on to his daughter, Lucy Cox. She continued the cave's success and built the Great Onyx Hotel at the cave, which offered overnight accommodations and delicious meals.

Not long after the Great Onyx was discovered, another interesting character came to the region. He is remembered only as Old Man Hackett. For the first two years that he lived nearby, he lived in the mouth of Long Cave, refusing to have much to do with anyone, and then rented a house in Cave City. People wondered why he was shipping out crates from Long Cave and some speculated that he might be mining the cave for minerals. The rumors flew and Hackett's appearance only added fuel to the fire. He wore ragged clothes, a long beard and wore his hair so long that it hung down to his hips. One story stated that he lived like a hermit because he hated women, having been jilted as a young man, and some were so scared of his strange behavior that they asked law enforcement officials to check him out. It turned out that he was a retired postmaster and tavern owner from Texas. Hackett prowled around the area for several years, digging holes to try and find a new entrance to Mammoth Cave. During one of his digs, one of his helpers was killed when a two-ton rock fell on him. This brought an end to Hackett's explorations and he eventually moved back to Texas. There, at age 90, he fell and broke his hip and in a fit of despondency, shot himself.

While Old Man Hackett was pursuing his mysterious underground activities, another caving enthusiast named George D. Morrison turned up in the area. He was a mining engineer and oil prospector from Louisville and also became fascinated with finding new entrances into Mammoth Cave. Morrison founded the Mammoth Cave Development Co. and took out options on land south of the Mammoth Cave property. He began running illegal surveys of the cave, trying to determine if the passageways went under land he had recently leased. He even sent people into the cave to listen for drills and to set off charges of dynamite so that he could watch for erupting ground or smoke. Mammoth Cave officials caught him on one occasion and he was arrested and fined $75 for trespassing. Morrison maintained that he was prospecting for oil but everyone, including the cave owners, knew precisely what he was up to.

Morrison later left the area to acquire additional money to fund his ventures but World War I stalled his plans and he did not return until 1921. This time, he found what he had been looking for all along -- another entrance to Mammoth Cave on his own property. Not only that, but he also discovered new sections of the cave that were even more beautiful than the older part. To make matters worse, his property stood between the old entrance and the primary tourist route, which meant that travelers had to pass his cave first. Morrison quickly improved the entrance and constructed a hotel that he called the New Entrance Hotel. He even started plans for an elevator that would take patrons from the lobby to the wonders below. The Mammoth Cave managers were furious, especially when Morrison began setting up roadside signs that called attention to his new entrance and began selling tickets that actually had "Mammoth Cave" printed on them. The location began siphoning off tourists from the original site and the Croghan estate (not surprisingly) sued for an injunction to stop him from using Mammoth Cave in his name and advertising. But when Morrison showed the jury his maps and proved that it was all the same cave and that tourists could visit either entrance, the court found in his favor. The Croghan's appealed the verdict and while a higher court supported Morrison, it did direct him to be more precise in his advertising.

Morrison's success was electrifying to the other cave owners in the area and those who did not have caves on their land opted for the next best thing -- they sold souvenirs of all types. Shacks and stands sold everything from bookends to paperweights, all made from polished cave onyx, much of which had been stolen from area caves in the dead of night.

By the middle 1920's, what became known as the "Cave Wars" were in full swing. Kentucky cavers acted ruthlessly and in highly competitive ways. In order to cut into their competitor's business, rivals lauded their caverns and often spread rumors about Mammoth Cave being flooded or that the Mammoth Cave Hotel was closed or falling down. The owners of caves often told visitors who came to see them that they shouldn't visit another nearby attraction for a variety of reasons, ranging from poison gases in the rival cave to a tourist being killed there in an accident. As more caves were discovered and developed, competition for the tourists became even more heated. Those who found a cave on their land borrowed heavily from the bank to develop it and to build a ticket office and curio shop. Then they roamed the countryside looking for tourists and herded as many as they could find into their caverns.

Sometimes the competition between the operating caves became more than just who did the most advertising. In this mainly Baptist area, shootings and killings were forbidden but just about anything else seemed to be allowed, including harassment, lying and tricks of all kinds. Some natives estimated that by 1925, as many as one-third of all of the visitors to the area were diverted away from Mammoth Cave and to the smaller caves by nefarious means. The owners of Mammoth Cave went to court several times to seek injunctions against the lies and huckstering -- one of the most popular stories being that all of the caves were connected and so it didn't matter which entrance you went into -- but all of the attempts to stop this failed.

On many occasions, violence and vandalism marred the countryside. Signs were torn down and destroyed, fires were set and even shots were occasionally fired. On a few occasions, the visitors themselves even got into the act. One incident involved rival caves that were located right next to one another. A fence separated the two entrances and as visitors filed into each cave for a tour, the owners encouraged them to throw rocks at the opposite tour group!

The ultimate high point in the Cave Wars came with the death and the strange afterlife odyssey of Floyd Collins, which began in 1925. It all came to an end a year later though when Mammoth Cave became a part of the National Park system.

THE MAMMOTH CAVE NATIONAL PARK

In the early 1920's, a group was formed called the Mammoth Cave National Park Association for the purpose of trying to get the government to grant national park status to the cave. By this time, many were starting to realize that the numerous caves in the area were undoubtedly connected. By turning the underground system into a national park, it would protect the entire region for future generations.

Most of those who started the association were businessmen and politicians, not the people who owned smaller caves in the area and who made their living from guiding tours through the attractions. Obviously, these people were opposed to the government coming in and taking over their property, but they lacked both the funding and the political clout to do anything about it. In 1926, legislation was passed that officially authorized the preparation of Mammoth Cave as a national park. Congress authorized the cave to receive National Park status that same year, however it was not made official until President Franklin D. Roosevelt signed the papers in July 1941.

The delay was caused by the refusal of the local people to sell their land. The national park was slated to absorb all of the land, both above and below ground, where the cave was located. This created a huge parcel of land to be sold to the government. It was the duty of the Kentucky National Park Commission, formed in 1928, to acquire the land but they met with nothing but opposition. The acquisition became a heated subject in southern and central Kentucky. While some sold their homes and land willingly, others were forced out by eminent domain. It did not make for a pleasant climate in the area and not surprisingly, there are hard feelings that still linger in the area more than 70 years later.

Many things have changed at Mammoth Cave over the years. In 1981, it was named as a World Heritage Site and nearly 2 million people come here each year to canoe, camp, hike and of course, to explore the passages of Mammoth Cave.

Other changes have not just been in the services offered in the park, but in the cave itself. At every moment, monumental changes are taking place underground that will have an impact on the future of Mammoth Cave. The underground rivers continue their journey through the rock, the calcium droplets of water slowly slide lower and lower, creating artistic fixtures of stone and cave formations grow in size that can only be measured by the eye over a span of hundreds of years.

In every moment, time marches on and brings changes here. However, some things remain the same, remaining lost and forgotten with time. They are the ghosts and spirits of Mammoth Cave.

HAUNTED MAMMOTH CAVE

There have been many stories of ghosts at Mammoth Cave, spanning several generations of visitors, guides and service personnel. This isn't surprising considering that caves can be very spooky places, filled with dark corners, shadowed crevices and odd noises. But are the stories of Mammoth Cave merely figments of overactive imaginations? That remains to be seen, although we should take into account that ghostly tales have been told about the place almost from the time when the first cave tours roamed the darkened corridors with only a small lantern to guide the way.

These eerie stories tell of unexplained sounds, strange lights, bizarre noises, disembodied footsteps and of course, apparitions and spirits. However skeptics maintain there are explanations for these things. A person's imagination can play tricks on them in the dark and footsteps and voices can seem ghostly when there are echoes from other parts of the cave. They also state that stories of encounters with ghosts in Mammoth Cave are told by tourists and visitors who have no previous experience with caves and with the natural phenomena that accompanies them. But there are others who would say that this isn't true. While many of the stories are indeed accounts told by visitors to the cave, others are not so easy to explain away. Many of the tales are experiences shared by park rangers, cave explorers, spelunkers and even geologists who are fully aware of what strange things a cave can do.

Believers in the resident ghosts can cite a number of reasons why the cave might be haunted. The long history of the place includes accidents from the days of the saltpeter operations, Native Americans who wandered into the cave and never found their way out, stranded travelers, missing cave explorers, tragic tuberculosis victims and even those who loved the place so much that they have never left --or so the stories go.

I will allow the reader to judge for himself.

I have visited Mammoth Cave many times in years past and while collecting ghost stories, I have had the opportunity to talk with many of the people who work here. I have also been able to find other accounts from those who have gone on the record about the resident haunts in years past. In my own experience, I have found most of the park rangers reluctant to talk about ghost stories, although I have found a few who don't laugh off the odd tales and who will share their own strange experiences.

One such ranger has served as a guide in the cave for a number of years. She told me that weird things often happen along the route leading from the historic entrance to the cave. One day, she had been leading a tour group into the cave and had stopped to point out a site along the passage. She paused to wait for everyone to catch up and noticed a man in the back who was lingering behind the rest. He was wearing a striped shirt, denim pants and suspenders, but that was all she remembered. After her discussion, the group moved further along the passage and she looked for the man again, but he was gone. There was no one else in the tour group who matched the description of this man, so she sent another guide back a little way to look for him. The man was never found.

Another story, told by an experienced tour guide named Joy Lyons, tells of a tour that was taken a few years ago in the company of a large group and two guides. When they reached a point on the trail called the "Methodist Church", they usually turned out all of the lights so that visitors could experience what the cave was like in pitch blackness. She was standing at the back of the group when the lights went out and she could hear the lead ranger talking about the experience. Then, she felt a strong shove against her shoulder. The assault was hard enough that she had to step forward to keep from falling over. She turned to another ranger, who was supposed to be standing next to her and she whispered to him to stop clowning around. A moment later, the lead ranger ignited the wick on a lantern and she saw that the other ranger, she had thought was close to her, was actually about 70 feet away. There was no way that he could have shoved her and then walked so far in complete darkness.

"There was no one near me," she said, "but it was a playful shove. There are a number of us who feel things in various parts of the cave. It's not frightening -- but it's something else."

Another account was passed along to author Arthur Myers by Larry Purcell, a science teacher from Bowling Green, Kentucky. He worked as summer guide at the cave for number of years and had some strange experiences of his own.

The strangest episode seemed to be connected to the ghost of Stephen Bishop, the cave's most famous guide. Bishop so loved the cave that he was once offered his freedom from slavery but refused to take it because if he did, it meant leaving Mammoth Cave. Purcell's encounter with what may have been his ghost suggests that he may still be exploring the cave today.

Purcell was on a tour one day and happened to be by himself as another guide was speaking to the group. The lights were all off and it was Purcell's job to turn them back on again. He said: "I was walking along and I saw a black man with a woman and two children. The man had on white pants, a dark shirt, a white vest and a white Panama hat. They were real enough so that I walked around them. I went and turned on the lights and there were no people there -- and there were no black people on that trip!"

And Purcell is not the only one to allegedly see Stephen Bishop. There have been a number of visitors who have reported seeing a man of the former slave's description and have assumed him to be part of a historic tour, perhaps playing the part of Stephen Bishop. When they have asked about the man, or have looked for him again, he is gone.

"I can tell you this," said one veteran ranger, who has guided literally hundreds of tours through Mammoth Cave. "I came here as a non-believer in ghosts. I've gotten a lot more open-minded about the subject as time's gone by."

An additional story comes from Charlie Hanion, a former cave guide who became a nature writer. He and a friend were leading a "Lantern Tour" of the cave (a historic tour designed to give the visitor an idea of how early tourists saw the cave) and as his friend was talking to the assembled group, a girl of about 14 years-old turned to Hanion and asked who the man standing near the rocks was. Hanion looked about 40 feet away and saw a man in old-fashioned, formal attire. He was dressed in a fashion that tourists from decades past would have dressed to tour the cave. The man quickly vanished!

"But the really weird part came the following week when we were on the same tour," Hanion added.

As the tour group reached the same point in the cave, a guide asked if there were any questions. A woman raised her hand and asked if strange things were ever seen in this part of the cave? The woman was a tourist and claimed to be a psychic. She pointed over to the place in the rocks where Hanion had seen the man the week before and she asked who that person was.

"It was the same spot where we'd seen it before. I didn't see it at all that time," Hanion recalled. He also admitted that while he hadn't seen anything, the entire experience gave him chills to think about.

Based on these accounts, it would seem that apparitions are fairly common at Mammoth Cave and this is especially true when it comes to the most famous ghost connected to the cave. It is said to be a fictional account but many wonder if the story might contain elements of the truth, especially those who believe they may have encountered the main character in the story.

In February 1858, an article appeared in *Knickerbocker Magazine* called "A Tragedy in Mammoth Cave". The story tells of a girl named Melissa, who confessed the entire tale on her deathbed, having succumbed to tuberculosis. Melissa was a southern girl who lived in the vicinity of Mammoth Cave and she had fallen in love with her tutor from Boston, a young man named Beverleigh. The tutor had ignored Melissa's affections and began courting a neighbor girl instead. Melissa plotted her revenge.

Having grown up in the area, she knew well the twists and turns of Mammoth Cave and with careful planning, she lured Mr. Beverleigh to the cave. She conducted him on a "tour" to the depths of the cave and to a place called "Echo River". Here, she vanished into a side passage and left the poor man to find his own way out. Days passed and Beverleigh did not return. Melissa had only meant the whole thing as a cruel joke and so in despair, she went back to the cave to look for him. She made daily treks underground, searching and calling out to him -- but Beverleigh was never seen again.

Melissa was later diagnosed with consumption and died a short time later, never recovering from her guilt over the tutor's death. Many believe that her ghost is still seen and heard in Mammoth Cave, desperately searching for the missing man.

While the story sounds incredibly melodramatic, the reader is warned not to dismiss it too quickly. According to Gary Bremer, a former Mammoth Cave guide, there may just be something to the tale.

Several years ago, Bremer and four others were in a boat on Echo River, an underground stream that lies deep in the cave. One of the men had left to get another paddle for the boat. Bremer remembered what happened next: "The three of us in the boat all heard a woman calling out. It wasn't screaming but it was as though she was looking for someone."

The next day, they asked some of the other guides if anyone else had ever had such an experience. One of the older guides told him about a murder that was supposed to have taken place in that area and told him the story about Melissa. Bremer had never heard the story before that time.

Strangely, it would not be his last encounter here either. A short time later, he was again on the Echo River, this time with a new employee who had never seen the river before. She suddenly turned and grabbed his shoulder. "Did you hear a woman cough?" she asked him.

Bremer felt a cold chill. Melissa had died of tuberculosis, he remembered.

The other employee would later verify Bremer's version of their experience and would also add that she had also heard garbled voices in the cave and on one night, believed that she heard someone whisper her name.

Not all of the accounts of Mammoth Cave come from parts of the cave that are accessible to the public. Many of the strangest tales come from Crystal Cave, which was once believed to be a separate cave and was once operated as a private attraction. This cave is located along Flint Ridge, now well within the boundaries of the national park. It is not, at this time, open to the public and yet the stories that surround this portion of the cave are too mysterious to not be included here.

Most of these legends involve the ghost of a man named Floyd Collins, the former owner of Crystal Cave. Collins was not only an avid cave explorer but an established businessman too, always on the lookout for new caves that could be developed and put into service as a moneymaking enterprise.

Floyd had grown up in the area around Mammoth Cave and through his early years, his family eked out a living with a farm on Flint Ridge. He had been fascinated with caves as a boy and spent most of his childhood crawling in and out of holes that were scattered over the farm. His life as a professional caver began in 1912 though, when he met Edmund Turner. The enterprising young man roomed with the Collins family for a time and he paid young Floyd to act as a guide and to help him find caves that could be explored and developed. Turner gave him more than just money though and instilled in Floyd a knowledge of cave formations and geology. Turner's discoveries and initial success only heightened Floyd's interest in developing his own caves and by World War I, he was spending little time on the family farm and was instead mining onyx and exploring the caverns of the area. In the winter of 1916 - 1917, he made his greatest discovery by accident.

One day, while slipping into a crevice that he described as "breathing" (meaning that air was coming out of it from a cave below) he uncovered a crawlway that led deeper into the earth. After two weeks of digging, he emerged into a huge cavern that was encrusted with white and cream-colored gypsum flowers. Delirious with excitement, Floyd rushed back to the house and even though it was well past midnight, he roused the family and rushed them to the cave while they were still in their night clothes. The stunned family members did not emerge until after dawn.

Floyd called this discovery "Wonder Cave" but William Travis Blair, his next-door neighbor, suggested that he call it Crystal Cave instead, referring to the wondrous gypsum flowers. Floyd's father, Lee, and his brothers helped him to enlarge the entrance and they smoothed the floors and made trails during what ended up becoming more than 12 months of hard work. While all of this was going on, Floyd was exploring new passages and chambers and continued to make discoveries that made the cave one of the showplaces of the Flint Ridge.

In 1918, the Floyd's opened the cave and hired a manager and with that, formally entered the Cave Wars. The family began prowling the highways looking for tourists because unfortunately, the cave was located off the beaten track and could be reached by an almost impassable dirt road. Floyd and his family fought for their share of the local traffic but the odds were against them, which was too bad. Crystal Cave was reportedly amazing and tourists were given an especially rare treat if Floyd himself showed them through. He often told them of adventures that were beyond the tourist trail or would, in his enthusiasm, reach over and break off one of the gypsum flowers and hand it to the astonished visitor. Those who came loved the cave, but few made the trip and Crystal Cave refused to make money, no matter how much work was put into it.

In the lull between tourists, Floyd continued to relentlessly explore the cave but this did nothing to alter the poor business situation. The cave was only occasionally profitable and the Collins' still had to rely on farming and other activities to remain in business. In 1920, Floyd even invested in a still and for a short time before Prohibition made legal whiskey to supplement the cave's income. Some say that he continued this after Prohibition was passed as well. The rough economic times, as well as family problems, caused a division between Floyd and his father, who wanted to sell off the cave and get out of the business. Floyd refused and in fact, the arguments between them stiffened his resolve. He was convinced that Crystal Cave's many passages led to connections with surrounding caves. He had already explored five or six miles of passageways and had uncovered many leads, some of which ran toward Mammoth Cave. He wanted to, like George Morrison, find a commercially exploitable opening -- and one that was found in the right place could even displace Morrison's New Entrance and ensnare the largest share of the tourists.

Floyd carefully researched his plans. He talked with old-timers and cavers about their experiences and looked over old charts and maps. From all of this, he concluded that the most likely spot for a new opening was just over the line in Barren County on the narrow piece of land that connected the Mammoth Cave Ridge with Flint Ridge at the latter's southeast corner. An opening here just might, Floyd thought, connect Crystal Cave with Mammoth.

Floyd recalled from his past explorations that a sand hole existed on the farm of Beesley Doyle. Since Doyle was only one of three farmers controlling this area, Floyd began negotiations with him, as well as Edward Estes and Jesse Lee, the other owners. Of the three of them, only Estes was a caver, often raiding local caves for the onyx, which he sold to tourists. Floyd offered to search their land for caves in return for one-half of the profits and the three farmers could split the other half. Only Estes originally balked at the deal but finally, prodded by the others, he also agreed.

Floyd began his explorations, starting with the hole on the Doyle farm. The press later called this hole "Sand Cave", but this was a misnomer. It was not so much a cave as a narrow, twisting crevice that led downward. It had been opened due to the collapse of a larger cavern centuries before and the passageway skirted the edge of an overhanging shelter's back wall. Floyd chose this route, which was covered with sandstone debris, because he thought it might be a shortcut to what he hoped was solid limestone below. He had no idea where it might lead but hoped for either a new passage to Mammoth Cave, a back door to his own Crystal Cave or even an entirely new cave altogether.

Floyd stayed with the Doyle's for the next two weeks as he began to dig out an entrance and to begin a descent into the crumbling passage. He returned home to his parent's house on weekends and his father constantly chastised him for the time and attention that he was paying to his new project. Not only that, Lee Floyd insisted, but the hole was dangerous and he warned Floyd that he was liable to get caught in it. His mother also chimed in. She confided to her son that she had dreamed that Floyd would get caught in a rock fall and would be rescued by angels. She was convinced that the dream had been a warning from God. She begged him not to return to the cave -- but Floyd did not listen.

At the beginning of his third week of work at Sand Cave, Floyd moved over to stay with the Estes family but left his work clothes at the Doyle farm because it was closer to the site. His progress in the cave was rapid, especially after his use of dynamite on Monday. On Thursday, he hauled some stalactites out of the cave to show to Doyle and Estes as evidence of the wonders that he was sure were waiting below. On Friday morning, January 30, 1925 -- Floyd Collins entered Sand Cave for the last time.

When Floyd did not return to either the Doyle or Estes homes by Saturday morning, it was realized that someone should go and check the sand hole and to make sure that he was all right. Unfortunately, he was not. While winding his way through the narrow passage, a rock worked its way loose from the shattered stone and fell on his left foot. He became wedged in against the wall and was unable to work himself out. He was lying on his right side and his right leg was locked at an awkward angle. His left arm remained free but in the cold dampness of the cave, it quickly became numb. During the night, Floyd had fallen asleep and when he awakened, he discovered that his lantern had gone out. He could only wait and hope that someone came to his aid.

When Floyd's family and friends arrived on Saturday, they immediately set to work trying to free him. They managed to work his upper body loose and to warm him up with a gasoline lantern but that was all. With Floyd still trapped, they began widening the narrow opening into the cave and removed two bushels of rocks but even this did not help. Floyd's brother, Homer, climbed down into the passage to spend the night with his brother as rescue attempts were called off for the day. Not sure of what else to do, Lee Collins offered a $500 reward to anyone who could free his son. It was becoming clear to the crowd that was beginning to gather outside that the rescue would not be a simple one.

By Monday morning, newspapers across the United States had begun to report his predicament. Hundreds of people congregated outside Sand Cave. Members of the Louisville Fire Department were on hand, as well as experienced cavers, concerned locals and many who simply meant well but had no real experience with such predicaments. Many of them tried to reach Floyd with supplies and comfort and while many of them made it, most turned back, paralyzed with fear at the narrowness of the passageway.

As mentioned, newspapers all over the country reported on the trap that Floyd had gotten himself into. A number of reporters tried to reach Floyd for interviews but the most successful was a cub reporter from the *Louisville Courier-Journal* named William Burke "Skeets" Miller, who later won a Pulitzer Prize for his coverage. Miller's nickname (for "mosquito") came from his diminutive size, which enabled him to slide down the narrow path and sit with Floyd where he was trapped. He made eight descents into the cave and conducted a series of interviews that were quickly relayed to his readers as a first-hand account of what it was like to be literally buried alive.

Days passed and began to turn into several weeks. There had been attempts to bodily hoist Floyd from the cave (he had requested it -- even if his foot was pulled off) and an assortment of wild schemes, but none of them had worked. The local attempts soon became a national crisis involving dozens of miners, the National Guard, the Red Cross and a number of engineers. Thanks to the inclement weather, the crumbling walls of the cave passage, and often just confusion, Floyd could not be freed.

Many would later claim that Floyd became secondary to the scene on the surface. Fascinated by the daily reports from the reporters on the scene, an estimated 20,000 onlookers streamed into the area. Some of them hoped to help or catch a glimpse of the now heroic Floyd but others simply wanted to exploit the event by selling food, drinks and souvenirs. The circus-like atmosphere reached its peak in mid-February and the steady stream of curiosity-seekers continued.

Finally, a group of men managed to work their way into the cave and began trying to pry loose the rock that trapped Floyd's leg. They had widened the passageway and as they worked, the rock finally came free -- then immediately slipped back into place wedging Floyd's leg even more securely into place. The worked it back and forth but it was no use. Then, to make the situation even more dire, a series of small cave-ins occurred, crashing down onto Floyd and cutting him off from the surface. His would-be rescuers, after discovering that Floyd was still alive, scurried back to the surface. From that point on, none of the workers would return to the cave, fearing that the entire shaft might collapse. Homer Collins was enraged that no one would attempt to save his brother and he clashed with the authorities. Eventually, he was banned from the site.

Since no one would go back into the hole, a new plan was devised. A vertical shaft was started a short distance away with plans for it to intersect with the spot where Floyd was trapped. Friends, family and volunteers worked feverishly and on February 16, the shaft finally reached Floyd. Tragically though, he had died three days earlier -- on Friday the 13th -- from exposure and exhaustion.

People all over America had been riveted to the story of Floyd Collins and his plight had been front page news in newspapers and the source of constant updates on the radio for weeks. The press had descended on the Mammoth Cave area and had turned the region upside-down. What was not reported so widely was the fact that it took an additional two months to finally remove Floyd's lifeless body from the cave.

The tragedy brought national attention to the Kentucky cave country, but it also created a backlash, leading many to wonder if the caves were safe. The tourist trade was temporarily affected, with the small commercial caves suffering the most. This was at the height of the previously mentioned "Cave Wars" and now the smaller caves were fighting one another for an even smaller piece of the pie. Even Crystal Cave, which should have still managed to draw business thanks to the Floyd Collins name, was hurt by the slump. As a result, Floyd's father, Lee Collins, was even more anxious to sell the place than he had been when Floyd was alive.

In 1927, he accepted an offer from Dr. Harry B. Thomas, a local dentist, to take Crystal Cave off his hands for $10,000. Dr. Thomas already owned two other commercial caves in the area, Hidden River Cave and Mammoth Onyx Cave. In the transfer of property, Thomas was authorized to move Floyd Collins' body from its resting place and re-locate it in Crystal Cave, where it would be given a new burial spot. The Collins family, of course, objected to this, but it was too late. Lee Collins had already signed the deal.

Thomas wanted to move Floyd's body because he was sure that it would be a huge moneymaker for Crystal Cave. He had the body exhumed and then placed it in a glass-covered, bronzed metal coffin, opening it for public viewing in June 1927. It was placed in the middle of the tourist trail leading to Crystal Cave's main concourse. Here, visitors could pass by and look at him as they walked deeper into the cave. He had a large granite tombstone placed at Floyd's head that read:

William Floyd Collins
Born July 20, 1887
Buried April 26, 1925
Trapped in Sand Cave Jan. 30, 1925
Discovered Crystal Cave Jan. 18, 1917
Greatest Cave Explorer Ever Known

Granted, the stunt was ghoulish but it worked. Hundreds flocked to see Floyd's body and in his death, he became the cave's greatest advertisement. The guides would lecture solemnly about the exploits of the "world's greatest cave explorer" while the tourists gawked at the white, waxed face of the man in the coffin.

The Collins family sued Thomas and the case was battled out in court for several years. In 1929, the courts ruled (hopefully reluctantly) that Collins' body could stay where it was. Dr. Thomas had the legal right to the macabre display. Floyd would remain where he was in Crystal Cave --- or at least that was the general idea.

At some point on the night of March 18, 1929, Floyd's body was stolen from its glass coffin and spirited out of the cave. The theft was discovered the next morning and authorities from three counties were enlisted to help in the search. The casket was dusted for fingerprints and bloodhounds, after being given Floyd's scent, scoured the surrounding area. Before the day was over, the missing body was discovered (minus the left leg), about 800 yards from the cave's entrance. It had been wrapped in burlap bags and hidden in the brush along the Green River.

The cadaver was back in its coffin the following day, a little worse for wear, although the missing leg was never found. The identity of the thieves was also never discovered, although many of the local folks had their suspicions.

The prime suspect was Dr. Thomas himself. Although he maintained that he could not guess the motives of the body-snatchers, there were those who believed that he had stolen the body himself in an effort to boost business at Crystal Cave (which it did). Others, however, blamed competing cave owners, jealous over Thomas' newfound success and some believed that the Collins family had nabbed the corpse, or had hired it done, and they had lost the body before they could get away.

Regardless, after the attempted theft, the casket was covered each night with a metal lid and was securely locked. As time passed, the body was shown infrequently, although tourists were still asked to pause at the casket and listen to a short spiel offered in memory of the fallen cave explorer. The body continued to be displayed on occasion as late as 1952, although it remained in the cave for years after, long after it was closed to the public.

Many years after his actual death, Floyd Collins was finally buried at the Baptist Church cemetery up on Flint Ridge Road. His grave can easily be found here today. The last time that I visited here, I found a plastic bag that had been left behind on his tombstone with a note that was inscribed "To Floyd". Inside of the waterproof bag were a handful of matches and a candle-- the best friends of an old-time cave explorer. Even after all of this time, Floyd Collins has not been forgotten. Could that be because his ghost is still around?

Over the past several years, Crystal Cave has not been accessible to the public, although it has been charted and explored by national park employees and by a limited number of spelunkers. The fact that these veteran cave explorers have encountered weird phenomena in the cave dismisses the idea that the ghost stories here are merely the result of the overactive imaginations of tourists who are unfamiliar with the ordinary happenings in a cave.

A few years back, a group of Mammoth Cave employees were on an after-hours excursion in Crystal Cave and they noticed an old whiskey bottle that was resting on a rock ledge. One of the men in the group picked it up and looked at it and then placed it back on the ledge where he had found it. The group walked on deeper into the cave.

Later on in the evening, one of the men was walking back toward the cave entrance and was just passing by the old whiskey bottle when he heard a strange sound. "It was just behind my ear," he stated. "I heard a sound as though someone had flicked a finger against glass... a clink. I turned around just in time to see the bottle hit the ground."

Another man who was with him jumped back in shock. He claimed that the whiskey bottle had not just fallen, but that it had come straight out from the wall and had just dropped! "The little clink was loud enough to make me look back toward the ledge," he remembered, "and as I did, the bottle actually came out and then went right down in front of me. It was very bizarre."

Could the ghostly activity in the cave be attributed to the ghost of Floyd Collins? If there were an identity to be given to this ghost, he would certainly be everyone's first choice.

Another tale from Crystal Cave is attributed to a former employee named George Wood, who filed it as a report back in 1976. He wrote that he and another employee, Bill Cobb, had spent a day in June checking springs for a study on groundwater flow in central Kentucky. They didn't make it to the last spring until after dark and it was located near the old and abandoned Collins house on Flint Ridge.

Cobb went to the spring while Wood waited near the truck. After a few moments, he heard the sound of a man crying out in the darkness. At first, he thought it was his friend calling for help, but the voice seemed too high-pitched. It was also so faint that he had to listen carefully to hear what it was saying.

The voice cried: "Help me! Help me! Help me, I'm trapped! Johnny, help me!" It called out over and over again.

As he stood there on the edge of the dark road, he felt a cold chill run down his back. He vividly recalled hearing and reading about Floyd Collins and how he was trapped in Sand Cave --- which was located just a short distance from where he was standing!

A few minutes later, Cobb returned and Wood asked him if he had been calling for him. The other man had heard nothing while at the spring, but after hearing Wood's account, admitted that he was spooked. In fact, they both were and didn't waste any time in getting back in the truck and driving off.

Could the spectral voice have really belonged to Floyd Collins? And if so, could the "Johnny" that was heard in the mysterious cry have referred to Johnny Gerald, a friend of Floyd's and the last person to speak with him before the cave collapse sealed him off from rescue? Is his spirit still trapped in the cave, or could the sound have been merely an eerie echo of yesterday?

The Cave Research Foundation (CRF) is an organization of highly educated and highly trained cave explorers that was founded in 1957. The members investigate and chart caves all over the country but Mammoth Cave is normally their base of operations.

Mel Park, a neurophysicist at the University of Tennessee and the operations manager for the CRF in the 1980's, stated in an interview conducted in the early 1990's that he was not a believer in ghosts. In spite of this, he did say that strange things often occurred in the cave that he could not explain. "You hear sounds sometimes," he said, "like conversations. Sometimes it sounds like a very active cocktail party -- but it's probably just a waterfall."

Other members of the CRF have also reported odd happenings over the years, although their explanations for the events are not quite as mundane as Park's.

A geologist named Greer Price worked at Mammoth Cave a number of years ago and he stayed at the Collins home on Flint Ridge, as it was leased by the CRF. Across the road from this house was the former home of Bill Austin, who owned Crystal Cave in the 1950's. The CRF had moved into the houses around

1970 and the Austin house was used as a headquarters and the Collins house for sleeping rooms.

Price moved into the house in the middle 1970's as the caretaker, working part-time for the park service and part-time for the CRF. He lived there during the dead of winter and was very isolated during the cold weather months. He had to walk a mile from the gate to even reach the house and he was the only person who had the keys to the site. Needless to say, he didn't get a lot of visitors -- at least living ones anyway.

"Some of the old time guides would look at me and say I was crazy," Price recalled years later. "They wouldn't live out there for anything."

In front of the house was a small shed that Bill Austin had once used as a ticket office for the cave. The first strange thing that Price noticed about the property was that the light in the ticket shed would often turn on by itself. He would sometimes get out of bed late at night and see the soft glow of the light from inside shining in the darkness. He wondered if the fact that the main chamber of Crystal Cave was located directly beneath the shed had anything to do with the odd goings-on. To make matters worse, the casket where Floyd Collins body still lay was located right under the house where Price slept at night. Even though the cave was closed to the public, it was still a thought that would give anyone the creeps.

Price also heard stories of rangers who had seen Floyd Collins, or at least an apparition who looked like him, inside of the cave. The figure wore a shirt from the 1920's and overalls and had a tendency to vanish whenever anyone came close to him.

He was also told about a CRF member who was listening to the radio in the Austin house one night when suddenly the regular broadcast cut out and a static-filled report came through, describing the attempts to rescue Floyd Collins. The next day, when the man asked others about the report, he was told that no such radio show had been playing on the station that night!

Price had other odd experiences at the Austin house, aside from the light in the shed. He explained: "One night, I was sitting up reading and I heard footsteps outside of the house. I know it was not my imagination because both of my cats raised their heads and looked toward the door. I hadn't heard a car drive up and there was no access to the place. I sat there for a few minutes and the footsteps stopped. The next morning, I went out and found footprints in the snow around the house and up to the door, but then they disappeared. There were no footprints going down the steps, and there was no evidence of a car having been driven in."

Dr. Arthur Palmer, a professor in the department of Earth Science at New York State University at Oneonta, was a long-time member of the CRF when he did an interview about ghostly happenings at the cave. "I'm a scientist," he said, "and I'm not susceptible to this type of thing. We weren't looking for ghosts but some of these accounts are fairly well documented, as documentable as these things get."

He spoke of an incident in 1973 when he and his wife visited Crystal Cave. "Collins' body was at that time in a casket in the entrance room. We had to walk past it. We were in a part of the cave that nobody for hundreds of miles knew how to get to, a totally uninhabited part of the park. Access was strictly controlled, so there was no possibility of anyone else being in the cave at that time."

Palmer was setting up his camera equipment to take photographs of some of the geologic features of the cave when he heard a sound from deeper in the cavern. It was the sound of banging, a very rhythmic sound that he described like someone taking a hammer and pounding on a slab of rock. It came about once each second, not random at all, but very steady.

"It was a very insistent, continuous pounding," he stated. "It was not a shifting of rocks, which would be a random clattering."

The scientist decided to make a quick retreat from the cave and as time passed, he wondered what he had heard there. "It was not until a couple of years later that it occurred to me that the noise was coming from the place where Floyd Collins used to come down and eat, and he would flatten his bean cans with a rock -- some of those flattened cans are still down there."

Dr. Will White, a CRF member and a professor of geochemistry at Pennsylvania State University, also had some odd experiences in connection with the cave.

Back in the days when Crystal Cave was open for business, there was an old army field telephone in the cave. It had once been used to alert guides that customers were coming to the cave from the ticket office.

"I was with a fellow CRF member, George Deike," White recalled, "and as we were going by the phone, it rang. We looked at each other, wondering what was going on, but we continued walking."

They walked about 100 feet deeper into the cave when the telephone rang again. White recounted what happened next: "We ran back and I picked it up and answered. It was one of those old-fashioned army phones with sort of a butterfly switch on it. What I heard sounded like a phone sounds when it's off the hook and there are people in the room. You can hear the sound of voices but you can't hear what they're saying. I said hello, or something like that, and on the other end there's this startled gasp and that was all -- no one responded. The line was now dead."

White and Deike went on into the cave, still puzzled over the strange experience, but on their way out, they traced the phone line out of the cave and all of the way to the old ticket office. They discovered that the phones were disconnected! There was no way that it could have rang in the cave and no way that anyone could have been on the other end of the line -- and yet it happened! Perhaps it was a telephone call from the other side!

So, are they really ghosts in famous Mammoth Cave? If the stories of witnesses and guides from almost the past two centuries can be believed, there are. Combine these accounts with hesitant reports from scientists and trained skeptics, who can't explain what they have encountered in the cave, and you certainly have an unusual situation on your hands!

But if nothing else, the cave is certainly ripe for a haunting and the legends alone draw thousands of eager visitors each year. The mystery, the history, the cave explorers who have never returned, the tragedy, the terror and the death have created just what may be one of the most haunted places in the world!

BIBLIOGRAPHY & RECOMMENDED READING

Allen, John - It Happened in Southern Illinois (1968)
Allen, John - Legends and Lore of Southern Illinois (1963)
Aron, Paul - Unsolved Mysteries of American History (1997)
Bingham, Joan & Dolores Riccio - More Haunted Houses (1991)
Borden, James D. & Roger W. Brucker - Beyond Mammoth Cave (2000)
Brehm, H.C. - Echoes of the Bell Witch in the Twentieth Century (1979)
Bullitt, Alexander Clark - Rambles in Mammoth Cave (1845)
Carr, Stephen - Historical Guide to Utah Ghost Towns (1972)
Childress, David Hatcher - Lost Cities of North & Central America (1992)
Clifford, Georgia McAdams - Indian Legends of the Mississippi Valley (1932)
DePeel, Kirk - Ghost of Moonville (1993)
Gavenda, Walter & Michael T. Shoemaker - Guide to Haunted West Virginia (2001)
George, Angelo - Mummies, Catacombs & Mammoth Cave (1994)
Godwin, John - This Baffling World 2 - (1968)
Guiley, Rosemary Ellen - Atlas of the Mysterious in North America (1995)
Hauck, Dennis William - Haunted Places: The National Directory (1996)
Hunt, Gerry - Bizarre America (1988)
Jameson, W.C. - Unsolved Mysteries of the Old West (1999)
Kafton-Minkel, Walter - Subterranean World (1989)
Lyons, Joy Medley - Mammoth Cave: Story Behind the Scenery (1991)
Magee, Judy - Cavern of Crime (1973)
Marengo Cave - U.S. National Natural Landmark (publication of the cave)
Marimen, Mark - Haunted Indiana 3 (2001)
Meloy, Harold - Mummies of Mammoth Cave (1996)
Missouri Historical Society - The Chatillon- DeMenil House (1966)
Monaco, Richard - Bizarre America 2 (1992)
Murray, Robert K. & Robert W. Brucker - Trapped! The Story of Floyd Collins (1979)
Musgrave, Jon - Anna Bixby: In Search of the Real Frontier Medicine Woman (1998)
Musick, Ruth Ann - The Tell-Tale Lilac Bush (1965)
Myers, Arthur - Ghost Hunter's Guide to Haunted Landmarks (1993)
Myers, Arthur - The Ghostly Register (1986)
Neely, Charles - Tales and Songs of Southern Illinois (1938)
Norman, Michael & Beth Scott - Haunted America (1994)
Norman, Michael & Beth Scott - Historic Haunted America (1995)
Olsen, Brad - Revisiting Lake Lahontan (World Explorer Magazine - Vol. 3 No. 1)
Platnick, Kenneth - Great Mysteries of History (1971)
Price, Charles Edwin - Haints, Witches & Boogers (1992)
Readers Digest - Great Mysteries of the Past (1991)

Readers Digest - Mysteries of the Unexplained (1982)
Readers Digest - Strange Stories, Amazing Facts (1976)
Reevy, Tony - Ghost Train (1998)
Roberts, Nancy - The Gold Seekers (1989)
Roberts, Nancy - The Haunted South (1970)
Rother, Hubert & Charlotte - Lost Caves of St. Louis (1996)
Rothert, Otto - Outlaws of Cave-in-Rock (1924)
Smith, Barbara - Ghost Stories of the Rocky Mountains (1999)
Taylor, Troy - Ghosts of Little Egypt (1998)
Taylor, Troy - Haunted Alton (2000)
Taylor, Troy - Haunted Illinois (2001)
Taylor, Troy - Haunted St. Louis (2002)
Taylor, Troy - Haunting of America (2001)
Taylor, Troy - No Rest for the Wicked (2002)
Taylor, Troy - Season of the Witch (1999 / 2002)
Thompson, George A. - Some Dreams Die (1982)
Trento, Salvatore M. - Field Gd. to Mysterious Places of Eastern North America (1997)
Trento, Salvatore M. - Field Guide to Mysterious Places of the West (1994)
Wagoner, John J. & Lewis D. Cutliff - Mammoth Cave (1985)
Walker, Stephen - Lemp: The Haunting History (1988)
Warnell, Norman - Mammoth Cave (1997)
Winer, Richard & Nancy Osborn - Haunted Houses (1979)
Yenne, Bill- Lost Treasure (1999)

Personal Interviews & Correspondence

Special thanks to the staff at Marengo Cave -- especially Susan Davenport -- who provide me with a detailed history of the cave and Wyandotte Cave as well. Contact them at www.adventureindiana.com for information on cave tours and other outdoor adventures. 1-888-70-CAVES

- ABOUT THE AUTHOR -

Troy Taylor is the author of 26 previous books about ghosts and hauntings in America, including HAUNTED ILLINOIS, SPIRITS OF THE CIVIL WAR, THE GHOST HUNTER'S GUIDEBOOK. He is also the editor of GHOSTS OF THE PRAIRIE Magazine, a travel guide to haunted places in America. A number of his articles have been published here and in other ghost-related publications.

Taylor is the president of the "American Ghost Society", a network of ghost hunters, which boasts more than 450 active members in the United States and Canada. The group collects stories of ghost sightings and haunted houses and uses investigative techniques to track down evidence of the supernatural. In addition, he also hosts a National Conference each year in conjunction with the group which usually attracts several hundred ghost enthusiasts from around the country.

Along with writing about ghosts, Taylor is also a public speaker on the subject and has spoken to well over 300 private and public groups on a variety of paranormal subjects. He has appeared in literally dozens of newspaper and magazine articles about ghosts and hauntings. He has also been fortunate enough to be interviewed over 300 times for radio and television broadcasts about the supernatural. He has also appeared in a number of documentary films like AMERICA'S MOST HAUNTED, BEYOND HUMAN SENSES, GHOST WATERS, NIGHT VISITORS and in one feature film, THE ST. FRANCISVILLE EXPERIMENT.

Born and raised in Illinois, Taylor has long had an affinity for "things that go bump in the night" and published his first book HAUNTED DECATUR in 1995. For six years, he was also the host of the popular, and award-winning, "Haunted Decatur" ghost tours of the city for which he sometimes still appears as a guest host. He also hosts the "History & Hauntings Tours" of Alton, Illinois and St. Charles, Missouri.

In 1996, Taylor married Amy Van Lear, the Managing Director of Whitechapel Press, and they currently reside in a restored 1850's bakery in Alton. In 2002, their daughter Margaret Opal was born and joined her siblings, Orrin and Anastasia.

ABOUT WHITECHAPEL PRODUCTIONS PRESS

Whitechapel Productions Press is a small press publisher, specializing in books about ghosts and hauntings. Since 1993, the company has been one of America's leading publishers of supernatural books. Located in Alton, Illinois, they also produce the "Ghosts of the Prairie" internet web page.

In addition to publishing books on history and hauntings, they also host and distribute the Haunted America Catalog, which features over 500 different books about ghosts and hauntings from authors all over the United States. A complete selection of these books can be browsed in person at the "History & Hauntings Book Co." Store in Alton.

Visit Whitechapel Productions Press on the internet and browse through our selection of over ghostly titles, plus information on ghosts and hauntings; haunted history; spirit photographs; information on ghost hunting and much more. Visit the internet web page at:

www.historyandhauntings.com

Or visit the Haunted Book Co. in Person at:

515 East Third Street
Alton, Illinois 62002
(618)-456-1086

Printed in the United States
122748LV00010B/43-45/A

9 781892 523310